LIFE ON MATAGORDA ISLAND

NUMBER FIVE
Gulf Coast Studies
Sponsored by Texas A&M University–Corpus Christi
Wes Tunnell, General Editor

LIFE ON
MATAGORDA ISLAND

By WAYNE H. MCALISTER

Illustrations by Martha K. McAlister

TEXAS A&M UNIVERSITY PRESS COLLEGE STATION

The paper used in this book
meets the minimum requirements
of the American National Standard for Permanence
of Paper for Printed Library Materials, z39.48-1984.
Binding materials have been chosen for durability.

Library of Congress Cataloging-in-Publication Data

McAlister, Wayne H.
　　Life on Matagorda Island / by Wayne H. McAllister ; illustrations by
Martha K. McAlister.
　　　　p. cm.—(Gulf Coast studies ; no. 5)
　　ISBN 1-58544-337-9 (cloth : alk. paper)—
　　ISBN 1-58544-338-7 (pbk. : alk. paper)
　　　　1. Natural history—Texas—Matagorda Island.　2. Matagorda
Island (Tex.)　3. McAlister, Wayne H.　I. Title.　II. Series.
QH105.T4M375　2004
708.764'121—dc22　　　　　　　　　　　　　　　　2003024640

CONTENTS

Preface *vii*

CHAPTER 1 Living on the Edge *3*

CHAPTER 2 Beach *36*

CHAPTER 3 Marsh *60*

CHAPTER 4 Unseen Fauna *100*

CHAPTER 5 Comparative Anatomy *125*

CHAPTER 6 Cardisoma *134*

CHAPTER 7 Predation *144*

CHAPTER 8 Death *166*

CHAPTER 9 Creatures We Have Known *176*

CHAPTER 10 Land *217*

Notes *235*

Index *239*

PREFACE

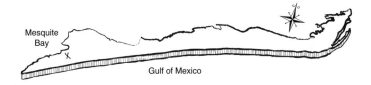

Mesquite
Bay

Gulf of Mexico

Sand grains move this way
Now all tumble back again.
Time duped to false start.

AN INAUSPICIOUS BEGINNING. It had rained all night and was
raining still. Despite several tarps and a couple of dozen large garbage
liners, all lashed into an irregular sodden hulk on the trailer, many of
our things were getting soaked. I had taken special care with my
books—two heavy bags tucked around each box—but between rain,
road splash, and shifting load they would not stay dry through the trip.
Our computers were on the truck seat where they stood a better chance.
My mood was rapidly darkening to match the weather. I knew it was
too late, but given half a chance, I would have called the whole thing off.

It was not supposed to be this way. We had been planning this move
for over a year. A multitude of bothersome details was taken care of.
The girls were on their own. We had no binding obligations, no pets
to give away. We could afford to make the shift. We enjoyed good
health. Nonetheless, the day arrived all too abruptly.

Day before yesterday I turned in my final course grades at Victoria
College as I had done for the past thirty years. Ordinarily, that would

bring a feeling of satisfaction and the anticipation of a relaxing summer break. Instead, we had decided to shatter tradition. Tomorrow I
was due to put on a U.S. Fish and Wildlife Service uniform at my new
duty station on Matagorda Island. At the moment I wanted nothing
more than to stay in my accustomed rut.

Ultimately, Martha had made the decision. She always does when
we come to something that really matters. I fret, deciding pro one day
and con that sleepless night, repeating the cycle for days. A dozen times
I ask what she thinks; she holds to her conclusion. Finally, I decide and
proclaim what we are going to do, inevitably agreeing with the solid
judgment she has already rendered. Ostensibly, I lead and she follows;
in truth, it is the other way around. Happily, she is usually right.
Woman's intuition, I guess. For sure, without Martha's unwavering
resolve, I would never have wrested myself from my cloistered bailiwick and ventured into a new career in a strange environment. Not at
my age.

What did I have to lose? A lifetime on the rural homeplace, familiar trails, a naturalist's acquaintance with every tree and hundreds of
resident creatures, daily communion with the Guadalupe River, the
spiritual umbilicus forged of childhood memories followed by over
half a century of mellowed reveries, security. Well, I was not really
giving all that up. We were not selling the land, just leaving it for a
while. I was, however, checking out of the teaching circuit for good.
They had been gratifying, stimulating, and fun years. What better way
to feel that the productive interval of your life was well spent than by
guiding and instructing young people through their first two years of
college? I worked through three generations of kids and relished the
prestigious WGA status that went along with my position. WGA?
World's Greatest Authority. For my students anyway, on any biological topic or career decision, I was their chief usher to the greater world;
a relationship as important to me as to my students.

Now I was giving that up, leaving academia, stepping down. I was
not certain what would be required of me on the island, but it was a
sure thing that I would not have a lifetime of background and experience to fall back on. I would rather give up my Ph.D. than my WGA
degree, but it did not work that way. No wonder the spring rain so easily dampened my humor.

What did I have to gain? As a retired professional biologist and
educator and a dedicated naturalist, I was heading toward a potential

paradise. Matagorda Island is an undeveloped ribbon of sand lying off the central Texas coast, strategically situated at an important bottleneck in the Central flyway. As the great blue heron flies, the island is only fifty miles from my home. Matagorda lies just downriver where it shields the placid Guadalupe estuary from the ceaseless pounding of the Gulf of Mexico. If I got homesick, well, Guadalupe water tempers the salinity of San Antonio Bay and deposits flecks of my homeground in the salt marsh on the bay side of the island. I could always go down and resuscitate in the brackish effluvium.

And after all, if the venture did not work out, we could always pack up and hie back to the homeplace.

The entire island is part of the Aransas National Wildlife Refuge complex, so it retains its natural flavor and is not overrun with people. It really is an island; there is no causeway. All that appealed to the naturalist in me. My specific job was to develop an environmental education program and to host visiting groups. That aspect tugged at my schoolteacher's roots. Martha and I would live on the island, isolated even more than we were on the banks of the Guadalupe. That lifestyle appealed to us both. Her only desire was to go beachcombing as often as she liked. We were taking her bike for that very purpose. So, there was every reason to be excited about our prospects.

For better or worse, we left. Martha drove the Trooper to the Aransas Refuge outside Austwell, where she would park and catch the workboat headed to the south end of the island. I would follow with our load of gear.

I banged our gatepost trying to get the big truck and trailer onto the main road. Then I set off in the steady rain for Port O'Connor, where I was to board a barge headed for the old military dock on the north end of Matagorda Island. En route I did not have much time to think. The idiosyncrasies of the borrowed truck, including a driver's-side wiper blade in tatters, and the insistent yank and drag of the large trailer kept me busy.

They were loading the barge when I arrived. With a jerk of his forearm a deckhand motioned me to drive up the distressingly narrow runners that spanned the mean-looking gap between dock and deck. I thought he was going to give me some hand signals to get me aligned, but he had turned his back, apparently considering the feat too routine for further attention. I made it, thanks to wide tires and plenty of boyhood experience at handling vehicles on the farm. I cut the engine and set the brake, already exhausted. Then I simply sat awhile, wondering if I was actually doing this, feeling slightly queasy from the rhythmic rocking of the vessel that was about to finalize my move from the mainland.

The barge, a hundred-foot-long rectangle, was mostly open cargo deck bounded by an insubstantial knee-high rail. A small wheelhouse perched above a rear corner. Everything about the vessel was massive: gigantic bolts, thick oily cables, an enormous winch. A palpable throb emanated from huge engines in its rusting bowels. The deck was filled with pickups and fully loaded trailers, a Suburban lacking a wind-shield and consumed nearly to its chassis with sea rust, half a dozen pallets of fifty-five-gallon petroleum drums, and assorted chunks of heavy machinery that seemed designed for brute destruction. The barge, as I later learned, had belonged to a rancher on the island who used it to ferry eighteen-wheelers across to pick up cattle and move them to market on the mainland. The FWS used it now to transport heavy equipment back and forth. On my maiden voyage the historic scow bore its original name, Miss Matagorda. A few years later it of-ficially became the Norman von Hoevel, in memory of the cigar-smok-ing pilot and former ranch hand who was today taking me across and who would prove to be my ready reference to insular days gone by.

With a rattle of giant chains and a hearty exhalation of diesel smoke, the engines growled into a new tempo, and we were on our way. We went down the Intracoastal Canal, east through the cut between the spoil islands and plowed into the Ferry Channel that angles across Espiritu Santo Bay. The slap of the low swells against the square bow emphasized the apparent impregnability of our stolid craft. Perhaps because there was no immobile reference point nearby, I felt less move-ment aboard now than when we were idling in port. It seemed to me that the channel markers and petroleum platforms were flowing dream-ily past us; that we were the only steady feature in this fluid, airy world.

The day began to open up. The overcast lifted, the horizon receded, stable landmarks faded, my face screwed into a continual squint. Al-though I could make out the thin white line of the island ahead and the radio antennae and water tower at Port O'Connor behind, I was encompassed, overwhelmed by water, sky, and light. I felt small. Our progress was slow but insistent. ("This here tub only goes straight on," Norman told me. "Yew can't hardly make her dido. It don't stop none too quick neither, lessen you run aground.")

It took an hour and a half to make the eleven-mile crossing. Eventually, everyone dozed: lulled by monotony, stultified by humidity, drugged by diesel fumes. When we thumped heavily against the slip on the island, I jolted back into reality and confirmed once again that I really was doing this. The continent was gone. There was only Matagorda Island, my new world.

I got the truck engine going, waited my turn, caught the vague hand signal, and drove out onto the crushed-oyster-shell landing. That was it. All personnel busied themselves debarking the rest of the load. Without realizing it, I was getting my first lesson in island etiquette: take care of yourself.

It takes awhile before a newcomer gains acceptance as an islander. Although there are no longer any old-time residents on Matagorda— no *real* islanders—the people who come out to work here daily do constitute a definite clique: not unfriendly, but reserved and distant, traits that are exacerbated by the people's isolated, close-knit daily lives. I suspect that island duty selects for a clannish personality, a propensity to coalesce into a social unit that serves as a buffer against the harsh, open terrain; the separation; and, incidentally, the occasional outsider. The best way to transform from outsider to islander is not to force it but to just let it happen. It was not too long before Norman took me into his confidence, Mickey became my gossip trunk line, Joe allowed me glimpses of his quirky inner sanctum, and Joyce let me see her cry. There was one other unexpected but inevitable concomitant of my acceptance. I, too, became suspicious of outsiders, for I was no longer one of them.

I ground the truck into gear and threaded my way through the maze of old air force buildings, across several cracked airstrips, and onto the one-lane road that runs the length of the island. The rain was done, the sky was clearing, and the sun was creating a steaming clambake atmosphere and causing me to pull my bare arm out of the truck window. T. E. Lawrence referred to the furnace of Arabia; I was entering the sauna of Matagorda Island. Muggy or not, the sunshine raised my spirits. Maybe I was doing the right thing after all.

The potholed road takes advantage of the linear topography of the island as it follows the slight rise that marks the inland edge of the marsh. Ahead of me Matagorda stretched in a slight southeasterly arc to a vanishing point in the hazy distance. Except for the road and an occasional line of posts that marked cross-fences, the vista appeared untouched by human hands. Neatly detached from the substance and turmoil of the mainland, virgin, unperturbed, suspended in time—an untouchable island universe reposed in all its natural splendor. I could not help but borrow from the vernacular of the astronomers who view the marvel of the galaxies. Dare I gaze upon it, let alone touch it?

Now and then I could see completely from side to side, maybe two miles across in the salt-white air. The sequence was always the same: bay, marsh, grassland, sand dunes, beach, the Gulf.

This was not my first trip to Matagorda Island. Martha and I had visited quite a few times, especially while Jim Shelton, a former student, worked here. So, the lay of the land was not new to me. However, now that I was coming to live here, everything seemed to take on a fresh significance. The naturalist in me was stirring. I wanted to know every plant, ferret out the haunts of every kind of animal, imbibe the smells, hark to the sounds, comprehend the sky, turn with the seasons. My schoolteacher side urged me to broaden my background—to learn about former landowners, past conflicts, current management plans, and whatever modern problems threatened the existence of this barrier island. Along the way I hoped to assimilate as much of the quintessence of this isolated windrow of sand as I could, and perhaps in so doing, to plumb new dimensions of myself. By the time I saw the tall palm trees and the outline of the hangar that marked the old Wynne Ranch site on the south end, I was riding an intellectual high, anxious to begin earning my WGA degree on Matagorda Island.

Martha was already there when I pulled up beside the house trailer that was to be our new home. She was beside herself to share the view, a spectacular sweep from bay to dunes and, as we were soon to realize, a superior observation post for Gulf sunrises, bay sunsets, barreling cold fronts, and every constellation that beams down on the Northern Hemisphere. The bedroom window was precisely aligned to receive a lovely onshore breeze and, incidentally, the crepuscular yammers of coyotes and the periodic thin wail of a whistling buoy far out in the Gulf. Flocks of brown pelicans, royal terns, and laughing gulls passed right by our windows on their way back and forth across the island. Long-billed curlews stalked crickets along the edge of the trailer's shadow. There was no yard; the grassland began at our doorstep. Not having developed an eye for them, I almost stepped on my first Matagorda rattlesnake within a few feet of the front door. No matter that an aging house trailer perched atop rusting metal leveling stands on a remote barrier island in the heart of hurricane country was not the most secure of domiciles. The island already had us under its spell. We were ready to accept its ugly moods along with its pleasant ones. Already in our third decade of marriage, we would forge yet another grade of togetherness here.

On our first night in the trailer, with the breeze gently lifting the edge of the sheet and the surf reduced to a relaxing white noise, Martha suggested that I begin a diary in case I might want to write of our experiences on Matagorda.

"You think so?" I responded dreamily.

"Yes. Didn't I just say so."

"Umm. We'll see."

So I did. And as usual, she was right.

This book winnows seven years of diaries, 1993–99. The end of the millennium seemed a satisfactory break point. (I am for 99/00 rather than 00/01 as culmination of the age; technically wrong, of course, but intuitively right.) Although it still hovers around natural history, this one is unlike our descriptive first volume on Matagorda Island.[1] By living here, we have learned a lot more about the hidden delights, the seasonal shifts, the thralls, and the challenges of existence on the island; and in its sublime isolation I have become better acquainted with myself. So, the format is looser and more personal. The manuscript was written entirely on-island.

How long will we stay? When we made the move, we thought we might last five years. We are already in our seventh winter. Perhaps, as Martha says, we'll just wait for a sign—joints getting too creaky, a Service decision we cannot live with, a hurricane that makes the choice for us. Or maybe I will finally succumb to the beckoning call of the Guadalupe River: Come back; come home. I think that when I do finally leave this island that I shall not return. Not because I fear that I would find my familiar roaming ground developed into oblivion; hopefully, its protected status will spare it that all too common fate. Rather, I believe that a return would awaken too many fond memories and that I would feel depressed, and I would chastise myself for ever having left. Better to leave and not look back.

I want to acknowledge the genial camaraderie accorded me by the FWS personnel with whom I have worked. I came here a rank outsider and was immediately accorded bemused family status. My superiors, especially Bret Giezentanner, Chris Pease, and Jennifer Sanchez, never failed to encourage me and back my every effort to bring an environmental message to visitors, even when things seemed to be conspiring against us. Felipe Prieto shared his knowledge of island ecology with me. I could not have kept the Conestoga rolling and the Environmental Center running without the ingenuity and expertise of David Stringo and Will Coppock, both of whom are past masters at improvising a "Matagorda fix" to keep things working. Norman offered me rare homespun insight into life on the island, past, present, and eternal.[2] And from the Texas Nature Conservancy, Michelle and Cathy shared the endless frustrations and headaches of making reservations and finding boat transport for visitors. We will never forget Joe and Joyce, who served as our unwitting role models while we adjusted to the delights and challenges of island life. There were many others, in and out of uniform, all great to consort with.

Finally, there is Martha. It was she who convinced me to come to Matagorda Island. She who enjoys it, tolerates it, and survives it with me. She who suggested that I write, saw to it that I did, and edited what I wrote. She who not only has put up with an isolated and often trying physical existence but has put up with me during those long intervals when we were the only two human beings in the entire world. Without her, my island universe would not be complete.

LIFE ON MATAGORDA ISLAND

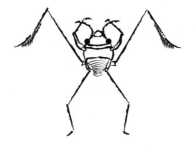

CHAPTER I

LIVING ON THE EDGE

Ah, wave signature!
Fresh fragile wiggle on beach
Where an ocean paused.

LIVING ON A BARRIER ISLAND is quite different from visiting one. A visit, temporary by definition, is planned for a pleasant time of year; a resident must endure all seasons. Sooner or later, residents have to learn to meet the island on its own terms. Those who resist eventually leave in despair or get rudely clobbered for their insolence. The island is not malicious, just so completely indifferent to human welfare that anyone caught athwart its inexorable path may well imagine malevolent treatment.

Both by nature and by mandate, Martha and I came to Matagorda Island in peace. We intended to abide by the same pacts that had served us well on the homeplace—bend when pushed; surrender the right of way when challenged; hold no grudge; enjoy each day; make do; live and let live. We actually had no choice; this insular wildlife refuge is, after all, dedicated to the preservation of the natural ecosystem. It is one of those rare instances where the needs and desires of people are not given top priority.

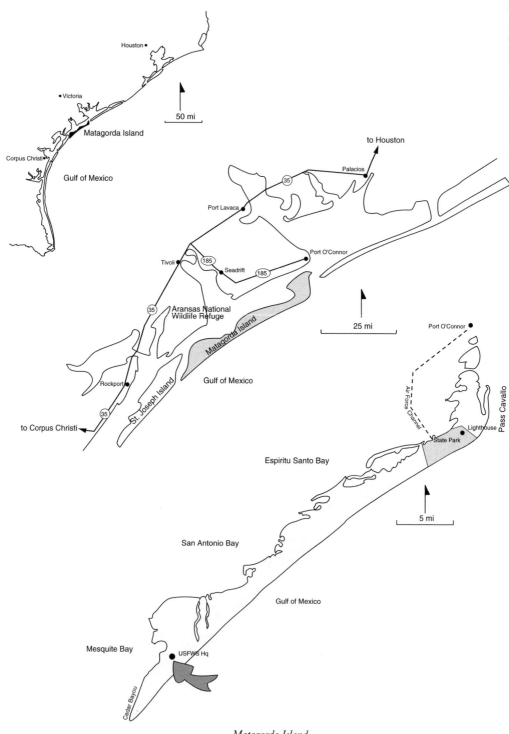

Matagorda Island

Even without a clear idea of the full commitment I was making, I willingly took the job with the understanding that we were coming to live astride the ultimate knife blade and that we would need to maintain our poise here as best we could without either cutting ourselves or dulling the blade's keen edge. It has been a stirring and satisfying balancing act.

Matagorda Island is on the edge in several ways, most obviously geographically. A thirty-eight-mile-long ribbon of sand, it lies 6 miles off the mainland in the upper part of the Coastal Bend, just where the coastline of Texas begins its droop to the south. This quiet stretch is 45 miles up the coast from Corpus Christi, the sixth-busiest port in the nation, and 120 miles down the coast from Houston, the second busiest. With a width of about two miles and an elevation averaging twelve feet above sea level, not counting the modest twenty-foot sand dunes, Matagorda is a last terrestrial outpost before the inclined continental shelf slides beneath the Gulf of Mexico. Our house trailer is situated at the old Wynne Ranch headquarters, near the island's grassy midrib four and one-half miles from the south end.

From our vantage we can see that we are surrounded by shoreline edges. To the west, Mesquite Bay separates us from the mainland. A dark streak across the bay is the line of dredged spoil banks along the Intracoastal Waterway. Beyond the spoil banks, across the waterway, a flat, unbroken line of wind-pruned live oaks tracks along Blackjack Peninsula, the heart of the Aransas National Wildlife Refuge.

Despite the constant threat of a spill in the heavily trafficked Intracoastal, with the Aransas NWR protecting one side and Matagorda Island the other, Mesquite Bay ranks as one of the cleanest lagoons along the coastline of a state not noted for its environmental perspicacity. The winter population of whooping cranes, a symbol of both "wild America" and of "ecotourism dollars," enhances the vigilance of those who use and those who patrol the surrounding waters. No one wants to be responsible for a mess-up here.

Although the Gulf piled up this windrow of sand beneath us, it is the bay that separates it from the mainland and so makes it an island. Mesquite Bay and the drowned river valley that was its prehistoric predecessor have cordoned this sandy ridge from the mainland since its inception five thousand years ago. The ancestors of the island inhabitants had to navigate across several miles of open bay, which thus became a biogeographical filter that winnowed out those not up to the journey and keeps the descendants loosely corralled here today.

A color-enhanced infrared satellite photograph of the Coastal Bend shows freshwater as a red cloud belching out of the Guadalupe River into San Antonio Bay. The cloud dilutes to a livid blush as river water swings south along the edge of Blackjack Peninsula and streams across San Antonio and Mesquite Bays to stain the marsh along Matagorda Island. The bay is caught in the act of hauling nutrients collected from the river valley into the salt marsh, the food basket of the island. This crimson trace of current also suggests how all manner of creatures that can neither swim nor fly—from jackrabbits to scorpions—might have wafted across the bay atop mats of flood debris.

At its south end, Mesquite Bay receives Cedar Bayou, the narrow tidal inlet that connects the lagoon with the ebb and flood of the Gulf. Roiling salt water flows in, stagnating bay water flushes out; and a jillion aquatic critters migrate between marsh and sea while fish, fishermen, and sea birds flock to exploit the traffic. Now and then the fickle channel clogs with sand until either a storm or a dredge restores its flow.

Out of all proportion to its small size and shallow bottom, Mesquite Bay defines, nurtures, and constrains our disjunct world. Mesquite Bay, not the Gulf of Mexico, determines our presence here. We come and go across the bay in a twenty-four-foot cabin boat powered by two 135-horsepower outboard motors, or we try to. Sometimes the motors will not start. Occasionally, one or both motors fail en route. For every projected trip between island and mainland, it is Mesquite Bay itself that makes the final decision: if the bay is benign, we can go; if it is treacherous, we must wait.

Wind is always a consideration when we want to cross the bay. A strong easterly can "blow the bay away from the island" and leave us stranded behind a series of exposed mudflats and oyster reefs. The motors churn up black muck, and we go nowhere. A hard norther brings plenty of water but at a price. Within a couple of hours the shallows can whip into a heaving washboard of ugly, white-capped chocolate waves three feet tall. Getting off the island headed into the wind is chancy. The boat, though difficult to steer, is made to take the pounding. The danger occurs when a deep trough is followed by a big wave that smothers the motors, causing them to cut out. Keeping a powerless craft under control while getting the motors restarted in that lurching mayhem is scary business. The most common fatal situation on the local bays is a wintertime loss of control and going overboard or, more likely, getting the craft jammed on an oyster reef or mud bank. Warm southern climate is no consolation. The bay water gets stingingly cold, and the wet wind is brutal. Hypothermia can kill in short order. So, when a winter bay says no, we listen.

We have yet to get caught in a hurricane here. When it comes, it will slam into Matagorda Island from the Gulf of Mexico. Still, the rising turbulence on Mesquite Bay, not the surge and backwash from the Gulf, will determine whether we can evacuate safely to the mainland. We must leave before the bay becomes impassable. We track any hurricane in the Gulf through weather reports, but we also watch the Intracoastal Canal for squadrons of shrimp boats racing for the protection of the Victoria barge canal at the head of San Antonio Bay. Shrimpers know when it is time to go to cover.

Less threatening but more frustrating is a quiet bay shrouded in fog. February, when cold air settles over warmer water, is our prime fog month. The thick swirls of mist, substantial enough to feel against your cheek and drip off your eyelashes, reduce visibility to less than a boat length. There is no more helpless feeling than being adrift in an encompassing sea mist, bereft of any bearing, haunted with a creeping panic, and tormented with the realization that but for your fog-blindness you are in familiar waters. Major trouble begins if you allow your innate pointer to override your instruments. Trust the compass! At least it knows the cardinal directions, if not the way to specific sites.

A foggy bay is telling us no, but the hushed, acquiescent ambiance tempts one to try anyway. What could go wrong beyond getting turned around a little? We got lured out a couple of times before we learned our lesson. Once we turned back before we were doomed; the second time we got so hopelessly disoriented we could hardly tell which way was up, much less which way was forward. We had to drop anchor and wait for the fog to lift. Only then, appropriately humbled, could we proceed.

We have seen Mesquite Bay in most of its moods. Like all edges in this coastal country, the bay is more often beautiful than beguiling. Three days after Christmas I caught an instant in my diary.

DECEMBER '93: *Up to a weirdly quiet morning; the onshore breeze has not come alive yet; the island gripped in rare cathedral stillness. Went down to*

put redfish entrails in my crab trap at the boathouse. The bay dark, motion-
less, gripped in the trance of a pervading fog. The water so still I could see the
flutter of ripple rings as acorn barnacles on the pilings kicked for their
breakfast. From the pier I saw a common loon—or at least its unmistakable
silhouette. It saw me but did not move, and neither did I. Everything—loon,
bay, fog, time, and I—were caught up in a common daze. Water and fog
merged so subtly and completely that the bird seemed levitated in the wet
ether. In one golden moment the loon broke the swoon: it let out one wistful,
indelible tremolo and plunge-dived soundlessly. (Or did it just melt?) Just one
short, winter-attenuated cry, but it caught the mellow tone and spellbinding
quality even in that. Was it just for me? Surely not. Nonetheless, loon, you
make it easier for me to be cheerful this Christmas, for I have been talking to
myself here for over a week.

We saw our first waterspout in Mesquite Bay. A silvery, sinuous column, too far off to discern its gyration, it dropped from a low-lying
cumulus cloud, and its foot danced across the bay in a spume of water. In the half minute before the column disintegrated, it traveled a
mile or more. We were both so enthralled that I did not even think
about my camera until it was over.

Another time, a small waterspout sprang to life a few yards off the
bay shore where I stood. I could hear the rush of air and see debris and
a geyser of water rising in a compact rotating column. But the vortex
quickly skipped onto the shore and began to wind down. Even that
short-lived little whirlwind wreaked a bit of havoc, for I saw it spit out
a bewildered least sandpiper with feathers in disarray.

One phenomenon we witnessed many times over Mesquite Bay
before we learned that it had a name. Summer weather conditions
must be just right: a medium-sized cumulonimbus cloud riding above
a draft of warm, dry air. As the afternoon wears on, the flat bottom of
the cloud darkens with moisture until it can no longer contain itself.
Rain begins to leak out in thin gray veils, but destined never to reach
the ground. Instead, this abortive precipitation vaporizes, consumed by
the warm air through which it falls. It is whisked back up, I suppose,
into the bowels of the weather machine that embraces this island.
There to try again and again until it gets it right. This is *virga* (streaks
in the sky), one more unexpected delight of Matagorda.

Finally, Mesquite Bay is where our sun goes to rest. Sometimes discreetly behind a curtain of winter clouds; other times aloofly through

a salt haze that gives it a cool, frosted glaze; often grandly amid blazing streaks of glory and a fancied blare of trumpets. Most commonly, it drops as an unadorned glob of molten metal and where it touches the bay spreads a blinding avenue farther and farther across the water until, in the blink of an eye, it is quenched. If the air is clear—rarely in this salty climate—a spectral green flash flickers on the horizon a split instant after the sun's rim disappears.

There are also notable moonsets that lay down a solid track of moonbeams on which it seems we could walk across the bay to Rockport without wetting our feet. One memorable evening Jupiter set in a stunning display complete with an inviting Jovian promenade.

Although our trailer is located about midway between two major edges—Mesquite Bay and the Gulf of Mexico—we cannot see the Gulf because of the sand dunes. However, on rare cold and clear winter mornings Matagorda Island treats us to a special vision.

JANUARY '94: *Up to a mystical dawn! This morning we can not only see the slumbering Gulf over the dune line, but we can gaze far out over the water to a crisply etched horizon. We gawk, babble, get the binoculars, and ogle some more. The entire sea has been raised. But nothing else seems amiss. The sand dunes are unperturbed, terns are working the low surf, and the petroleum platforms are standing in their usual spots. It is our perspective that is exalted. Something about the air, I suppose. Then, with the coming of the sun, the sea sank from view, and our world became real again. Our brief "Gulf illusion," as we called it, was gone. Too indescribable and unbelievable to share. We will just keep the secret between us.*

Though our presence depends on the bay, our world actually exists at the whim of the Gulf of Mexico. The sea made this barrier island, tends it daily, caresses it, occasionally menaces it, and doubtless will someday annihilate it. Sand piles are not made to last. Viewed from on high, the Gulf is a relatively small, nearly landlocked sea lacking the tidal range, the fetch, and the huge combers of the open ocean. However, from barrier-beach level, the Gulf transforms into an enormous, omnipotent, and often ominous entity, every inch an ocean in its own right.

Despite its allure and omnipresence, the Gulf of Mexico is less familiar to us than Mesquite Bay. We cross the bay, plumb to its bottom, navigate into all its recesses. We visit the Gulf daily, but always show it more respect. It is much more difficult and more dangerous to go out into the Gulf for any distance. On a good day we can venture waist deep into a gentle surf, but most times we are content to stand on the beach and gaze out into the grandeur.

The view can be ethereal or ugly. One day a translucent turquoise expanse stretches from beach to horizon, a day when no one would imagine the sea to be anything but perpetually benevolent and the world anything but round. But when the onshore wind stiffens and the swells run deep, though the open Gulf may hold blue green, the inshore water turns brown with a load of stirred sand. The dun color reaches from surface to bottom and begins as abruptly as a dropped curtain, precisely where the waves strike the offshore bars. As the wind continues, the entire visible Gulf turns dark. Exploding surf and fierce breakers with wind-whipped crests crash far up the beach and claw streaming gashes in the sand as they fall back. The island reels at the shock and roar, and the dune field begins to slump seaward. Humans, humbled for the moment at least, stand well back from this show of brute force.

And yet, on some quiet mornings there is no separate sea and sky, only an amalgam of hydrosphere and atmosphere melded through a perfect watercolor match of almost undetectable sea mist.

Through all its moods the Gulf retains many of its secrets hidden by depth and vastness or withheld by royal prerogative. We know it well, yet we know it not. *Mare incognitus.*

Although it was not my original intent, I have become quite familiar with the Gulf of Mexico by routinely jogging along its margin. There is no better nor more alluring natural track than a firm beach. Every other day, in all but the worst weather, I run barefoot two miles along the same stretch of sand, swing around, and return. The exercise not only sets my blood to coursing, but it opens up my mind and makes me receptive to the mood of the great body of water sprawled just off my shoulder.

I have run the beach in February with a blue norther numbing the rims of my ears and my breath riming my beard. I have run it in August with the hot moist breath of the Mother Gulf rattling in my chest and sweat pouring ineffectually from every pore. I have run it with the fuse of an incipient charley horse burning up my hamstring and with the pain of plantar fasciitis stabbing my heel. I have run it in thunderstorms when I was the most likely lightning rod anywhere around. Four miles a run, sixteen miles a week, over eight hundred miles a year—about the distance from Texline on the upper edge of the Panhandle down the axis of Texas to Southmost on the bank of the Rio Grande outside Brownsville. Me and Forrest Gump, running because we must. Me and Bernd Heinrich, running because we are gripped by the exhilarating *passion* of it. Six years and still huffing. It keeps the pipes open and the synapses crackling.

My heels strike the firm, moist sand in cadence with the throb of the surf, and I feel the pulse of the ocean through the bottoms of my bare feet. Every quarter mile or so I anticipate the shriek of a displaced willet or a flutter of startled sanderlings. When the tide is low, I jog along a strip of sand rendered hazardous by a slick of fecal pellets thrown up by ghost shrimp in such profusion that the soft little pills squish between my toes and pack into patties in my insteps. Other times I garnish the immaculate damp beach with a trace of yellow green footprints, compliments of the diatoms squeezed to the surface by my passing. When the waves come in nearly to the dunes, I push on through sinking sand and ankle-deep water.

On a rising tide the ocean sometimes spits up great blobs of sea foam, which are playfully batted up the beach by the onshore breeze. These animated puffs slide erratically and even leap up and somersault, enjoying their ephemeral freedom. I cannot resist breaking stride to kick at spindrift, and I am always amazed that although I can scatter the froth, the impact is utterly impalpable.

On days when the Gulf is cool and the island is warm, a dense fog develops at the interface. I ride my bike from the trailer to the dunes in bright sunshine, only to enter a chilling mist on the beach where I begin my run. Actually, the fog bank makes for an ethereal jog. I feel suspended in space and time, moving with ingrained rhythm but seeming to be on a treadmill. I use the feel of the sand and the sound of the surf for orientation, and I sense my two-mile mark kinesthetically.

I return to my starting mark pleasantly exhausted. There I indulge in a long, uninhibited leak to speed the loss of body heat. Almost instinctively, I direct the steaming stream toward the nearest ghost crab burrow, not out of malice but more of mischief, just an irresistible urge to wet on something. Because of my indifferent aim and the boundless absorbency of the sand, I doubt the resident crab is even aware of the insult.

In good weather or bad, when I come out of my runner's trance, I
feel as though I have experienced poignant, secret things that I could
not otherwise tap. This is no simple jogger's euphoria. The Gulf and
I have communed.

The Karankawas, the aborigines who once stalked this island, were
said on occasion to have stared unblinking and spellbound at the sun
rising out of the Gulf.[1] Perhaps. Much that is written about these Indians is apocryphal, but I tend to believe this account. I have done the
same thing, maybe for the same reasons, which at least in my case have
absolutely nothing to do with the anthropologist's arcane speculations
about religion or rituals. I do it spontaneously. I do it first out of simple
childish fascination. Also from an inherent wonder at things cosmic,
including this most fetching manifestation of the turning of the earth.
I do it for inspiration, whether my mood needs lifting or not. I do it
despite my knowledge of the damaging influence of ultraviolet radiation on my retinal maculae; I trust the heavy coastal atmosphere to
afford me some protection during my indulgence. I do it, I suppose,
because I do not have the willpower to resist.

Martha and I frequently drive to the beach to witness the spectacle
of sunrise—a good example of our simple but satisfying insular
lifestyle. The eastern sky is already aglow, the Gulf still dark, early
terns wheeling. We wait, and then it happens, abruptly. The bloodred
limb emerges from the slumbering sea, and the new day is ignited. I
can hardly view the spectacle without conjuring the preliminary, barely
audible strains and the rousing crescendo of full sunrise in Grofé's
"Grand Canyon Suite." If there is a bank of cirrus clouds hovering in
the east, our sunrise is transformed into a *sunburst,* a phantasmagoria
of glowing orange pink cobbles splintered by Day-Glo orange radiants.
On a clear morning we can look forward to the extra delight of a vivid
green flash flickering across the solar rim—the same apparition that
attends a clean sunset. After that magic moment the full body of the
sun clears the horizon quickly. It is an illusion, I suppose, but it seems
that if the sun moved at that initial rate all day, it would reach the
western horizon far ahead of its allotted time and so throw us all out
of kilter.

No matter, the spell is over. I glance aside, nagged by a purple
afterimage but filled with hope and enthusiasm. With this inspiring
beginning, how can I fail? Even in a world less cluttered, the Karankawas must have experienced the same jump start.

• • •

Matagorda is called a *barrier* island because it stands as a natural bulwark mitigating the clout of a storm-incensed Gulf against the ticky-tacky that people have imprudently erected on the coast. But a deeper significance involves neither humans nor storms. Watch the waves come rolling in, charging up the soft beach, dragging the sand about, even on a calm day. How does the island withstand this slight but ceaseless assault?

The beach is the key to the island's covenant with the Gulf. To understand that pact, you must first expand your vision of the beach to include the primary dune field at its back and the sandbars paralleling its front but submerged beneath the surf. They all work together as a shock absorber with sand as the resilient medium. The Gulf gives as well as takes. Waves and longshore currents bring sand even as they snatch it back again. The crucial aspect is the equilibrium—lots of energy expended to move lots of water and sand around, but in the end things looking pretty much the same from one day to the next. That is the special talent of this ultimate edge.

Look out, beyond the surf, to the swells rolling in off the Gulf. Focus on one. Picture it as an Olympic hurdler charging ahead: complete symmetry, athletic grace, supreme self-confidence, total concentration. Envision every glistening body part stretched taut in perfect synchrony, eyes fixed, cheeks puffing rhythmically, running directly down the barrel of a telephoto lens.

Suddenly, as the wave reaches the shallows, its toe scrapes the bottom, gouging up a mound of sand. The clean roll of water is thrown askew, its bottom hanging back while its top pitches forward, the smooth surface erupting into a foaming breaker. The master runner has tripped trying to clear the hurdle. Now he stumbles ahead in broken stride, arms flailing to regain balance. Both wave and runner have lost a lot of their initial poise and momentum.

In the midst of his throes the faltering runner tips the next hurdle and is further debilitated, even as the weakened wave breaks heavily over the next sandbar. The final hurdle comes all too soon. It throws the reeling runner sprawling on his face, and he skids to an ignominious stop. The tiring wave heaves across the innermost bar, laps up the inclined beach pushing a thin ridge of sand to its fore, and it too goes flat and drains away, its once proud vigor totally exhausted.

The barrier island has distracted the Gulf into tossing around tons of water and sand in such confusion that the waves make landfall with scarcely enough strength left to scribble a sinuous signature in the wet sand.

But the dance is not done. Sand that dries above the reach of the waves is picked up by the wind and bounced across the backbeach until it encounters an obstruction. Small piles become large piles, compounding until sand dunes with smooth, characteristically contoured windward and leeward slopes result. A sparse but tough assemblage of plants soon takes root and holds the dune field in place. The dune line protects the interior of the island from salt spray, sand blast, and wind erosion, and it holds back all but the most determined storm surges.

But these are secondary services. The main contribution of the sand dunes to the integrity of the island is their passive role as a sand bank, ever ready to accept a deposit or approve a withdrawal by the beach, which then hands the sand along to the hardworking offshore bars.

When the weather is fair and when the onshore breeze drives the water into shore at an angle, the waves tend to take extra sand from the bars and leave it on the beach. The wind picks up this sand and drops it in the dunes. During tropical storms and winter tempests, and times when the water meets the shore head-on, the waves gouge out chunks of beach and sap the bases of the dunes. The beach narrows, and the dunes lower as sand shelves into the surf to rebuild the bars.

In the wintertime, when northers enhance this movement of sand from dunes to surf, we see a spectacular display of fluent geology. The smooth dune crests quiver with spumes and curtains of norther-whipped sand. The dry grains coalesce into writhing streamers that form a wildly racing, ever-changing network suspended ankle high, ghostly pale above the dark, wet beach. Standing with the maelstrom hurtling toward us, we experience the illusion of moving rapidly forward; turning the other way evokes an even more giddy effect. A video camera produces a remarkably deceptive image.

Uncountable zillions of grains, cubic yards, tons of sand must be displaced from dunes to surf before a norther tires. It is truly a haunting vision, a phenomenon the geologist refers to as "saltation" but that we prefer to call "ghosting."

This remarkable cutting edge of the island is the geological analog of a waterfall, its relatively steady outward appearance the result of continual internal movement—in this case, reciprocal rather than one-way motion. The Gulf is appeased; the beach persists. So natural, so beautiful, so sensibly compromising. So neat that you have to be there to notice it at all.

Tidal passes at each end complete the margins of the island. Passes are important natural conduits between Gulf and lagoons, affording interchange of water, nutrients, sand, sea life, and pent-up energy. Pass Cavallo on the north end separates the island from Matagorda Peninsula, a long sand spit reaching down from the mouth of the Colorado River. This pass figured prominently in the early cultural history of Matagorda Island, admitting, and often wrecking, ships from the days of La Salle through the era of the Morgan steamers. The early port of Saluria and the Confederate Fort Esperanza both rose and fell on Pass Cavallo. A hurricane got the port. First the Yankees and then the sea took the fort. The durable lighthouse still stands as a historical monument only because it was moved inland from its original location on the shore of the pass.

The draft of Pass Cavallo was reduced when a great natural logjam on the Colorado River was dynamited in the 1930s, giving the river separate access to the sea. It was diminished again in 1963, with the opening of the Matagorda Ship Channel through Matagorda Peninsula four miles north of the natural pass. After that, seemingly immortal Pelican Island split apart and then disappeared from the mouth of the pass. In 1961, Hurricane Carla reshaped the channel and shifted its submarine bars, and the J-hook grew out into the tidal current. Through it all the pass persisted. Now humbled to mere recreational boat traffic, Pass Cavallo still helps maintain accord between island and Gulf.

Cedar Bayou to the south performs, on a smaller, more fickle scale, the same functions as Pass Cavallo. With many recollections, from Jean Laffite's sleek brigantines to the cumbersome hand-drawn ferry that hauled across Captain Peter Johnson's mule-drawn stagecoach, this shallow channel sometimes divides and sometimes unites Matagorda Island and St. Joseph Island.

Moving here, we crossed edges less material than the geographical ones. There were, for instance, "the elements," raw forces of nature that we were unaccustomed to meeting head-on. We came from a countryside with shade trees, rocks, logs, streams, songbirds. Matagorda Island offers only open, seamless sky, omnipresent sand, interminable wind, blazing sun, distance distended to a salt-hazed vanishing point, croaking herons. At first, the stark openness fostered a sense of unmitigated *vulnerability;* a weird paradox of claustrophobia and agoraphobia—of being tightly restrained in a wide-open place!

That sort of lingering distress eventually passed. Now I no longer walk around consciously fearful or thinking about imminent evacuation, yet neither am I totally relaxed. Call it apprehension or wary respect, a telling reminder that I am *on* this island but not *of* it. Have I failed to adapt? I rather fancy that admission of vincibility is a vital step to accommodation. I came here to enjoy the island's glory side; for that privilege I readily submit to its other side.

There is a rather surprising opposite side to the vulnerability coin that took awhile to expose itself. I am not sure it is healthy, but I am convinced that the opposing face shows itself more and more as we extend our tenure here, and there does not seem to be much that I can do about it. I call it "island syndrome"—the ever-increasing contrary tendency to regard the island as *more* secure than the hazardous mainland. We first noticed the effect during our monthly trips ashore for supplies: traffic, lights, noise, smoke, dust, flu, hurry, and everywhere, people in the way. The very place where we had spent most of our lives now was threatening to crush us. When we got back to our island, we heaved a sigh of relief, and we put off the next trip as long as possible. The island had become our escape, our hermitage, our retreat from the clangor and dregs of civilization; but it also meant that we had lost some of our ability to cope "on the other side." And that was not the end of the creeping syndrome.

We became increasingly alienated from the greater world. (I say "we." I am much more afflicted than Martha is.) Nothing really seemed to matter except what was happening on the island. No world or state event, no catastrophe, no celebration—nothing really registered except the mundane events going on right around us. In compensation, little things began to loom large. I would lose sleep over a balky generator, develop inordinate concern for an inflamed joint, worry about getting my monthly report done on time, or fret when the sandhill cranes did not appear on schedule. These mattered immensely. A natural response to prolonged serene isolation? I suppose so. An estimable response? Hardly, but there it is. And by consequence, when I am on this island, the rest of the world simply does not exist. A separate island universe for sure.

We were warned that we might contract "island fever," in its various forms a common ailment of insular residents. Sure enough, we are both victims. Again, I think I am more sickened by the malady than Martha is. If I may self-diagnose, mine is a psychosomatic disease that derives from isolation in paradise exacerbated by a propensity for a sedentary lifestyle.

I prefer to visit one place twice over two places once each; one place a hundred times rather than a hundred new ones; intimacy and every-dayness over casual acquaintance and constant stimulation; home to anywhere else. Here I can satisfy vicariously any dim stir of wander-lust, for world-class long-distance travelers periodically pause at my doorstep. Observing a group of migrating red knots hungrily probing for coquinas in the swash puts me into contact with the Queen Eliza-beth Islands in the high Arctic, the spectacular spawn of horseshoe crabs in Delaware Bay, and the bountiful mudflats of San Antonio Oeste on the wild coast of Argentina; a span of ten thousand ventur-ous miles in a blink of my mind's eye. Why should I go anywhere else?

So, I soon bonded with my sublime surroundings. That union in-evitably spawned strong feelings of respect bordering on the devout. In this day of multiple environmental threats, respect prudently wells into concern. In isolation, concern easily slides into paranoia and the culmi-nating symptom of island fever: "Stay off my island!" It is a jealous, possessive, and unseemly attitude and one that is especially misplaced and frustrated on a wildlife refuge open to the public. However, I sub-mit from my biased vantage, the compulsion is not really an abnormal one; indeed, it may be quite natural. I fight it, but I expect no cure.

Here comes a mob of noisy aliens onto hallowed ground. How am I to react? I respond by stifling my flicker of anxiety and welcoming them ashore. Invariably the people prove amiable, interested, respect-ful of the island, and fun to talk with. Despite myself, I have a great day. Yet, when they leave, even though I experience a rewarding sense of accomplishment, I am glad they are gone. I will go through the same agony next time, for apparently the disease, once contracted, is lifelong.

On a barrier island your mood is influenced by the very air itself. The combination of high temperature and high humidity with sea-level altitude, forms a stultifying mix that takes getting used to. The contents of the salt shaker congeal into a solid lump. Matches will not strike, and mildew grows while you watch. Tableware rusts; breadbox-size propane refrigerators need weekly defrosting; cellular telephones commonly lose contact with their base station; radio messages break up. Electrical contacts misfire in the salty atmosphere; computers turn morose, windshields wear a perpetual glaze, and motor vehicles balk for a dozen corrosive reasons. You need to acclimate physically and immunologically as well as emotionally.

Wind, generating waves and currents, lifting sand and pushing weather, is the chief mechanical force that forms, maintains, and disrupts a barrier island. But wind is also an "edge," a daily factor to contend with. Wind that cools the skin and that chills the bones; wind that can titillate or sandblast; wet wind and dry wind; occasional wind and interminable wind. Wind that holds the mosquitoes at bay; wind from the most aggravating direction when you handle paper or fold up a tarpaulin or just try to get an arm into a jacket sleeve. Wind that will not be ignored.

Northers arrive with an unimpeded rush, pushing water against the island, crashing over the oyster-shell ridges, and chilling all with their wet gusts. We generally have a day or so of gale-force southeast winds that vent into the low pressure that precedes a norther. These come off the Gulf, and they not only warn us but warm us. Then the norther pounces, causing the mercury to plummet. Although we are usually spared truly frigid conditions, the wet wind and the sharp contrast in temperature chills to the marrow. Some of my most vivid memories of Matagorda Island involve weathering a hard norther in our insubstantial house trailer perched three feet off the ground with its bottom insulation in shreds.

JANUARY '95: *Just after good dark the norther slammed into the trailer like a freight train. We rocked alarmingly but finally settled down to a minor jolt each time a fresh gust came across. I could hear our milk boxes and water carboys stored underneath go rattling off into the grass; they will be far and wide tomorrow. Fortunately, we were forewarned by the southeast wind, so I had tied a tarp over the outside of the front door and tacked a wool blanket inside. Windows and electrical outlets have got their winter seal of duct tape. Still enough cracks for the wind to set up an unnerving banshee howl, like the beast was going to be amongst us at any moment. Heater is running, but it quickly began to lose ground. We opened the oven and turned it on high, then stood beside it to absorb what heat we could before it dissipated. Not much help. Already down to forty-eight degrees Fahrenheit inside; too cold to concentrate on anything deeper than numb fingers and prickly ears. Colder below; a knee-deep layer of refrigerated air seeps up through the floor. Even our harvest mouse boarder looked cold when he emerged from his retreat. So, without need for preliminary discussion, we entered into what has become our routine last-ditch defense: we got ready for bed. For me that meant pulling on long johns, donning two pairs of socks, and piling in. Martha still insists on a shower. I tell her I am in my "winter mode," which means nothing but emergency contact with water. She claims if I do not shower, I cannot snuggle, but the cold changed her mind. I knew it would. Nothing like a head-to-toe embrace beneath a heavy pile of blankets to make life seem not just barely livable but well worth living! We drifted off to the penetrating thrum of a metal tie-down strap vibrating in the wind and a loose piece of duct tape snapping against the window. Let this old norther blow; all it is doing is giving us a special form of togetherness.*

Then there is "The Wind," a force the Caribs deified as "Hurakán." Norman said "hurry-cane." The Anglo pioneers in this coastal country caught the baleful and exotic flavor of these big storms with "West Indian cyclones." By any name, the implication is the same for all coastal residents: Watch out!

We moved to this barrier island with our eyes open. The bad news was that it lies smack in the storm belt where a hurricane can be expected every four to five years and a supertempest takes aim every twelve years or so. Our evacuation route includes nine miles of open water and roads with stretches at or near sea level. The good news was that Matagorda Island, because of its broad, grassy interior and substantial dune fields, was judged relatively safe from all but a powerful right-hand landfall—the worst punch a cyclone can throw. Although the back side of the island has been flooded by storm tides at least a dozen times in the last century, the substantial dune ridge has prevented a general washover, even during the ferocity of Hurricane Carla, which slammed straight into Pass Cavallo with winds more than 170 miles per hour in 1961.

All this aside, when we moved here in 1993, we unknowingly brought with us an impregnable defense that no statistician or historian can factor into an equation of doom—phenomenal good luck. We have been threatened only once, in 1999, when Hurricane Bret wavered at the last moment and made landfall below Corpus Christi. Bret ended a decade without a hurricane anywhere along the Texas coast, and it has been over three decades since the immediate Coastal Bend was savaged by Carla. The trouble with luck is that you never know how long it will hold and there is no sure way to keep it stoked.

Although I do not see much predictive value in the homespun philosophy of "the futher we are from the last hurry-cane, the closer we be to the next 'un," I am not complacent. If we stay on, our luck will run out, and a rickety house trailer on a barrier island is no place to challenge a cyclone. We have no such intention. If it looks grim, we will stash our books on a high shelf in the generator house, grab up the computers, leave the rest of our belongings to fate, and hie across Mesquite Bay.

Cyclone—born of the same transient heat of condensation that fosters gentle dewdrops and wispy ground fog. Like the diamondback rattlesnake, it impresses this coast with a singular, tantalizing psychological dimension.[2] The willful storm can maim, kill, devastate. Less brutal but more agonizing is the *threat* of a cyclone—the realization that you are trespassing where the surly counterwhirling winds traditionally roam, that nothing you build can be regarded as permanent, that none of your possessions are safe, that no plan you lay can take the fickle beast fully into account; that you and yours are in a jeopardy of your own making, *that you are asking for it.*

Yet, the menace of a cyclone is not all bad. Where the monotony of the sea and the weight of the air can seduce the most determined intellect into prolonged narcosis, the dread of a cyclone is an edge that keeps the mind alert. The lives of human residents of the area would be more drab without the threat of their magnificent storms. For all the anxiety and wreckage that cyclones lay on the land, I would not for a moment have them quashed any more than I would have rattlers eradicated.

I do not say this from armchair vantage. I have been there, several times, although not within range of a tidal surge. The first time, I was at an impressionable age, so I can relive the event. I can see the windmill wobble, begin to lose its blades, splinter, and then explode; the heavy barn door somersaulting on edge across the yard; the air filled with chicken feathers, tree branches, fence pickets, and roof shingles. I can hear the awful, unremitting roar of the wind, recoil to the sting of the rain as we broke from the shuddering house to a recess beneath the heavy trestle at the river, feel Aunt Stell's grip on my hand tighten while the storm clawed at our refuge. Scary at the time, but over half a century later I cherish that memory. It was a genuine experience in

Nature at a receptive time, and it purged me of any latent hubris toward the out-of-doors.

Once great storms were unnamed. They arrived unannounced to any who lacked the acumen to read the haze in the air, the swells piling against the wind, and the water rising outside its designated time. They so terrorized coastal populations as to become enduring landmarks in time. "Well, I can't recollect exactly, but it was before Beulah."

Today we demean and even commercialize hurricanes. We name them with gender-proper etiquette, hem them in with an "official" season, nitpick them according to wind speed and surge height, dissemble them with statistics, dog their trails and try to predict their tracks, raise awareness while whipping up panic, oversell everything from milk to batteries, vie to provide television coverage of the misery and mayhem, and judge their every nuance in terms of human lives and human dollars while playing down human arrogance.

Cyclones are a dominant part of what little wildness remains along this overpopulated, overmanaged, overdeveloped, overcoddled, overforecast coastline. Like the presence of the tsetse fly in parts of Africa, the threat of cyclones along the Gulf Coast keeps great tracts of land from being totally engulfed by the surrounding human population. They belong. Give them their space. Let them be.

We learned stoically to meet the other elements. Rain, for instance, is more impressive inside our trailer than outside. The weather-beaten metal roof is paper thin, its seams leaky, and in one spot I put my foot right through the ceiling while applying roofing tar. But it was a rare hailstorm that really did our roof in. Before that, we caught leaks in coffee cans; afterward, it took five-gallon buckets harvested from the beach. During one week of deluge we had eleven plastic buckets strategically located and a twelfth ready for quick rotation. We needed to empty them periodically—including a night shift—to keep them from overflowing. Drip strings tacked to the ceiling directed the water into containers on the floor without creating a waist-high splash. It still sounded like we were living inside a waterfall. Books and computers were covered with garbage liners. Light bulbs in ceiling sockets mysteriously filled with water.

Despite our best efforts, the particleboard floor got soaked and soon heaved and hardened into ankle-deep folds ever ready to trip the unwary. By some act of providence the roof above our bed held until one heavy downpour finally breached even that sanctum. When I think of rain on Matagorda Island, I think of the long drumming night spent not daring to turn from my flat-on-the-back position, a five-gallon container clasped between my knees to catch the stream of water dribbling from the ceiling. Martha thought it was funny; I was only mildly amused. Better than total frustration, anyway. We used our pet phrase for the situation: "If you are going to live on a barrier island, you have got to make certain adjustments."

Thunder comes in two basic varieties, I think: startling and soul lifting. I have heard louder, more reverberating thunderclaps in the limestone canyons of the Hill Country, but I have never jumped as high as when the sky explodes on this island. I suppose the personal exposure here makes the difference. Such violent thunder accompanies fast-moving weather fronts and is usually short-lived. The squall lines barge across the island to lose themselves in the Gulf of Mexico. I recorded our first such experience.

OCTOBER '95: *The afternoon had gotten calm and sultry, a warning of something impending. No wind out here, you take notice. Sure enough, a band of purple gray clouds heaved up in the north, flickering with lightning. The weather came at us in a hurry, and soon we could hear and feel the throb of thunder. The cloud bank quickly loomed over the ranch house and poised to pounce, while the sun, low in a clear sky, cast an intense golden light against the dark, rumbling backdrop. A sudden wind gust brought us out of our trance, and we retreated into the trailer as the squall line blasted across, headed for the Gulf. Out the south window we watched the weather liven the bluestem into a rippling sea. Then, at an instantaneous flash-blast-and-tremor, we saw a red fireball erupt a quarter mile away. Before we could react, the same thing happened again just to the west, and we heard other detonations around us. Lightning bolts were stabbing down and igniting the grass. The initial compact, ruby red domes flared into orange red flames, and our astonishment turned to concern when we realized that we were surrounded by half a dozen spreading grass fires. Before we had fully decided to get into the pickup and drive out of danger, a hard shower quenched the hot spots. Within half an hour the black tempest was out hammering the Gulf, and we were left with the acrid smell of wet-grass smoke, a spectacular sunset, and the feeling that we were not just lucky to be safe and sound, but fortunate to have shared in this special time.*

For me anyway, soul-lifting thunder comes from both within and without. Late in a summer afternoon, after a withering day, a stupendous thunderhead rises out of the Gulf, its billows and turrets swirled with every shade of gray. Garnished with subtle pastel highlights and cleaved with dark chasms, the roiling cloud mass is capped with a signal windswept anvil. Cool sheet lightning skips repeatedly across high crevasses, and the great cloud begins to mutter to itself. I am far enough away to feel secure from its violence, close enough to hold the promise of a cooling shower, situated just right to be enthralled with its awesome power and majesty. Each time the cloud rumbles, I quiver, not in fear but in ecstasy.

On a barrier island sunshine ranks among "the elements." Of course, it powers the ecosystem, generates the weather, and moderates the winters, but the sun's rays are also an important edge to contend with. I frequently ask visitors what they regard as the most dangerous aspect of Matagorda Island. Rattlesnakes rank high, followed by hurricanes, alligators, stingrays, and undertows. I point to the sun, and although they still hold tanned skin in esteem, most people seem to get the message. Indeed, some realize that they are already sunburned from their half-hour boat trip to the island.

Sunshine is a force that I, with red hair, blue eyes, and freckles, had to take into serious account while considering this position. All my shirts are long-sleeved, and I never wear shorts. I always wear a hat outside, and Martha made me a neck drape that buttons onto my Service cap, giving me a jaunty French Foreign Legion air. My spectacles are coated with a film that absorbs ultraviolet rays. My beard is not just for convenience or show; it protects my face from the sun. On the beach, where solar radiation comes from above and also ricochets off the sand and water, I slather on sunscreen and wear cotton gloves with the fingers cut out to protect the backs of my hands while retaining dexterity. Despite all my precautions, I have developed keratitis on my left forearm, which I absentmindedly expose in the truck window while driving. Although Martha does not flaunt her advantage, her brown complexion renders her as deftly fit for this island as a sand crab.

One of the most depressing images I have ever seen is a satellite photograph taken at night showing the entire nation ablaze with lights. Every metropolis either shows itself individually or is fused with its suburbs and adjacent cities into a luminous reticulum. It is easy to trace the east and west coasts, the outline of the Great Lakes, and the arc of the Gulf of Mexico. Locally, I can pinpoint Houston, Victoria, and Corpus Christi. Happily, there are dark voids, and Matagorda Island lies hidden in one.

Darkness is not conventionally thought of as an elemental force, but here it definitely ranks at least as an elemental *presence,* something to be reckoned with. Here, night is more than an interlude holding days apart; it has a substance of its own. This insular darkness seems more than a mere absence of light, far deeper than the earth's shadow. It is as though we are *immersed* in a palpable silken liquid that immobilizes but does not suffocate.

Except to view the constellations, I do not move around much outside in the dark, for then mosquitoes are on the rise, and rattlesnakes are on the move. At least, there is only a vanishing likelihood of a criminal lurking in the night. (I am always chagrined when I try to show city-bred, mugger-conscious youngsters the constellations, to find they are at first reluctant to brave the dark even for the much-anticipated star show. Prudent perhaps, but a shame.) Out here, for us at least, the darkness itself is not inherently scary. It does not foster demons or bring on an uncontrollable bout of shuddering. Rather, it is a delicious experience, a time to gently touch body to body, to talk quietly, to pull the sheet up against the onshore breeze, and finally to lapse, hover in transcendence, and then drift away into that secure black oblivion.

Sand is so ubiquitous on a barrier island as to also merit elemental status. Not sand in its geological and ecological roles, piled in dunes or spread across the backbone of the island. But grit in your food, around the back of your neck, beneath your eyelids, between the sheets, on the floor minutes after it was swept. Until you quit trying to brush sand away, you have not adjusted to the island.

To reside on Matagorda Island, you must be prepared to live in a time warp, to cross a paradoxical temporal edge where the human dimension exists on a treadmill, surrounded by cycles, caught up in an endlessness where both anticipation and procrastination lose their meaning and advance is offset by stark indifference. In contrast, real time on the island marches resolutely ahead to the measured beat of a distant drummer. Sediment fills the bays, the island shuffles to the south, the continental shelf creaks downward, sea level wavers.

Martha and I have been here forever, it seems. Yet, this chain of barriers along the coast has existed for only about five thousand years, an eye blink of planetary time, and it will likely not last beyond a second blink. Eternity and oblivion side by side.

When I taught school, I consulted my wristwatch a hundred times a day. Within a week of moving to Matagorda Island, I took my watch off, first because the sweat and sand beneath the band were aggravating, then because I realized that the hours and minutes had become irrelevant.

Time moves slowly out here, so slowly that there is plenty of it to squander. I had to reframe my notion of progress, to regard a day as successful with nothing more to show than the realization that I had done no harm. (Wasn't it John Steinbeck who asked so poignantly why it is that progress always looks so much like destruction?) Certainly, I do not rise each morning with the definite intent of doing nothing, but if that is the way things play out, then it is no big deal. Tomorrow will do.

Early on, both Martha and I were concerned with what we called "the problem of sloth." Our apprehension was well founded, for we did indeed cross a definite edge from a relatively active lifestyle to a decidedly passive one. I left bustling undergraduate academia; Martha left a busy homemaker's ambiance. We descended abruptly into this estranged insular environment.

The quandary was not how to avoid boredom; with our mutual interest in the out-of-doors, we could never exhaust the intrigue of this coastal paradise. Rather, we had to beware of settling in too completely—of letting the salt air, high humidity, soporific sea, and pleasant natural surroundings envelope us in a lotus-eater's swoon. Out here it is *too* easy to escape. First hours, then days and months fly by in empyreal succession. Procrastination comes naturally, and it can become addicting. Intellectual stagnation is a constant threat. Listlessness—before you know it, your life is slipping away and you either do not notice, or worse, you do not care. Of course, you can take Thoreau's view to heart and consider idled hours to be the ones best spent. But even Henry David worked much more industriously than he admitted.

So, we had to adjust. We both read. Martha enjoys cyberspace (but with no telephone lines, no "information highway"), her digital camera, beachcombing, and all sorts of handcrafts. I am more limited and more susceptible to aimlessness. Rambling in Nature is my abiding love, and I continually need to beware of pleasuring too much here. On a pretty morning, I just cannot stay inside. To justify my indulgence, I strive to share by conducting the environmental education program (in which Martha works side by side with me) and by writing. I have already reached the stage where I enjoy watching kids make everyday discoveries on the beach or in the marsh fully as much as I like uncovering something new there myself. I feel good when a group leaves the island better informed and more concerned about the barrier ecosystem than when they arrived. They will be our stewards one day, if they and the island last so long. Maybe I have set a few of them on a compassionate track. I like to think so.

Despite good intentions, I quickly lost track of days of the week, including weekends, holidays, and my days off. Calendar days faded, and even the months seemed inconsequential. Mail a week late made no difference. Out here we could afford to substitute harmony for punctuality, so we synchronized with the natural rhythms. Tick marks are everywhere: daybreak, day length, phase of the moon, reigning constellations, track of the sun, pulse of the tide, first blossoms on the woolly globe mallows, spring and fall appearance of ruddy turnstones on the beach; whether the meadow frogs are calling, the barn swallows have arrived, the coffee sennas have set fruit. First scissor-tailed flycatcher today; it must be about mid-March.

But natural indicators are cyclic. To mark time in untrammeled nature, the human mind needs a *chronology,* a tally of annual cycles set into a sequence. Then one can recognize perturbations, discern trends, cherish memories, look ahead. That used to be a function of the tribal elders; out here my diary suffices. Then there is my Matagorda Stonehenge.

Having moved into the center of a nearly uninterrupted horizon, I thought of tracking the sun. As the Wynne Ranch headquarters includes an airstrip in the shape of a cross, I chose the center of the intersection as my reference mark. On March 21, I stood at the designated spot and watched the sun clear the sand dunes across the slumbering grassland. I set a post on a sight line a hundred yards out in the bluestem to be my equinox marker. Two weeks later I went out in the predawn and took a reading to double-check on Copernicus. Sure enough, the sun rose approximately one diameter north of my post.

When the sun hesitated on June 21, I sank a second post, and I was gratified to find that it lay tolerably close to 23.5 degrees north of the first post. Again I was elated when, on September 23, the rising sun crowned my equatorial post again. The final post was erected on December 22, and it, too, was close enough to 23.5 degrees south to keep up my faith in celestial mechanics.[3] With the sun reliably corralled between the tropics of Cancer and Capricorn and precisely skewered at the equinoxes, I felt a twinge of that pride and power that must have exalted the high priests when they confirmed their control of the sky.

Visitors are fascinated with my rudimentary tracking device, what Martha calls my set of Druid posts. For all its simplicity, it elicits a flood of questions that underscore how little we know—how much we have forgotten—about our everyday world. Does the sun *really* move back and forth like that? Why does it always stop right there and turn around? Why does the sun go north in the *summertime* and not in the wintertime? What do you mean, "celestial equator"? What is a Druid? Why in the world did they name it Cancer? How come there aren't two equinox posts? What does "solstice" mean? Would sunset be as good a mark as sunrise? And so on. I am no high priest, but I hold exalted WGA status. I speak and the sun obeys. And all the while, on Matagorda Island the memories pile up and time marches on.

Near the end of a fun day, while visitors are waiting for the boat, I like to ask them what they enjoyed most about the island. Kids will immediately mention the beach or specify ghost crabs, alligators, or some other creature that excited them. Adults are more reflective, and an amazing proportion of them finally say that it is the quiet, the isolation that most impressed them. "I envy you two, living here in such splendid solitude."

We do indeed lead a removed, if not truly idyllic, lifestyle. However, pleasant though it is, it takes some getting used to. Adult visitors claim they yearn for the secluded life, but I suspect they really mean they enjoy a brief respite. Many maintain that a day on Matagorda Island is a delightful opportunity to be alone in nature. Yet, Martha and I are with visitors every moment they are afield, and for safety reasons we stress that none should strike out on their own. They are nicely separated from the civilized world, but they definitely are not alone. I doubt that one in a hundred ever has spent an entire day without seeing another human being, nor is the experience easy to imagine in other than a fanciful way. Living a significant portion of your life alone is a different, somewhat eerie existence; and it is not all serene.

First, Matagorda Island is no mythic Walden. It is a national wildlife refuge and state natural area, with management goals and controlled access by the general public. A work crew comes across from the mainland five days a week, and other governmental personnel arrive now and then. Except during the dead of winter and the high heat of summer, we host a stream of visiting groups at our Environmental Education Center. Occasionally, a graduate student spends some time here doing field research. On most days, if I cruise the shoreline, I encounter several people fishing. And of course, Martha and I have each other.

Ordinarily, everyone leaves at about four o'clock in the afternoon, and we are alone until the next weekday morning. If we have no group scheduled, we see no one except distant fishermen on holidays and weekends.

When people leave, the sudden quiet falls like a curtain. It is both relaxing and a bit unsettling. Suddenly, we are truly alone, not just to do our own thing but to survive, each to tolerate our own personality as well as that of our partner in a forced togetherness that has got to work if we are to endure. There are other times, ranging from a few days to nearly two weeks, when there is no one else. Those are the times when you really discover whether you have in fact adjusted to life on a barrier island.

Of the five major barrier islands on the Texas coast, only two, Matagorda and St. Joseph, are still functional islands. The others, islands no more, are connected to the mainland by causeways. It is amazing how definitely and how poignantly even a small unspanned body of water like Mesquite Bay can create and hold apart two worlds. Access by people, arrival of supplies, evacuation in emergency—*everything*—has to come across the water. Boats break down or simply do not arrive and depart on time. And boats are at the mercy of the weather. Inclement weather exacerbates the gap between continent and island both physically and emotionally.

With our moods already depressed by a dark and wet February day, it is, if not actually discomfiting, at least bizarre to realize that we are the only human beings on Matagorda Island. Literally, we are out of sight and out of mind. We might as well be the last two people on earth. We are, indubitably, together/alone.

At Christmastime, Martha leaves to visit kin. I am invited, but I decline. Other FWS personnel are glad for me to keep up official presence on the island over the long holidays. Consequently, I am no longer together/alone; I am alone/alone.

The experience is at once delightful, sobering, and otherworldly. I have an undisturbed, uninhabited, intriguing universe to explore and cavort in according to my whim. I am familiar with this barrier. I know many of its secret places, the haunts of most of its fascinating creatures, and I know to beware of its beguiling moods. Perhaps it is rash, but I feel not the slightest twinge of fear or sense of peril while alone here. I spend my days afield, happily absorbed in the moment, and I while away an appalling amount of time doing nothing in particular.

ONE WINTER DAY IN SOLITUDE: *A perfect day with nothing to show at the end except what was here at the beginning. No dirt displaced, no streams detoured, no trees felled, no animals killed. No discontent with this day of sloth, no sense of deprivation for lack of worldly acquisition. Nothing to buy and nowhere to buy it, so even thinking about money is to squander my wealth of time. No schedule-seeking frenzy. Insistent quiet rather than incessant noise. Spiritual rather than material satisfaction. A different sort of in-place progress, a delight that takes some getting used to.*

Yet, when I try to commune with this island during these solitary intervals, I am engaging in soliloquy. No matter the intimacy I strive for, I remain manifestly apart. Too many civilized generations, too much artificial clutter, too many hours comfortably ensconced separate us now. Even here on a wildlife refuge where they are not threatened, all the animals keep a wary eye on me; and it is well that they do, for my species is a perfidious one.

It is just as well, I shrug. I do not really aspire to be a working part, a happenstance, an unconscious entity, unnoticed while here, unremembered when gone, driven inexorably by the need to prove my fitness against an unseen scale, ever striving just to exist, one of the wild bunch.

But if I am content to be a cognizant observer, it is still bothersome to appreciate how utterly inconsequential I am to all that goes on here. Although individual animals may skitter at my appearance, the barrier ecosystem—this world of sea and sand that I so admire and yearn to comprehend—is totally indifferent to my existence. It managed before

I arrived; it tolerates my presence; it will continue unperturbed when
I leave. Worse than my being abhorred or loved, the island simply does
not care, never has and never will.

Still, in utter solitude here, I occasionally yearn to belong. No matter. I will settle for the role of arm's-length guest and be as polite as I
can. Have I been in solitary here too long?

It is not my relationship with the island that concerns me while I am
alone; it is my relationship with myself. Inevitably, involuntarily, a sojourn of solitude becomes an interval of penetrating introspection. I
find myself thinking overmuch about me. For better or worse, I am the
only companion I have. I must contrive to get along.

After only a day or two, I habitually talk aloud to animals, to things,
and to myself. Sometimes I think I lapse into a weird nonverbal
thought pattern, just an uninterrupted and uncontrollable stream of
consciousness. I can hear myself think. Often I feel disembodied and
raised on high where I can look down and see myself, and I judge how
I am behaving. Some days I do not like what I see, and those are the
only days I feel lonely.

Am I letting what remains of my life dribble away among these
sand dunes? What am I searching for here? What am I trying to accomplish? What *can* I accomplish out here apart from humankind?
Need I achieve anything? Why not just *be?* I scribbled in my diary
during my second week of isolation.

DECEMBER '95: *No dawn on this, the last day of the year. Totally overcast
with a cold, slanting rain. Puddles inside the trailer. Cooped up. Feel stiff.
Tried chatting with the harvest mouse who has moved into the trailer for the
winter, but he seemed not to be in a garrulous mood, for directly after
nibbling crumbs, he retired into the couch. He will sleep the day away;
perhaps I should do the same.*

*Finally did get out for a round in the pickup. Not much to see. The island
is a sodden brown, the sea an uninviting gray, the beach lifeless; everything
looks extra grim through the smear of the windshield wipers. Just to verify
that there was a larger world out there, I flipped on the truck radio and
happened to tune in the traffic report from Houston. Ten seconds of that
frenzy was enough. I snapped the radio off with my conviction reaffirmed: I
am here partly to ensure that I am not there.*

*Cheered, I watched a peregrine toying with a raft of green-winged teal
and saw a coyote catch a mullet. Then spent the rest of the day reading,*

writing, and shivering. Got dark early. After hot soup, I mulled over New Year's resolutions but concluded that there was no need to commit to change. I will just muddle on.

Tried to hang on until midnight but could not. Am I getting jaded? What difference out here anyway? Another day, another month, another year, a fresh diary. Even the harvest mouse, who surely will never see another New Year, remained through the chilly night, I think, in the bowels of the couch with wet nose pressed to warm belly, a rhythmically heaving featureless ball of fur. I have unintentionally corrupted that mouse by providing him with room and board. He, in turn, has perverted me with his euphoric, bulbous-eyed vision of the everlasting present. I suppose that my aspirations for the New Year are no more consequential than his. If we both wake in the morning and regard each other across the breakfast table, we will be off to a good start in our respective directions.

If you are going to live on a barrier island, self-dependence comes with the territory. Emergencies spring first to mind, the many "what ifs?": chest pains, a broken leg, a rattlesnake bite. Our first line of defense is common sense—we try to lead a healthy lifestyle and keep an eye out for hazards. Norman once told me matter-of-factly, "Well, yew don't want to plan to have no trouble when yew're out cheer alone. If yew do, well, yew jest gotta deal with it." It is not quite as bad as that. We do have a telephone number posted on the wall that is supposed to get us a helicopter from Corpus Christi within half an hour. Fortunately, we have never had occasion to try.

The little annoying things demand self-reliance: the generator coughs and quits, the pickup refuses to start, the water pump dies with a horrible grinding whine and a shower of sparks, first the commode backs up and then the drain field overflows, the front door blows off its hinges, the last light bulb flashes and goes dark, there is no more toothpaste. The island is no different than the mainland—things tend to go wrong on Fridays or holidays. Even on a weekday there is no convenient Wal-Mart. Norman had uncomforting advice, "Well, yew jest make do'er do without."

I am not all that good a fixer, but I have made quite a few silk purses from a rubble of sows' ears. The maintenance men speak of a "Matagorda fix," which means wiring, welding, nailing, duct-taping, or just brutally forcing something together until you can get a spare part. And if ingenuity is not up to the task, you do in fact "do without."

When we are without electricity, we make do with oil lamps. Without running water, we have bathed in a pool with a ring of curious alligators in audience. With the pickup down, we walk, sometimes for miles, occasionally in the dark, always attended by mosquitoes. Without heat, we bundle up to our eyeballs. Without civilization, we go primeval.

We seldom host a group of adults without one or more members (always women; the men take certain basics for granted) asking us about groceries. We keep a list and take it when we go shopping; we buy large quantities; we rely more on canned and dried food (including milk) than frozen, because it is a long, chancy haul to the freezer. We buy lots of produce and glut on it while it lasts. No garden here; well water is too salty, and deer are perpetually hungry. Martha makes bread, and I catch lots of fish; we sometimes have them so fresh that their jaws are still snapping spasmodically in the offal bucket when the hot baked fillets come to the table.

When we go across for groceries, about every three weeks, each item gets handled a minimum of eight times between grocery shelf and kitchen counter. For durability we shift from plastic bags to cloth ones. Cold stuff is carried in picnic ice boxes. Forget ice cream and the like; it will never make it. The trip involves, besides our private vehicle, a pickup on the mainland, the boat, and another pickup on the island, none of which is entirely reliable. Every sort of mishap is possible: a sack dropped into the water; a bag tipped over in the jolting boat, spilling its contents into the bilge; a satchel left in the pickup, sure raccoon fodder. An item is not really guaranteed until we consume it.

Our move onto the island brought blessings in disguise, most significantly a forced leap to simplicity. We had to leave much of our "stuff" behind. Only when pressed to cull did we realize how much was mere encumbrance. Once outside the mainstream we felt relieved of the inadvertent, mindless drive to grow, acquire, achieve, appear, glut, compete. Our regimen of restraint became an avenue to a different, less invasive sort of fullness. In the end, we are enriched rather than deprived by our pared-down lifestyle. And by being forced to live gently on this island, we simultaneously press with a softer touch on the larger environment that must succor our meager needs. It is a good feeling.

The first step to restraint is awareness. Take electricity. Although we could survive without it, even at this remote outpost we need at least minimal electrical power to lead a productive existence. We have a small propane generator for the house and a solar panel to run a water-pressure pump, a cellular telephone (which works at the whim of the atmosphere), and a reading light. Without telephone lines, there is no Internet, no fax machine, no bother. I wish we were all solar, but the Service regards additional collecting panels as too expensive, and wind generators would be hazardous to our streams of migrating birds.

The generator is housed in a small building all its own outside the back door, and although we have grown to ignore the sound of the thing, our ears prick up instantly at the least waver in its steady roar, and when it does falter, I hustle to give it an assist. Living under its dominion, we have come to regard it with the same resignation as the ravages of old age—it is better than the alternative. I ritually turn the infernal machine on in the predawn and off at bedtime. I minister to its every need: oil, filter, plugs, coolant, fuel; and coddle it through bouts of corrosion, worn brushes, and general malaise. In return we have power for lights and word processors on an isolated barrier island.

But not for flagrant use. If we turn on the microwave and coffeemaker at the same time, the generator snaps us into reality by throwing its overload switch and deadening the entire house. If salt air glazes the rotor or fire ants nest among the circuit breakers, nothing happens when I crank up in the morning, and our whole day hangs up. At night when I shut the generator down, I watch the lights in the house quickly damp and blink out as the roar sucks in on itself and the metal house ceases to vibrate. I stand there in the dark, weaving a bit off balance from sudden lack of sight and sound. Whatever else, we do not take electricity for granted. Or windmills and water, or propane and heat, or even sea breeze and its coolness.

When I return after being off-island, I head for the beach. There the sand underfoot, the sucking thrum of the surf, and the roll and aroma of the sea quickly complete my purge. I experience the contrasting sensations of being completely drained and fully revitalized; at once relaxed and refreshed. As far as I can see into the white salt haze up and down the beach, tranquillity reigns. "This beach is not pristine," I tell visitors. "Look at all the trash and you can see as much. But it is undeveloped, and in today's world that is as good as it gets."

As good as it gets. In fact, our trashed beach on Matagorda Island is the ideal, the yardstick against which the deleterious effect of human presence is measured on other Texas barrier beaches. Mercifully, this innocent strip of sand has never known the dreadful, ungoverned seethe of humanity that attends Spring Break and the Fourth of July along other sections of the Texas coast. No tacky concessions, blaring radios, obscene beach parties, lowest common denominators. Its forebeach is not rutted and hard-packed by the weight of traffic or sifted and effectively sterilized by cleaning machines. Its sand dunes are still in place, unburdened, unfenced, and unscathed. Its wild residents are abundant, diverse, and tolerably naive. For how long? Hopefully, as "forever" as it can get. This is, after all, a national wildlife refuge.

Yet, even from this remote coign of vantage, I worry. I do not stump around in a dark funk, but neither can I afford to stroll in unmitigated bliss. World powers exist in uneasy truce, democracies are not forethoughty, new technologies rise and spread before being adequately plumbed for harmful environmental side effects, land managers often think they are wiser than Mother Nature, public attitudes change, memorandums-of-agreement lapse, laws get reinterpreted, people beget more people.

And Matagorda Island is not as isolated as it seems. It lies downhill from everywhere, so it can be seriously affected from a distance. Dams on local rivers impede the flow of freshwater, nutrients, sand, and sediment to the bays. The big jetties up the coast hold back the natural longshore flow of sand to the island and throttle the normal ebb and flood through Pass Cavallo. The local bays get overfertilized and polluted with runoff from chemically doped agricultural fields, shrimp farm outfalls, and municipal storm sewers, which, especially in the summertime, consume dissolved oxygen, creating dead zones and succoring smothering populations of toxic red and brown microorganisms that foster more zones just as dead. Shrimp trawls scour the bay bottoms mercilessly while oyster dredges chop at the live reefs and trappers overexploit the population of blue crabs.

The tide of ecotourists is rising to ominous proportions, its desire to witness Disneyesque Nature accompanied by its demand for human access and convenience. Everywhere, houses are going up and people are moving in. The popularized dictum that humans and Nature can coexist without significant sacrifice by either quarter is the hopeful but doomed slogan for the Corpus Christi National Estuary Program and similar well-meaning coalitions. Until someone in charge admits that there are simply too many people on the Texas coast—whether they be environmentally aware or heedlessly exploitative—Nature will continue to take a beating.

While there is time, it would not hurt to give this heretofore fortunate island an additional edge, something in reserve, a hedge against the day when humans decide that Nature is not doing a good enough job of caring for this exposed strip of sand.

How about a patron saint; a benefactor; an elder with exclusive knowledge who is not reluctant or restrained in spreading the unvarnished word to the masses; an oracle confident enough to speak predictions in plain language rather than in suggestive vagaries; someone untouchable by chambers of commerce, real estate dealers, or local politicians; a secular Assisi, with compassion updated from concern for soulful-eyed animals to a hard-eyed vision of entire coastal landscapes and of barrier islands in particular; a zealot who, when challenged, only gets more resolute?

I recommend St. Pilkey, Orrin H. Pilkey, Jr., coastal geologist, Duke University, Durham, North Carolina. He has already lent his knowledge and wit to a slim Good Book on the stewardship of the Texas shore.[4] There and elsewhere he has preached a simple credo that I paraphrase: The best way to manage barrier islands is to leave them alone. He has much more to say, all of it from the shoulder, including the simple declaration that people should not live on barrier islands. Although I stand in patent violation of his residency dictum, my environmental messages are apostolic. At any rate, even when things seem to be going well, it is not a bad idea to have that extra edge—a mentor, of whatever persuasion, who is on your side.

When I am on this lovely island, it is difficult to imagine that it really might be threatened in any significant way by the seemingly distant modern world. Consequently, I have few entries in my diary addressing that possibility. Once I did register my concern to Norman. As usual, without any hesitation that might indicate deep forethought, he blurted out a response and I scribbled it down: "It really don't make no difference if'n people tear it up today. Yew look out chonder tomorrer and the island will still be thar like always, even if'n the people ain't."

Neither erudite nor comforting; charmingly enigmatic. I am not sure what St. Pilkey would make of it.

CHAPTER 2

BEACH

Pelicans glide low
Mighty comber rears on high
Sea erases birds.

IT SEEMS TRIVIAL to say that the beach is made of sand, but I always do so—holding up a handful and letting it dribble through my fingers.

"Where does beach sand come from?" I ask a class. Fingers point to the surf in a bored, any-fool-can-see gesture. "Yes, but how did it get out there? The bottom of the Gulf is not an endless bed of sand; it is mostly ooze. The sand lies in a narrow band just offshore. So, from where?"

Sullen silence. They know if they wait long enough, I will tell them, or at least drop a clue, and they will not have to think.

"From back there," I point, living up to their expectations. "*Way* back there." They turn and look inland, as though expecting to see a wall of sand advancing. A few eyes light up. The uplands, weathering, unimaginably slow disintegration of the primordial bowels of the earth. "Igneous, sedimentary," I say, and a student or two nod vaguely, acknowledging that they have heard those words somewhere before, but never outside and, of course, never associated with a beach.

"So, we have sand—grains of pulverized rock—accumulating among the hills. How did that sand get offshore here?" Hands go up, because that is easy. Rivers, flowing water, downhill; no problem. So, sand came downhill with the water. How did the water get uphill to bring the sand down? Rain. They are warming up now. From where the rain? Clouds. And the clouds? Atmospheric moisture, condensed aloft. (They *do* know things, if you can just get at it.)

Where did the moisture come from? Silence again. Then, surprising himself, someone explodes: "Evaporation!" From where? Pause, then a bolt of comprehension comes to several at once: "Out there, the ocean!" But that is *salt* water! Is rain salty? "No, no, the salt stays behind; just the water evaporates." (They would make their science teacher proud.) Finally, what caused the evaporation; what lifted the water to get this cascade of events started? Long pause. Then, from way in the back comes a hesitant, querying voice: "The sun?"

"You mean, sunshine is what hauled those tons of sand out there into the surf?" My incredulous tone shakes their faith. They shuffle uneasily and go silent. "Well, you are right" (knowing looks; dignity instantly restored). "*Solar power,*" and I jab a finger dramatically at the source.

They think our story of sand is ended, and they are anxious to get into the water, so I have to be quick to keep their minds on the topic. How come just sand? Where are all the rocks and sticks, all the mud and clay that come down the rivers along with the sand? Well, logs get snarled up and eventually rot. River flow slackens on the flat coastal plain, and the gravel drops out. And the mud, silt, and clay? Fine stuff stays suspended until it reaches the quiet depths well out at sea, eventually drifting down to coalesce as ooze. Sand grains, however, are just right in size and density to be transported by water and dropped wherever the current slows. So, clean sand, winnowed of debris, accumulates offshore.

But sand offshore is not a beach. What puts the sand beneath our feet? "Waves," comes the quick response, and all eyes focus on the next incoming wave as though they can see its load of sand grains. Right; what causes waves? After some discussion they get it right— "the wind." Now they anticipate me. "What makes the wind?" one student asks, mimicking me to a T. Now they are enjoying the game. However, they are coming to the end of their meteorological background.

"Do you feel the onshore breeze against your cheek right now?" I ask. Hot air rising off the island, cool air racing in off the water to fill the void—voilà, wind! So, what really causes the offshore breeze? "The sun," they say it assertively now. And so, what causes the wind that generates the waves that bring in the sand that forms the beach? In unison—"*solar power!*" And I point again for emphasis.

The waves bring in this *neptunian sand* (who was Neptune?) and sculpt the beach to high-tide line; even further during storms. But sand goes well above flood tide; it is spread across the backbeach and piled into the dunes. How did it get there? Easy, the wind. Yes, but there is something more afoot. Wind does not easily carry wet sand. Well, it can carry dry sand. Yes, what . . . "The sun, the sun dries it out. Then the wind whisks it inland!" Right on. So, the backbeach and dunes are made of *aeolian sand* (who was Aeolus?), piled there by good old *solar power.*

Any questions? None. They know from my tone what is coming next unless some egghead dares to prolong the session. These are, after all, high schoolers, past masters in the art of reading a teacher's body language. We have only been together half a day, and they are already picking up on my mannerisms. For a few minutes anyway, they have thought in logical sequence, plumbed unrealized reservoirs of knowledge, discovered connections, and better yet, enjoyed the mental exercise.

"OK, take a half-hour surf break." They are gone.

Viewing beach sand at 40x magnification, I am dazzled with a colorful show of gems: rutile, hornblende, feldspar, pyroxene, garnet, staurolite, tourmaline, olivine, biotite, zircon, magnetite. Light from beneath the microscope stage shows each mineral luminous with its own color or a sharply etched silhouette. The surfaces of the particles are glazed, and their edges are rounded by the ceaseless grinding in the rock-tumbler action of the waves.

The general size of the sand grains is important to the texture and appearance of the beach. Matagorda Island is banked with "fine sand," the grains averaging a quarter millimeter across: a stack of four grains spans one millimeter, the thickness of a dime. Such small, smooth particles fit together tightly, leaving little room for water in between.

Martha and I quickly noticed that when we tried to dig in the wave-washed sand of the swash, the shovel blade slipped easily in, but opposed extraction with a stubborn, sucking resistance. The saturated sand, once dug and piled aside, shifted and writhed animal-like in its haste to settle back in place. Standing barefoot among the waves, we were soon ankle deep in hungry quicksand; wriggling toes only speeded our descent. No danger here of being dragged down out of sight, but such liveliness in a medium we regard as utterly passive is a bit disquieting.

We were encountering *thixotropy,* the tendency of a semisolid gel to transform into a soupy sol when agitated. More plainly, the mush of submerged sand changes to a gritty syrup when stirred. It has to do with particle size and released water films. Besides startling beach-combers and disappointing sand-castle builders, thixotropy affects the mechanics of insular shock absorption and the ease with which burrowing creatures move through the sandy depths.

When a wave washes up the beach, very little water can seep into the saturated sand. Most of it slides back, so the waves engage in a continual planing action, wearing the beach into a broad, sloping surface. Such a fine sand beach, with the grains tightly welded together by the trapped film of water, is characterized by a band of firm wet sand just above the waterline, perfect footing for beachcombers, joggers, bikers, and (unfortunately) automobiles, as well as the stuff from which lasting castles can be molded. And, as one might expect with physical qualities so different from the thixotropic sand of the swash, it is attractive to a different host of burrowing creatures.

As each wave collapses over the last bar, it pushes a thin sheet of water with its load of liquefied sand up the beach as far as its strength will allow. Most of the water drains back; some sinks into the beach. At the line where a wave front expires, there remains a sinuous stroke parallel to the waterline: a *wave signature.* Interlacing and erasing each other, often punctuated with fairy ring impressions of burst bubbles, each minuscule ridge of sand and finely minced shell reflects the eccentricity of that particular wave as faithfully as a fingerprint.

On hands and knees to examine a signature, I witness a meticulous sorting of sand grains, shell fragments, and sand dollar spines along with ghost shrimp fecal pellets, smears of dark organic matter, and sheets of clay and silt. The lighter silt and organic particles wash back to sea, while the heavier stuff remains. If moist grains of sand at the waterline could be marked, I could see that as they are lifted and jostled by successive waves, they tend to migrate south along the beach by infinitesimal increments. With prodigious patience and persistence, the sea is moving this island, a grain at a time, southward.

The waves heave miracles onto the beach daily: a beer can without a visible pinhole and with an intact tab, yet filled with pure seawater; a spindle of wood so smoothed that a computer-driven robot could not improve its symmetry; shell frit that a centrifuge would have considered homogeneous, cleanly separated into half a dozen quanta.

As you proceed from the wave-washed swash zone up the inclined forebeach, the sand gets progressively drier and looser. As the sand dries, there begins another round of winnowing, even more fine scaled than before. The wind picks up the most buoyant bits and bounces them up the beach, the lightest ones as far as the dunes. Dune sand is therefore perceptibly finer than beach sand. (Aeolus is more exacting than Neptune.) At the apex of the forebeach slope lies the strandline, marked by an accumulation of shells and assorted tidal debris. Beyond stretches the backbeach, an expanse of dry, shifting sand cluttered with storm-tossed refuse of natural and human-made origin, and merging with the outlying dunes.

So, there is not one beach here but several; successive bands aligned with the waterline and passing through fine gradations of sand texture and moisture as well as a subtle array of chemical components. It would be amazing if this physical imprint were not mirrored by partitions in the ranges of the highly specialized creatures that populate this demanding habitat.

From the human point of view, the barrier beach is a paradox: appealing to visit but appalling to live on. Think about what it takes, besides good weather and low surf, to make a day's excursion enjoyable: shade, dark glasses, sunblock, a hat, water, food, and, finally, a good shower afterward. Take all of those crutches away and consider existing on the beach full-time, good weather and bad. The prospect is grim; even the Karankawas did not try. No wonder that on a daytime visit to the Matagorda beach, the shoreline seems destitute of residents. Birds, fish, and an occasional jackrabbit or coyote do not count; they are visitors, like us.

There are in fact, full-time dwellers on the beach. But to survive in this hostile site, they share two features that keep them hidden from us. They are small so as to make negligible demands on food and space, and they spend most of their time under the sand to avoid the elements and predators. Some live truly subterranean lives; others are active on the surface in spells tuned to the tides and the sun. Few creatures can stand the rigors of the beach year-round. The Matagorda beach hosts about thirty-five species of smallish residents (not counting those tinier than the sand grains): *psammobionts*—creatures of the sand. Of these, about a dozen are abundant. All are fascinating.

To find and study psammobionts (to pronounce it, drop the *p*), I use not binoculars but shovel, sieve, and pocket magnifier. I need to have a sharp eye for beach zones. The surest place to make a quick strike is the swash, where little lives are most cushioned. Water makes the difference, for that universal solvent brings all the amenities: oxygen for gills, food for mouthparts, a rinse for wastes, lubricant for easing subterranean movement, transport for larvae, steady temperature for constant activity, and salinity for healthy metabolism.

Still, even in this optimal wave-swept part of the beach, life is patchy. I frequently sift out nothing more than bits of shell. In a strip of swash that looks to me homogeneous as far as the eye can see, there are, apparently, subtle nuances: proportions of shell and sand, amounts of suspended organic matter, the angle the waves make with the shore. Differences of consequence to lives forever teetering on the edge. Of course, that unequal distribution means that I occasionally hit pay dirt. The sieve comes up loaded; I am stunned by the numbers of scrambling bodies all frenetically trying to get back to the security of their dark and wet womb.

At the time that the tide is actively on the move, either up or down, the smooth sand of the swash occasionally erupts with hundreds of little knobs. They spurt up from the sand into the moving water in patches of hundreds at a time—a startling sight to behold. Each half-inch, wedge-shaped clam—for clams they are despite their uncharacteristic liveliness—goes skidding and tumbling with the wave for a dozen feet before it slides to a halt, upends, and hastily noodles down out of sight.

For half an hour, while the flood or ebb tide is at its peak, millions of coquinas (*Donax variabilis*) respond to a common cue. Perhaps they feel tell-tale vibrations of the traveling tide; perhaps they get an advance hydraulic perception through the water film in the sand. Whatever they

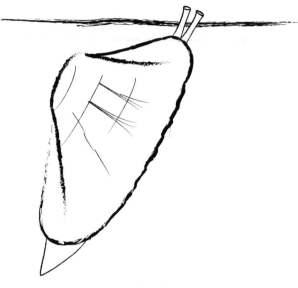

Coquina

sense, their response keeps them near the fore of the wave line, optimally situated to glean suspended matter and assorted animalcules. Indeed, they are absolutely dependent on the wave-induced agitation. In stagnant water, they cannot suck in enough nutriment to maintain themselves.

None of our visitors go to the beach without digging up coquina clams. We watch them jostle about in jars of seawater, extending their yellow siphons and pale foot. Everyone gets to hold coquinas in a palmful of wet sand and thrill to the tickles as the brazen little clams try to dig their way home.

Everybody marvels at the varied colors: sky blue, pastel shades of lavender and pink, rich yellow and coral, and bland white. Many beachcombers collect the shells; they aptly call the paired valves "sea butterflies." Why, alone among all the colorless psammobionts, are these clams so brightly and diversely pigmented? Experts offer no suggestions, but I have a suspicion. Coquinas, living just beneath the surface of the sand, are frequently uncovered by waves. Birds, keen eyed and with color vision, are among their arch predators. In the traceries of refracted light, surface sparkles, and the iridescence of rocking pods of foam and bursting bubbles, perhaps the colors of coquinas might well be effective camouflage.

There is another angle. Visual predators such as birds develop a "search image," a mental target on which they focus for quick prey recognition. Faced with multicolored clams, the birds may zero in on the more common colors and pass over individuals decked in other hues. So, color variation among coquinas might be a means of dulling the birds' perspicacity.

Coquinas are regarded as a *keystone species* in the swash: they are of exceptional importance to the well-being of the living community of which they are a part. They merit this status because they are perennially present and very abundant and because they are prey items for many associated creatures. In the summertime the number of adult coquinas peaks; double handfuls can be scooped from their clusters without seeming to diminish their multitude. In the fall adults appear to grow weary, many lying uncovered and moribund on the sand where ring-billed gulls and hurrying flocks of red knots snap them up. Others migrate to deeper water where they spend the winter. By springtime, after a brief interval among the plankton, speck-sized coquinalings begin to show up in the sand.

Early in our explorations of the beach, we found fingertip-sized pellets of crushed coquina shell, apparently the end result of some predator's repast. Finally, we saw a willet suddenly gag, open wide, and regurgitate just such a pellet. These birds stalk the lower swash, snapping up tardy coquinas entire and letting their remarkable gizzards do the rest. American oystercatchers likewise consume small coquinas, but they position larger clams hinge-down in the sand and open them with a stab from their stout beak, then deftly pluck the soft innards. Legions of sanderlings also feed on coquinas, but these little birds take only the tiniest clams.

We have dug up a moon snail with a coquina clasped in its muscular foot and watched by flashlight as a ghost crab worked at the seam of a coquina with its large pincer until it pried open the shell and plucked out the meat with its small pincher. Blue crabs and speckled crabs gain quick access by snipping off the edge of the shell. Gulf whiting and pompano snap up coquinas tumbling in the waves; southern stingrays suck them out of the sand; and schools of black drum, so close in that their backs are exposed, root avidly for the clams in the backwash. Both the ray and the drum have special teeth designed for crushing clam shells.

Visitors seldom sieve the swash sand without encountering several scuttling little creatures they aptly call "sand bugs." These cute bugs are actually mole crabs (*Emerita portoricensis*)—one of the most highly specialized inhabitants of the beach. An adult female is about three-quarters of an inch long, pale gray and football shaped. With legs kicking and rear appendages whirring rapidly to turn the sand into a thixotropic slurry, she is perfectly streamlined to skid backward through the sand. There are few field demonstrations more intriguing than dropping a mole crab into a scooped-out hollow in the wet sand, pouring in a cupful of water, and watching the little crustacean disappear backward. The quick grab needed to recapture it gives an added respect for the abilities of the shorebirds that routinely feed on mole crabs.

Mole crabs scuttle up and down with tides, settling near the high-water line, where they dig in, coming to rest at a forty-five-degree angle, always facing the sea. The pair of stubby front antennae joins into a straw that barely clears the sand and serves to exhale water drawn from below and passed across the gills. The second pair of antennae is long and hairy, kept carefully coiled out of harm's way when a wave comes crashing in. Then these appendages are quickly flicked out to stream in the gentler backwash, where the hairs form a net fine

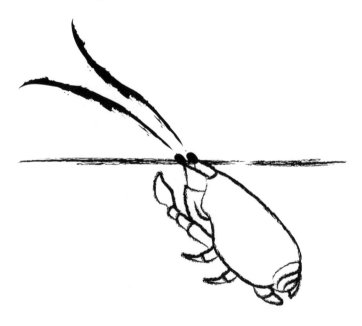

Mole crab

enough to snare phytoplankton and even bacteria. The loaded antennae are drawn in and licked clean, ready to be recast on the next backwash. Like coquinas, mole crabs feed only in streaming water, so despite pleas from students, they never go back to school or home aquaria.

The ordinary vision of a snail shows it sliding along the inside of an aquarium glass grating off the film of algae or perhaps munching the edges of greens in the garden. So, it comes as a surprise when I hold up a moon snail and proclaim it to be one of the most important predators on the beach. A carnivorous snail? I only add to the disbelief when I show, in my other hand, the shell of a disc clam with a neatly beveled hole drilled right through it. The moon did *that*? How?

The moon (*Polinices duplicatus*) is a fairly large snail with a globular shell as much as three inches in diameter. Moon snails spend most of their time plowing through the sand just beneath the surface of the swash. Passage through the sand is eased by extending the large, fleshy body mass and bending a mucus-covered flap back over the shell. If disturbed, the animal spews out water from internal canals and quickly collapses into its shell. It is in the extended phase that the moon becomes a tiger.

Whether a moon cruises at random or smells out its prey is not known for sure, but when it contacts a hapless clam, it clasps the bivalve in a curl of its muscular body. After probing about for a spot that suits it, the snail extends its fingerlike proboscis and begins to rasp the clam's shell, using a remarkable mouthpart called the radula. This apparatus works like sandpaper, with rows of hard prickles working back and forth. The tip of this grinding machine is rotated, creating a round excavation. After the moon abrades awhile, the proboscis is raised and a glandular papilla is sponged over the site, releasing a shell-softening secretion. Then the proboscis goes back to work, followed by the papilla and so on until the shell is breached. At last, the slender proboscis slides inside and begins to snip at the soft flesh of the clam, feeding the bits directly into the gullet. The moon can finish up its leisurely meal, "licking the plate clean," without ever opening the valves of the clam. How neat can you get!

Low tide exposes clusters of squatty, half-inch-tall "volcanoes" on the swash, the active ones intermittently spurting fountains of sand and water. Around most turrets is a ring of pellets like a cast of chocolate sprinkles. Clear signs of some subterranean creature, but what?

Even longtime coastal residents, fishermen included, shrug and mutter, "Worms, I guess." I wore out my back and my patience digging into these holes, to no avail. Whatever was down there sank into the soup well ahead of my shovel. Then I heard of a hand-powered siphoning device that would suck up a core of sand along with the elusive sand dweller. I made one from PVC pipe, dubbed it a "slurper," and now use it to reveal one of the least-known common animals of the beach.

What comes up in the burp of sand is a four-inch-long, translucent white creature with a shrimplike rear and crablike front, complete with weak pincers. This is a ghost shrimp (*Callichirus islagrande*), a crustacean with closest kin among the hermit crabs. Every feature of its elongate body reflects a subterranean existence. Among the many bristlelike appendages beneath its abdomen are three pairs modified into paddles. These paddles, each pair held together like cupped hands, whir in fevered unison to eject sand and to generate a water current through the burrow. Thus the sand volcanoes.

Through the unpigmented exoskeleton one can clearly see the internal organs: dark intestine, bright orange fat bodies, yellow ovaries, and the rapidly beating heart. The mouthparts are fringed with little hooks and delicate hair brushes designed to clutch grains of sand and scrape off the smears of organic matter and colonies of algae and bacteria. Small eyes and long sensitive antennae confirm that the ghost shrimp lives in a dark world of chemical and tactile sensations.

Although they never voluntarily surface, ghost shrimp are important members of the swash community. Their tunnels, which may go three feet deep, aerate the substrate, and ceaseless excavation recycles nutrients and releases wastes. Tiny pea crabs (*Pinnixa* spp.) and bright orange copepods (*Clausidium caudatum*) also frequently live in the burrows. A single ghost shrimp may produce 450 fecal pellets a day, each a little cylinder of organic matter and a seething mass of bacteria—a potential "second harvest" for other members of the community. I have seen ring-billed gulls glutting on windrows of ghost shrimp pellets accumulated at the waterline. Pulverized by the waves, the fecal suspension is sucked up by coquinas and netted by mole crabs.

Despite their secretive habits, ghost shrimp are routinely caught by several predators. Black drum, sea catfish, and southern stingrays use the same tactic as my slurper to suck the crustaceans out of their tunnels. I have seen a sharp-eyed willet once in a while snatch a ghost shrimp that was busy clearing its burrow of sand.

Many other creatures appear in sieve boxes in the swash. Sand-digger amphipods (*Haustorius* sp.) are abundant, mini-pillbug-like crustaceans that kick their way through the shallow sand slurry. Squatty surf crabs (*Lepidopa websteri*), pearly white and lustered with violet iridescence, appear among the mole crabs. Auger snails (*Hastula salleyana*) extend their extraordinary foot to serve as a fleshy surfboard. Rice-grain-sized dwarf olive snails (*Olivella minuta*) leave twisting trails that end in tiny bumps (where the snail is) in the wet sand when the tide is out. And no marine environment is complete without its host of worms. The swash supports red threadworms (*Lumbrinereis parvula*), shimmy worms (*Nepthys bucera*), bloodworms (*Glycera americana*), sand parchment tube worms (*Onuphis eremita*), and a seethe of tiny palp worms (*Scolelepis squamata*), each kind with its own ecological tale to tell.

Late summer afternoons I jog the beach knee deep in a swarm of zooming bodies: tiger beetles, disturbed from the sand. I have found eight species of tiger beetles on Matagorda Island, but only one (*Cicindela dorsalis*) lays exclusive claim to this band of beach from the waterline to four feet up the wet forebeach.

Beach tigers are three-eighths of an inch long, long-legged and big-eyed, cream colored with a tracery of brown lines over their backs. Under a hand magnifier their sickle jaws look fearful, but they neither bite nor sting when handled. They are hard to see on the beach unless they move, and when they do move—they can run, leap, and fly—they are so fast that predators other than robber flies do not even bother to give chase. Despite their wariness, we discovered that if we sat quietly, the beetles began to settle nearby, and we could watch them at length.

JULY '94: *We had been sitting barely five minutes before beach tigers began appearing from nowhere to alight at arm's length. Much better behaved company than an Independence Day crowd of people! Several were mildly interested in a wiggling toe, but soon they seemed to forget us and went about their customary fitful business. Each one moves continually in sudden, rapid dashes punctuated by abrupt stops, reminding us of the halting gait of snowy plovers. During the motionless instant the beetles look all around. They are incredibly alert to all movement, including passing shadows, in their immediate surroundings.*

They seem to have only two things in mind: food and each other. They scurry along the waterline after each retreating wave, searching for bits of wrack, pausing briefly to dig like terriers in the sand after a palp worm or snatch at passing shore flies. We watched a cluster of beetles munching on the tentacle of a stranded Portuguese man-of-war, unfazed by the potential of causing a coiled stinging cell to explode. Two others were busy snipping at dried flesh inside a coquina shell. Another happened upon an uncovered sand-digger, instantly snatched it up, and went racing off with the prey struggling in its jaws while several other beetles noticed and gave chase, like a passel of chickens competing for a tasty morsel.

These beetles are acutely aware of each other. Mostly, each one seems concerned with keeping a bit of personal space between it and its neighbor, but the males pack a powerful libido, and they accost all comers until they strike a receptive female. Then they adroitly mount and the two go off, the larger female nonchalantly toting her partner as she proceeds in typical start-and-stop foraging behavior. Only aching muscles break our séance; we never tire of watching these comical little critters.

I record the appearance of the first adult tiger beetle on the beach about the second week of May. By June they are incredibly numerous. Their numbers wane in September, and they disappear during October; the adults, that is. The population lives on, of course, and we did not discover where until one winter day.

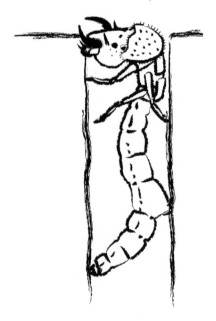

Tiger beetle larva

JANUARY '95: *A revelation on the beach today! We noticed another sort of little hole on the backbeach, quite different from that made by beach hoppers. This one is perfectly circular, hardly more than a pinhead in diameter and with a semicircular spray of tiny sand pellets off to one side. Lots of holes! I excavated one carefully with my knife blade. The tunnel went straight down for three inches. At the bottom we found what we dared to hope for—a large-headed, big-jawed, contorted little grub with a curious hump on its rear end—a tiger beetle larva for sure. So we have closed their cycle, which appears completely confined to the beach. Adults on the forebeach in summer; larvae hidden on the backbeach during the rest of the year. Another Mata-gorda secret in our pocket.*

As they grow, tiger beetle larvae enlarge the diameter of their shafts slightly and deepen them considerably. Full-term grubs lodge eight inches deep. No matter their stage of development, these budding beetles already display a version of their tigerish heritage. They wait patiently at the top of their warren, humped back propped comfortably against the inner wall, iridescent green head flush with the surface, beady eyes and sensory hairs alert to any creature that comes past. With snap-trap quickness, the tiger beetle larva pops partly out, snatches its prey in ice-tong jaws, and instantly drops into the safety of the depths to consume its meal.

I have several times gone to the beach near sunset to see what the adult tiger beetles do at night. The result is always the same. I choose a likely candidate and watch it exclusively, following its wanderings. Finally, the insect moves up the forebeach a bit and slows down, even-tually coming to a halt. There it stands while the light begins to fail. I see it; then I do not. I blink, refocus; it is still there. I blink again, and it is gone. That ends the quest. I have read that these beetles burrow into the sand at night, and ours likely do just that, but apparently not on the open beach. I suspect that they fly to the dunes and shuffle into the sun-warmed sand amid the sea oats stems. Next day, when the sun has warmed the air and sand, they reappear as magically as they van-ished.

Do individual tiger beetles return to a homestretch of beach day after day? One July morning we used felt-tip pens to dot ten beetles from one site green and ten more from a nearby site pink. That after-noon we returned to find six green tigers and four pink ones still hus-tling along their respective grounds. Next day two greens and one pink

were back in place, and we found a second pink beetle running among
the greens. On the third day, we encountered a lone pink tiger displaced twenty-five yards along the beach. It was the last. Clearly, our
experiment was too paltry to do more than pique curiosity. Did our
marked beetles rid themselves of their colors, die of natural or ink-
induced causes, loom unusually large in the eyes of predators, or simply wander out of our purview? It adds to the intrigue of this island
to be unsure.

The strandline is the daytime home of one of the signal members of
the beach fauna. Turn a piece of wrack there anytime except dead of
winter, and you will set off a veritable explosion of leaping white flecks.
Beach hoppers (*Talorchestia* sp.), hundreds if not thousands! Ours may
be an undescribed species.

Beach hoppers are akin to sand-diggers. Both belong to a group of
small, mostly nondescript crustaceans called amphipods. They look
like abbreviated shrimp. The branch that includes the hoppers has
taken up a terrestrial mode. They still breathe with gills and so require
very moist air, but they will drown in water, and the females do not
even release their eggs into the sea.

Our hoppers have large, silvery gray compound eyes that detect
bands of polarized light in the sky and the positions of sun and moon.
By sky watching they are able to keep themselves from wandering off
their favored band of beach. On summer days beach hoppers dig in
beneath surface debris along the strandline and emerge at night to forage for any sort of rotting organic matter. When they find a rich source
of food, such as a dead sand dollar or a hank of decaying sargassum,
they excavate around and beneath the windfall and bury it below a
heap of sand. Under this cover they can feed at leisure all day without
danger of drying out. In cool weather each hopper digs a short, vertical tunnel with a distinctive oval opening in which it may spend several days until the beach warms up.

In the summertime we have been on the beach at dawn when the
hoppers were finishing their nocturnal ramble and digging in for the
day. We would lie on our bellies to take advantage of the sun's low rays
illuminating the little fountains of sand kicked up while the hoppers
dug. They work headfirst, scratching with front appendages and kicking the sand out the rear beneath their bodies, like a dog digging a
bone. Before settling down for the day, they shove up a sand plug to
assure privacy and a moist retreat. Hoppers perform this ritual afresh

every morning, for they do not return to a prior abode. Abandoned tunnels may remain intact for several days, which explains why I frequently come up empty when I dig after hoppers.

Hoppers do not routinely share quarters, but in March "consenting adults" do cohabit. The nuptial tunnel is about twice the normal depth, and the pair is curled together in a slight enlargement at the bottom. Invariably, they are of maximum size (body length about half an inch) and opposite sex. There is no larval stage; females carry their eggs and hatchlings in a brood pouch beneath their abdomen. The little ones hatch out as miniature adults and begin to appear by the jillions beneath the wrack in April.

I agree with the kids I send to catch one with only fingers: beach hoppers do not just vanish when disturbed, they seem to translocate in true transponder fashion—to beam elsewhere. It takes the combined magic of a good lens, high-speed film, and the flicker of a strobe light to determine what really goes on when a hopper hops. With this apparatus you can see the little creature tense, crouch, and then spring up and away by suddenly extending its curled abdomen. It tumbles slightly in midair as it performs a parabola before gracelessly whomping onto the sand, bouncing a time or two and skidding to a stop. The critter scrambles to regain its composure and sets up for another launch. Despite their remarkable agility, hoppers are routinely caught by birds and snatched by tiger beetle larvae.

Although flies can be found scattered all across the beach, the strandline is the realm of an astounding mass and great assortment of them. The adults are not restricted, but their eggs and larvae are. Amid the windrow of decomposing sargassum, putrefying carcasses, and assorted bird plops, crowds of tiny maggots writhe in ecstasy. And so the passerby stirs up a whir of wings: black anthomyiid flies, ashy-winged shore flies, dark seaweed flies, gray flesh flies, metallic green blowflies, and ankle-nipping stable flies.

Most of these flies survive winter on the beach as pupae nestled in the sand and debris. The adults begin to emerge in early spring, each species according to its tolerance of and preference for rising temperature. On cool mornings, when the flies are torpid, sandpipers and sanderlings avidly peck them up. A significant eruption occurs in June when freshly metamorphosed anthomyiid flies and shore flies coat the strandline in a buzzing gray carpet. That is precisely the time when Wilson's plovers' eggs hatch on the backbeach. Precocial plover chicks follow Mom and Dad, but they get no handouts. Little balls of fluff on pipe-stem legs scamper about harvesting the rich bounty of flies. The timing of the two events is not just fortuitous. Without the flies the chicks would likely starve.

When we first began to familiarize ourselves with the Matagorda beach, we noticed what we eventually named the "scribble zone." Actually, it encompasses two separate belts, one on the upper forebeach just above the strand and the other in moist swags on the backbeach. In these zones we could always find little traceries of dry sand grains dribbled over the moist surface of the beach. These were our scribbles, surely the work of some tiny subterranean denizen, but we were a while running it down.

On hands and knees, with a 10x magnifier, I could see that a scribble was made of sand grains lifted into a ridge and dried out so it had a paler tone than the moist sand below. Hardly as wide as a pencil lead, each ridge wandered for an inch or so, gave off a stubby branch or two, and ended as abruptly as it began. A dissection with the tip of my knife blade revealed a horizontal tunnel beneath the ridge. Within their zone the scribbles were closely spaced and numerous, often forming a continuous granulation, an eye-catching, but for the moment, inexplicable feature of the beach.

We swept clean a section of scribble zone and washed down a second section. Then we waited and watched for an hour. No scribbles appeared at either site. We gave up and returned that afternoon to find both areas covered with fresh scribbles. I tried turning my knife blade parallel to the sand and quickly shaving off a ridge to reveal the underlying tunnel. On the very first try I saw a black speck hustling in consternation along the roofless, suddenly sunlit groove. In triumph I lifted it still kicking on the tip of the blade and deposited it into a vial containing sand. I tried the same tactic a dozen times and finally captured two more specks.

Back at the trailer we put moist beach sand into a clear container, dropped in our three specks, closed the lid, and waited. Next morning there were scribbles on the sand! Through the side of the jar we could see not only the underlying horizontal tunnels but also a heretofore undiscovered set of vertical pipes that descended about an inch below the surface where they ramified in a series of side branches and chambers. Our three specks were still busy fashioning these lower galleries. Occasionally one knocked off work and went scurrying nimbly along the maze of tunnels, performing a deft body-doubling turnaround to change direction. Next step, the binocular microscope and books.

It took only a moment under 40x magnification to recognize our speck as a miniature beetle. The optical micrometer gauged it at just under three millimeters long. Our beach beetle, as we came to call it, is dull black with a pale band across the middle. This band is a pair of short wing covers, and that, along with the elongate body and beaded antennae marked it as a rove beetle of the family Staphylinidae. After considerable eyestrain I took it to the genus *Bledius,* but beyond that both my abilities and my books failed me. Our beach beetle might well be an undescribed species. No matter, we are more interested in its existence and behavior than its name.

What do the little rove beetles do down there? Inspection of surface sand grains reveals an encrustation of blue-green algae and a fester of diatoms, a virtually unlimited food resource. There are also succulent growths of green algae and spongy clusters of bacteria, more potential foodstuffs. All except the bacteria need sunlight, so they are concentrated in the uppermost layer. Presumably the surface tunnels—the scribbles—are gouged out while the beetles are feeding like miniature moles. If they tire of veggies, the insects could scarf up a nematode worm or ciliate protozoan, but the structure of their mouthparts suggests a vegetarian diet.

Beach beetles do emerge from their subterranean retreats on occasion. In May and on sultry afternoons in August we have encountered swarms of adults flying low over the beach, likely engaged in prenuptials. From the lower galleries we have sifted eggs, larvae, and pupae. At mating times, multitudes of these little insects scuttle about

Black beach beetle

on the sand, and western sandpipers consider them worth pecking up. I have also found a small predaceous carabid beetle inside the scribble tunnels, so even such cramped quarters are not immune from invasion.

A high tide or heavy rainfall may collapse and soak the passageways, but it certainly does not kill the beach beetles; within hours their scribbles appear on the clean surface. Like all other psammobionts on the beach, their response to a storm is to hunker quietly in their retreats until things calm down. Then they dig out and take up life anew.

All across the beach from the high-tide line to the edge of the dunes there occur round holes centered on a radiation of scratch marks rimmed with a semicircle of sand pellets. The sand throughout this area is covered with the unmistakable eight-ply stitch marks of scuttling ghost crabs (*Ocypode quadrata*). The crabs are abroad at night or on cloudy summer days and sunny winter afternoons, foraging across their domain, which extends out into the swash.

The holes lead to tunnels that go down at a forty-five-degree angle away from the Gulf, so the entrance is inclined to catch the onshore breeze. In the summertime there are often two entrance passages joining in a Y, apparently to allow a draft through the lair. Otherwise, most burrows are simple slanting shafts with a lazy L or J shape at the bottom. The blind end, where the occupant spends the day, is comfortably enlarged. Usually there is only one crab to a burrow.

Holes are small near the water and get progressively larger toward the back of the beach and on through the sand dunes into sparsely vegetated areas on the seaward half of the grassland. Small ones will not admit a pencil, but you can roll a golf ball down the large ones. The diameter of the domicile is correlated with the size of its occupant, and the depth is related to its location. Crabs dig down to wet sand just above the water table; they find this after a short excavation on the lower beach but at progressively greater depths toward the dunes.

Well adapted to land life, ghost crabs have a cluster of special hairs at the base of one pair of legs that, pressed against wet sand, can draw in enough water (leaving the salt behind) to keep the gill chamber moist and maintain water balance. Animals that live well back from the sea, with deep burrows that go down to the water table, may exist indefinitely on absorbed water; those that live on the beach, however, conveniently visit the shallows to wet their gills during every sortie.

Ghost crabs are opportunists—they consume anything edible that they can get at, a distinct advantage for a creature on a sandy waste

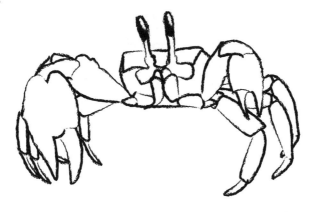

Ghost crab

largely dependent on unpredictable offal from the sea. When they sally forth for the night, crabs that live on the beach make directly for the strandline and forebeach to sample the smorgasbord provided by the waves. Any bit of organic flotsam will do, animal or vegetable, still reflexing or bloated by decomposition. Stranded jellyfish may be picked at in place, but detached fragments are often dragged across the beach and into a burrow, leaving an enigmatic trail for the beachcomber to puzzle over. Several crabs may dig in directly below a big chunk of carrion and emerge to dine communally right at home.

During the warm months, a ghost crab may forage far up and down the beach during a night and dig a new home or appropriate a vacant one wherever the morning light finds it. Excavating a shallow burrow in the moist sand is a relatively easy task for a crab. In the dunes, however, a burrow may descend through four feet of packed sand. With such investment in its lair, the tenant becomes more possessive and sedentary. Inland ghost crabs typically return to the same burrow unless provoked to move. Although they wander widely, they seem always to know where home base lies. They have good eyesight and surely must use local visual landmarks. But ghost crabs are mostly abroad at night, when, even on the reflective sand, their vision must be limited. It seems unlikely that sensitivity to magnetic forces or to polarized light would be effective over so short a distance. Maybe there are significant chemical cues.

In desperation, I think, some investigators have suggested that the crabs have a kinesthetic sense that unerringly brings them home without the need for external bench marks. Somehow, it is proposed, the crab's nerves and muscles take unconscious note of its every movement as it leaves its burrow and wanders about, all the while keeping a running account of a physiological reverse azimuth pointing home. When called upon, the system then reads the recorded muscle activity in reverse to bring the creature back again, at top speed and in a beeline transect, rather than retracing its original path. This would explain why crabs on the beach—which are visually orienting—always run away from me when I approach, while those among the dunes, which are obeying their inner urge, sometimes scamper nearly between my legs on their arrow-true dash for their burrow. Yet, I remain skeptical about muscle sense as a homing mechanism.

Although a dozen things about a ghost crab's anatomy fit it for a life on the beach, the burrow is its real ace in the hole. Here ghost crabs retreat to escape the elements: dehydrating or chilling winds, solar radiation, extreme temperatures, or whatever combination makes for a depressing day to a crab. In winter they close the entrance with a sand plug and squat for weeks at a stretch at the bottom of their warren in uninterrupted torpid vacuity. On summer days they plug the passageway to seal themselves in a cool, moist chamber. For storms, when the entire beach is inundated, ghost crabs take no emergency precautions. They merely hunch in their chambers, even if these collapse around them, and wait for better times.

Whenever we have visitors stay overnight in the summertime, we take them to the beach at night to watch the ghost crabs by flashlight. As far as a light beam extends, it reflects off pale bodies along the waterline and out in the swash. The ghost crabs are there, wetting their gills and hunting coquinas. An occasional individual will stand its ground against a careful approach with the light and eventually begin foraging. The crab moves stealthily, lightly vibrating the tips of its vertically oriented pincers against the sand. Either by feel or taste or some combination, the crab senses something. Immediately it grapples with its pincers and finally lifts out its prize, usually a coquina but occasionally a surf crab, mole crab, or sand tube worm.

The crab manipulates a clam until it can force the valves open. Then it busily picks out the flesh and transfers it to the mincing mouthparts with its small pincer. Soon it will drop the cleaned shells and start off on a fresh hunt. In autumn, when coquinas become lethargic, ghost crabs locate buried windfalls and spend entire afternoons harvesting the bounty. Areas of forebeach ten feet across will be pocked and scratched after such ghost crab banquets.

Once I came across a pair of least terns defending their scrape with its clutch of two eggs from the advances of an adult ghost crab. The three parried repeatedly until finally the crab gave it up. The crab might not have handled an egg, but it could have killed a pipping chick.

Ghost crabs have so accommodated to the shore that they cannot swim and are at considerable risk in the shallow surf. They crouch and cling to the bottom but are occasionally lifted and tossed about by the waves. At such times they are prey to aquatic predators. Nevertheless, a ghost crab that feels threatened on the swash, and with its route up the beach cut off, will readily take its chances by scuttling into the sea. Soon, however, if it has not met mishap, it will reappear not far down the beach.

Adult crabs are fast enough to outdodge mammalian predators and formidable enough to wander with impunity among shorebirds. They duck into their lairs to escape potential surface predators, but sometimes their retreat becomes a trap. In autumn and early winter, when the crabs begin spending more time in their burrows but still emerge often enough to leave a scent trace, they begin to suffer a sustained assault. For weeks on end, the beach is riddled with mounded excavations and liberally sprinkled with bits of ghost crab exoskeletons. Each night keen noses snuffle for occupied burrows. The sand is easily excavated, and the crabs offer no resistance and so become an easy meal. Next morning the tracks and dig marks are easy to read. Feral hogs, coyotes, raccoons, and badgers—in descending order of depredation— take a heavy toll of ghost crabs. Finally, winter storms erase lingering olfactory cues, and the remaining ghost crabs drift on, secure in their winter languor.

JULY '95: *I noticed a thimble-sized pile of dry sand on the beach at high-tide line, not like anything I had seen before. Probed beneath it with the hand trowel and found a small tube leading straight down, like a tiger beetle larva's work, but too close to the water. It continued about four inches. I finally uncovered a squatty, turquoise blue "beetle" huddled at the bottom. Only after I got it into the palm of my hand and held it up in the sun did it unfold its legs and try to escape, and I could see that this was no beetle but a gnomelike little crab! The blue of its carapace was complemented by a pair of*

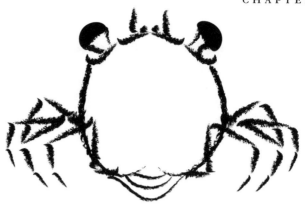

Ghost crab megalops

*huge, powder-blue eyes held up on periscope stalks. Those enormous optics
betrayed the nature of the cute little beast—a megalops (huge eyes)—a late
developmental stage common to all crabs. But which crab? No paddles on the
hind legs, so not a swimming species. Had I at last found a ghost crab
megalops? Put this one into a small jar of wet beach sand where it immediately burrowed out of sight. Four days later we noticed it scuttling around on
the surface, as neat an elfin ghost crab as you ever saw! It had shed its
exoskeleton and assumed its final appearance beneath the sand. We took it to
the beach, wished it well, and covered it with a smidgen of sand.*

We find ghost crabs paired at night on the forebeach in the summertime. They press belly to belly and nose to nose, the male on top, the
much smaller female upside down underneath. By late summer we
encounter females carrying large wads of gray eggs beneath their
"aprons"—their curled abdomens. When the eggs are ripe, the mother
crabs release them to the sea at high tide. The sand domes of megalops
appear erratically on the forebeach in July and August.

Surely the greatest attrition among ghost crabs occurs during the
several weeks the defenseless larval stages float among the plankton at
sea. Cabbagehead jellyfish probably sop up jillions. Once the survivors
metamorphose and make landfall on the beach, the insect-sized
crablings need to dig in rapidly to avoid predation by shorebirds, tiger
beetles, and established members of their own species. Throughout
their hazardous first year little ghost crabs are picked off by gulls and
willets by day and by raccoons, coyotes, and larger ghost crabs by night.

As they increase in size and experience, their survival rate rises. By becoming more nocturnal, they escape the notice of birds. By growing larger they are better able to hold their own among their brethren.

No beach minicourse is complete until all visitors hold a ghost crab in their hands and gently touch one stalked eyeball with their index fingers to observe what the crab does in response. If you do not know, you really must try it for yourself.

CHAPTER 3

MARSH

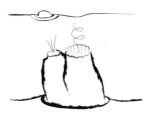

*Perpetually
ready to take on the world
Pinchers gaped, blue crab.*

AFTER A MORNING ON THE BEACH, an afternoon on the bay side of the island brings into sharp contrast these two shoreline environments separated by only a mile of barrier sand. Here on the "back side" things appear more laid back. There is no churning surf, no open beach, and often no onshore breeze. The heavy air is permeated with an odor of decay and vibrant with the whine of saltmarsh mosquitoes. Waist-high cordgrass grows along the bank, sending underground runners out to sprout in the shallows and obscure the waterline. In the skim of water among the grass stems minnow-sized fish wriggle, sending up plumes of smoke-fine silt as they dive for cover. Hermit crabs, laboring under their purloined shells, stitch trails across the mud. The fringe of shore grass is flanked by a sequence of varicolored greens that march across the low shore. The prostrate and tangled plants are ever ready to snatch at ankles, their crisp leaves crunching underfoot with the snap of a fresh dill pickle.

A distinctive coterie of animals inhabits the marsh. There are crabs, of course, but not the same kinds that live on the beach. If I were to transpose a ghost crab from the beach and a fiddler crab from the marsh, I would be lowering a sure and rapid death sentence on both. Each crab is so adapted to its home environment that it is equally misadapted to alien surroundings. The insects, worms, clams, snails, amphipods, and a host of lesser organisms also differ. Indeed, the entire marsh community is as characteristic and as marvelously attuned to the sultry bay side of the island as the beach community is to the windswept Gulf side.

Because of their mobility, birds move easily from one margin of the island to the other, but even among birds some species tend to stay put unless tides or weather forces them to move. The beach is the favored domain of gulls and terns, with bullet-shaped bodies and strong wings tapered to bat the constant wind. The marsh is populated by a sprangle of long legs with splayed toes, sinuous necks, and stabbing or probing bills. This is the realm of the waders, herons and egrets and the like, with broad wings and a fold-up anatomy that gets them airborne only with effort. Once on the wing they are graceful but not agile. Herons occasionally fish on the beach, and gulls readily settle on the marsh, but each is then transient and not completely at ease.

What sand is to the beach, *muck* is to the marsh. Anything lacking the buoyancy of a bird sinks to its hocks trying to get across this mire. You can go up to your thighs in water that is hardly knee deep. The black ooze will suck shoes or rubber boots right off your feet. You can easily lose your balance, especially while standing on one foot trying to recover or replace a shoe, and go completely down. You may suffer nothing worse than a thorough mud caking, but things can get serious if you encounter mud shell—oyster shell covered with sediment, the animals long dead but the shells still sharp edged. In that case you may suffer bad cuts on hands, feet, and knees, abundant bleeding, and a good chance of infection.

Salt marsh fringes the entire back side of Matagorda Island. Ooze, with its tangle of low vegetation, varies from a few yards to over half a mile wide, depending on the reach of high tide. The sharp margin of the beach extends thirty-eight miles from Cedar Bayou to Pass Cavallo. But with innumerable inlets, fingers, islets, peninsulas, mud banks, oyster reefs, lakes, and washover channels, the marsh presents a convoluted edge; it twists and turns for over eighty miles between the two tidal passes.

Over the marsh and across San Antonio Bay the smudge of live oak copses cloaks the mainland six miles away. From there it is another twelve miles north to the palmetto-strewn delta of the Guadalupe River. That stream has already picked up the discharge from the San Antonio River by the time it threads sluggishly around its last, water hyacinth–clogged meander and finally discharges into Guadalupe Bay.

It seems incredible that such a relatively small and distant influx of freshwater could have a tangible influence on the marsh here, but it does. I can catch some marsh water in my cupped hand and taste the impact of the river. The water is *brackish*—neither fresh nor saline, but something in between. Despite the daily influx of seawater through both tidal passes, runoff from the mainland manages to establish a graduated range of salinities in the bays, from nearly fresh at the delta to full strength seawater at the passes. Heavy rains can turn the entire bay and marsh nearly fresh for a while, and droughts can run the salinity well beyond that of the open ocean. Most of the time, however, creatures of these back lagoons and marshes can find the salt concentration that suits them best.

Some kinds, like comb jellies, take on the same salt concentration inside their bodies as that of their environment, and if they strike an unfavorable gradient, they must move or curl up and die. Others, like gulf killifish, can osmoregulate—maintain a constant internal salt concentration even when the salt content of the water around them varies. In all cases, however, creatures are better off living at their optimal salinity. The more they drift from that comfortable spectrum, the more their body is stressed and the less efficient they become at conducting their normal business of surviving, growing, and reproducing.

The river has other, subtle but still significant influences on the marsh. Many of the particles of silt and clay that give color to the river settle to the bottom of the bays, but the finest bits are transported to the back side of Matagorda Island where they filter gently down amid the marsh plants to become the most recent layer of ooze. As the plants proliferate year after year, the bulk of their dead remains increases, they compress the soft substrate, and the entire vegetable mat begins to sink. Continual arrival of sediment allows the marsh to keep its head above water, so to speak, even if sea level rises slightly. There is a knife-edge balance here as dynamic and as vital as that between the Gulf and the beach.

The river also brings a haze of suspended organic matter, energy-laden nutrients scoured from its watershed. From particles of decomposing sycamore leaves to carbonates leached from Cenozoic sea floors, everything is trundled downstream as a thin soup that is greedily imbibed by members of the plankton. It is also sieved, sucked, and gobbled up by the infauna, the creatures that burrow in the bottom. Even some fishes, like mullet and menhaden, filter the spare gruel. The rest, from blue crabs to red drum and raccoons to snowy egrets, share in the feast by eating the eaters.

Even in this subtropical climate, the salt marsh has seasonal cycles of activity, from the doldrums of summer to the spring and fall passage of migrating birds. Less well known but fully as important is the seasonal migration of aquatic creatures. Blue crabs, white and brown shrimp, red drum, and flounder all lay their eggs in the Gulf of Mexico, and there they hatch. Their larvae ride the flood tides through the passes and spend their juvenile lives feeding and hiding in the marsh. These mass movements of homing larvae, the gulfward immigration of adults, and the developmental cycles of resident marsh species such as oysters and speckled trout, are oriented and choreographed to times of plenty in the marsh. Usually that means spring and fall, when the rivers release their maximum discharge from recent rains. These natural seasonal pulses of freshwater set the tempo for the bay and marsh, thus knitting one more link between the fresh and marine systems.

I cannot see these links between river and marsh, but I am persuaded that they exist. The results are all around me: a plenitude of nutrients; a comforting pad of sediment; a forest of green stems and skeins of green slimes; an abundance of nooks and crannies chocked with protoplasm packaged in all manner of tasty sizes and shapes; ripples, soft splashes, and burps of activity from every quarter; moderate temperature; salubrious salinity; green films bubbling with oxygen; ample water; lavish sunshine. And this whole potent, vital concoction is flushed, rinsed, invigorated, mixed, and stirred into biochemical motion by the rise and fall of the tide. Even though our local tidal range is piddling, it maintains the pace-setting quality of tides the world over by instilling vigor among the denizens of the marsh. Is it any wonder that the natural hydroponics of a salt marsh generate life more exuberantly than does any other natural ecosystem on earth, not excepting rain forests and coral reefs?

I can as well call this scene an *estuary*—a grand coming together of the best that freshwater and salt water have to offer. But what's in a name? That which we call an estuary by another name would smell as effluvious: food basket, nursery ground, wellspring. The bounty of this marsh, where life is most diverse, most abundant, and most fecund, feeds the bulk of the barrier island ecosystem.

Whether I use binoculars to watch a marsh hawk snatch an unwary marsh rice rat from amid the maritime saltwort or get down on hands and knees to observe a myriad of shore flies contentedly sponging the sticky wetness from a mat of blue-green algae, I miss much of the real seethe that churns inside this marsh. For that I need a microscope and a dole of imagination, for I must enter an alien world.

Everyone is at least vaguely familiar with the natural cycle: life, death, decomposition, life renewed. In the bowels of the marsh—down in the muck—the role of decay looms so large that it obscures the definition between life and death. In a marsh, where life is so prolific and death so ongoing, the less digestible parts of plants (and to a lesser extent, of animals) rapidly pile up and are immediately coated with a slick of bacteria and fungi. These invisible but potent microbes begin to break down and soften the resistant vegetable tissues; and their activity impresses the muck with the cloying redolence of a diaper pail.

Thus tenderized, the once-ignored vegetable pieces become attractive to a host of appetites with nimble nipping mouthparts, the "choppers and mincers" of the marsh: grass shrimp, mud crabs, fiddler crabs, isopods, amphipods, killifish. They snip out microbites until there is nothing left but shredded fibers. This particulate matter the tides distribute throughout the marsh. All this bothers the microbes not at all. Indeed, the maceration has enhanced the surface area over which they can spread their busy colonies. The rate of decomposition simply accelerates.

A bacterium, however, being so vanishingly small, has no room for mouth, teeth, or internal organs. It accosts its food by secreting digestive enzymes outside its unicellular body. There the chemicals reduce the most resistant foodstuff to a mush that is then absorbed by the microbe. A mushed-up bit of organic matter coated with live-and-working bacteria and fungi is called *detritus*. In a particle of detritus, not only is the original nutriment in the plant tissue exposed and rendered edible, but much of it is transformed into microbial protoplasm—a toothsome morsel for any detritivore that comes along.

In a marsh there are plenty of hungry candidates: nematode worms, cumaceans and ostracods, fiddler crabs, angelwing clams, plicate hornshells, barrel bubble snails, chironomid midges, and red thread-worms. Detritus gets vacuumed up, sieved out, and gobbled down nearly as fast as it is formed. Indeed, this half-dead, half-live, smelly, seemingly insignificant, and thoroughly unappetizing looking sludge is the principal organic power source that drives the livelihood of the marsh and, in turn, much of Matagorda Island.

Once eaten by a juvenile brown shrimp, say, a detrital particle is not finished. As the dark wad threads along the shrimp's intestine, it is scavenged of some of its vegetable and most of its microbial content, but not all. Inedible fragments are coalesced from hundreds of ingested particles and finally ejected as a neat cylindrical fecal pellet the size of a pinhead. Immediately, such pellets are colonized by legions of bacteria and fungi, which are as avid over this once-digested mass as they were for recently deceased plant tissues.

Soon the fecal dropping is squishy and slick with a seething population of microorganisms. Along comes a mysid shrimp, which grabs up the delicacy and proceeds to devour this "second harvest" with gusto. Again the organic matter passes through a gut, and the depleted leavings are extruded as feces. After microbial infiltration of this frugal waste, a capitellid worm makes a tertiary harvest. The progressive decomposition continues until the last calories are drained and the detrital mill has ground the original foodstuff into little more than a mineral stain on the substrate. Eventually, a probing root hair will encounter and absorb the stain. Bellies have been filled, the food chain charged, the water cleansed, a fastidious miracle wrought.

Then there are the desulfovibrios, the *really* alien bacteria, so exotic that atmospheric oxygen is to them a violent poison. They live sealed in the oxygen-free, nutrient-rich, utterly black viscid world beneath the surface of the muck. There they consume organic matter by primordial biochemical pathways so contorted that toxic sulfuric acid and hydrogen sulfide leak out as by-products. The hydrogen sulfide permeates the muck with the odor of rotten eggs and stains the entire substrate black by combining with iron particles to form ferrous sulfide.

Several kinds of worms are adapted to withstand this ooze. When they burrow to the surface, oxygen in the air gains access to the depths and converts the black ferrous sulfide into brown ferric sulfate in a sort of worm-induced rust formation. When I turn a shovelful of semisolid muck, it appears black with dendritic brown traces outlining the paths of the worm burrows.

Aside from dictating the limits of the surrounding zones of vegetation and stirring the suspended materials in the water, a rising tide quickens the entire marsh. Oysters gape, set up their feeding currents, and spit little fountains of pseudofeces into the air. Snapping shrimp pop, ghost shrimp clear their burrows, and grass shrimp appear from nowhere. A dozen kinds of worms and clams rouse from their crypts in the sediment to whatever dim level of consciousness they ever muster. Burrowing sea cucumbers unfurl their conveyor-belt arms, while acorn worms begin to exude their curls of sludge. Amphipods skitter, ostracods dart, and bubble snails plow their way along the bottom. Saltmarsh periwinkles slide up the stalks of grass ahead of the rising waterline, while saltmarsh grasshoppers and an assortment of spiders head for the leafy canopy. Striped hermit crabs, mud fiddler crabs, marsh crabs, and blue crabs all begin to stir. Little fishes wriggle excitedly, some with their backs exposed, each anxious to be among the first to probe the advancing waterfront for goodies. Bigger fish follow little fish, and the birds arrive in squadrons to ensure that the upper echelons of the food chain get stoked.

When the tide goes out, it exposes a perimeter of dark mud between the grass line and the retreating waterline. The sun quickly bakes the surface into a cracked crust where only flies, small beetles, and tiny shore bugs routinely scamper. The other residents of this tidal flat have sucked down into the cool, moist interior, sometimes retreating a foot or so to contact the soupy interface between sediment and groundwater.

Least and western sandpipers, Wilson's plovers, dunlin, dowitchers, greater yellowlegs, and willets know to work the cracks and the edge of the flat near and just beyond the waterline, where the substrate stays moist enough for the subterranean fauna to remain within pecking depth. Willets and plovers are sharp eyed enough to pick up cryptic surface clues or slight movements to detect their quarry. Dunlin, dowitchers, and most sandpipers rely on their sensitive bill tips to signal the position of buried prey. These probers can forage with their eyes closed, and indeed when I use binoculars to watch them working, I frequently see that on the downward thrust their eyes are tight shut, probably for protection from mud and water.

When I dig where these birds have been poking, I am astounded at the evident sensitivity of their bills. Some of the mudworms and midge larvae that wriggle on my sieve are little more than minuscule red curlicues of protoplasm, so small that I cannot feel half a dozen of them moving in a drop of water on my fingertip. Yet the birds detect and extract them with apparent ease. How many of these writhing fractional calories must it take to adequately stoke the frenetic disposition of a least sandpiper for a day? Whatever the outcome of the calculation, it would likely rival the more publicized metabolic equation for a hummingbird. Multiply the result by the number of shorebirds at work and be further amazed at the productivity of this seemingly lifeless expanse of mud.

JULY '95: *Hot today, but the tide is out, and I do not want to miss an opportunity to check the mudflat.*

Lots of delicate wagon wheel imprints, each with radiating spokes and a tiny hole for a hub. Some a bit larger than the others; a scant palm width across. I dug beneath several of these and collected some flaccid, bright yellow worms that squirmed energetically for a while and then went still in my container of water. Finally realized that these were not worms at all but severed clam siphons! So I began to dig deeper. Sure enough, about eight inches down I consistently got constricted macomas (Macoma constricta). *Pretty white shells cleanly upswept to the right at the rear end. The clams lie horizontally on their left side, so the incurrent siphon, when it emerges, is directed neatly upward along the curvature of the shell. When water covers the flat, this flexuous tube is pushed to the surface of the mud and extended like an animated vacuum cleaner to snuffle for detritus. Repeated extensions and withdrawals scribe the wagon wheel. Neat!*

Smaller wagon wheels, easily covered by a half-dollar, are made by Culver's sandworms (Laeonereis culveri) *reaching out as far as they can for organic matter. A quick slice with the shovel catches them still descending in their tubes. This is easily the most common medium-sized polychaete on the flat—the shortest distance between detritus and shorebirds.*

Western sandpipers were getting sandworms only a few yards from where I was squatting. They have a keen technique. When a bird grasps one end of a worm, the bird rears back gently, pulling the worm partway out of its tunnel. Then the sandpiper relaxes and quickly shifts its grip further along its prey. Again it leans back. I can see the worm stretch thin, but before it snaps, the bird apparently feels the tension and slacks off. Directly, the sandpiper gets the entire worm free of the mud, gobbles it down, and immediately begins to probe for another. I judge that a busy bird—and all seem continually busy— gets one sandworm every thirty seconds.

Tiny piles of black fecal pellets mark the excretory pores of capitellid threadworms (Heteromastus filiformis). *The more I look, the more I see. These thin, maroon worms burrow everywhere, even in the anaerobic, sulfurous layers. They snap so easily that I seldom get a whole one in my collecting jar. I am not sure even a sandpiper can do any better. It does not seem to matter much to the worm. A head with only a quarter body just keeps right on trucking.*

In water beneath my microscope a threadworm continually coils and uncoils like a watch spring while its proboscis regularly everts into a bright spherical balloon. At home in the ooze, the worm moves by expanding its balloon, which then acts as a temporary anchor while the remainder of the body is drawn forward. It then deflates, burrows ahead, reinflates, and repeats the process. Threadworms do not have to forage for food. They just eat their way through their endless universe of fortified muck. Their guts extract organic matter and compact the indigestible remainder into chains of little mud balls that I can see queued up in the intestine awaiting expulsion.

From interesting to bizarre! I noticed small coiled pats of extruded mud that looked like they had been squeezed from a buried toothpaste tube. Within a few inches of each mound there was a shallow funnel half an inch across and about as deep in the surface of the substrate. Took me awhile to realize that the toothpaste and the funnel were at opposite ends of a U tube, and to get at the critter responsible I needed to dig about six inches down between these two surface marks.

What I unearthed was truly weird: wormy but no true worm; about as long as my little finger; nearly colorless except for five thin white bands running the length of its soft, squirming body; a flowerlike spray of wiggling tentacles on one end; no obvious head, eyes, legs. Although the thing looked slick, it was prickly to the touch and even stuck briefly to my fingers like Velcro when I tried to drop a specimen into my jar.

Looking under the scope I quickly verified my suspicion—a burrowing sea cucumber (Leptosynapta inhaerens)! *How many naturalists are fortunate enough to count such intriguing creatures among their backyard fauna? In a dish of water they convulse with peristaltic waves, like so many disassociated lengths of intestine. The mouth is at one end, surrounded by a ring of twelve tentacles lined with little fingerlike processes. Each tentacle continually reaches out with grasping motions, curling outward and downward like a hand with probing fingers. This is the way the sea cucumber picks up detritus that slides into its feeding funnel. A loaded tentacle bends into the mouth, where it is swept clean.*

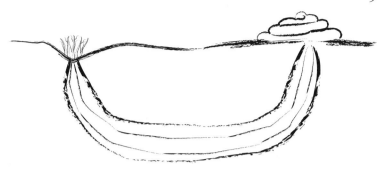

Burrowing sea cucumber

When I rack to higher power, I can see that the skin of a sea cucumber is thickly embedded with tiny anchor-shaped ossicles. These account for the animal's burrlike feel, and they allow it to maintain its position inside its burrow.

MARCH '96: *A flock of American avocets foraging in a mere skim of water at the edge of the marsh on a falling tide. They march forward in a ragged line. Each bird hunches over and trots ahead on turquoise legs, working its unique upswept bill rapidly from side to side, delicately scooping up the organic pap that coats the bottom, then pausing to gobble greedily before hurrying forward to keep up with the advancing group.*

These birds do not seem to be looking or feeling for food, and they are not sifting it from the muck; they are simply swallowing the slippery bottom-stuff entire. They must leave it to their digestive systems to glean calories and pass the dollop of inert material.

I went out with a hand net and did some skimming of my own. Poured the barely palpable ooze into a dish and let it settle, then scanned it with my binocular microscope. I had no idea that I would be three days working through the miraculous menagerie hidden in the slush! Scanning the surface of the muck beneath an inch of water under 20x is exciting—like being inside a submersible cruising the silent flatness of the abyss!

Movement everywhere. Hairlike strands poking out of pinholes and whipping in the water. The most abundant sort is paired. The pairs are neatly spaced, each couplet just beyond touching distance of the next pair; a scad per square inch. These are the dual feeding tentacles of mud whipworms (Polydora ligni). I can see floccules of organic matter sticking to the whips, then zipping along the conveyor belt of cilia and into the worm's mouth.

*There is another kind of paired whip scattered among the mudworms.
This duo is shorter but just as busy picking up particles. A second pair of
filaments occasionally emerges from the same hole and stands passively
upright in the water. These are fleshy gills decorated with bars of copper
green, and they give the hidden worm its name—bar-gilled mudworm*
(Streblospio benedicti).

*Spent nearly an hour trying to identify the numerous very thin solitary
whips poking up among the mudworm tentacles. Nothing seemed to work.
Then it dawned on me: these were not polychaete worms at all. They are
oligochaetes! Finally took them to Naididae. Close enough.*

*More worms. This time not annelids. Nematodes. A virtual seethe of them
whipping through the muck everywhere. And an occasional wormy maggot—the larvae of long-legged flies* (Dolichopodidae). *Finally, down nearly
at protozoan dimensions, a swarm of actively cruising acoel flatworms.*

*And swimming things. At least three kinds of copepods. Several varieties of
large, twirling ciliate protozoans. An occasional hurrying ostracod. And the
peculiar little crustaceans called tanaids* (Leptochelia rapax). *These ordinarily live in flimsy tubes in the ooze, but when displaced, they bob to the
surface of the water where they get trapped in the clutches of the surface film.
There they struggle helplessly, showing their every detail to my lens.*

*Early on I noticed that the silt sample was laced with short strands of
blue-green algae, riddled with banana-shaped, motoring diatoms and
packed with detrital floc. This entire sediment literally is working alive
with animal-things and plant-things, ready calories for those who can
glean them.*

*Deft action with fastidious bills prevents the avocets from taking in too
much mineral muck. A discriminating gut sops many of the usable calories
from the slurry before the remainder is squirted back into the water to begin
another round. A remarkable transformation of goo into bird. Such mundane
alchemy is what keeps me rooted on this island.*

The commonest finger-sized holes in the tidal flat are made by ghost
shrimp (*Callianassa jamaicense*). Although they are different from the
ones that inhabit the surf, the animals look much the same and lead a
comparable lifestyle. Here, where burrows are more permanent, ghost
shrimp dig deep, branching, interconnected tunnels. When I dig into
one entrance, fountains of water squirt up from half a dozen surrounding holes. The slurper is still the best tool. I wait for the rising tide.
When the first skim of water fills the holes, the ghost shrimp begin to

clean house. An early morning sun sidelights the emerging stream of water, and a quick draw on the slurper usually sucks up a surprised ghost shrimp.

There are less numerous finger-sized holes in the mud, recognizable by being more precisely rounded and leading into a dark tube that plunges straight down. At the bottom, sometimes over two feet into the ooze, lies one of the most impressive denizens of the tidal flat.

I prefer to await a rising tide so I can view the burrows beneath several inches of water. Soon, what appears to be a small, flesh-colored elephant's trunk complete with a pair of prominent nostrils pokes up an inch or so out of one of the round holes. If the light is right, I can see a burble of water swirling around the busy nostrils. I need to do a quick dig to see more. I go up to my armpit in the muck before my fingertips contact the chalky edge of a fragile shell. After a careful retrieval I wash my treasure to reveal the white, sharply ridged, neatly tapered shells of an angelwing clam (*Cyrtopleura costata*), a favorite of beachcombers. Subterranean colonies of these animals usually go unnoticed in the marsh, except for their siphons (the "elephant's trunk"), which draw in and expel water.

Other members of the infauna commence to do their thing when the tide rises. Razor clams, jackknife clams, and dwarf surf clams suck in their share of suspended and deposited organic matter. Red-gilled worms, the larger ones ten inches long, rise to scrap what they can from the softened upper sediment. Bamboo worms, so named for their characteristic segmentation, begin to draw detritus into the bottoms of their thin vertical tubes, while plume worms poke out of the tops of their crook-shaped parchment tubes to hawk anything edible that drifts by. Trumpet worms scratch their way through the sediment with a battery of stiff golden setae and use thin tentacles to drag detrital particles into their exquisitely manufactured home—a mobile case shaped like an inverted ice-cream cone with a crystalline wall one sand grain thick, the particles so precisely cemented together as to make the great wall of Machu Picchu seem haphazard by comparison. The aptly named medusa worm rises to one end of its U-tube and extends a writhing tangle of tentacles across the bottom in search of organic particles. Meanwhile, bloodworms, clam worms, and yellow paddle worms, all possessing an eversible proboscis equipped with wicked ice tong–like jaws, cruise the upper sediment or lie in ambush for any soft-bodied creature that wanders by.

Crustaceans—the insects of this brackish world—are everywhere. A net drawn on a rising tide can harvest a clicking and leaping mass of brown shrimp, white shrimp, and grass shrimp mixed with scuttling blue crabs and lumbering striped hermit crabs. A fine-mesh hand net may snare arrow shrimp, broken-back shrimp, and a variety of amphipods and isopods.

Any seine haul will likely come in heavy with a windrow of clear, amorphous comb jellies. "No, they are not jellyfish." And, I tell kids for the hundredth time, "They won't sting! Pick one up, like this." About the time the kids get the courage to feel the strange, gelatinous consistency of a comb jelly, I notice a sea nettle—a true jellyfish of the stinging variety—in the midst and warn them. Immediately, they lose interest in touching anything remotely jellylike.

It takes patience, but they learn more than it seems. Just being here, seeing, shuddering, hesitantly touching, getting wet and dirty and mosquito bitten, making little personal discoveries, being with a WGA who gets as excited as they are—it is all so much more meaningful and lasting than sitting slouch backed in air-conditioned comfort watching a nature program on television. For all concerned, including Matagorda Island itself, this is time well spent.

A seine pulled across the flooded mudflat, even one tugged and twisted by enthusiastic but comically inept kids, always yields fish: bay anchovies, tidewater silversides, gulf menhaden, spots, pinfish, black drum, lizard fish, gulf killifish, long-nosed killifish, sheepshead killifish, Atlantic needlefish, bay wiffs, personable little naked gobies, baby

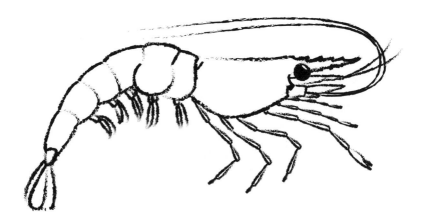

Grass shrimp

southern flounders—perfect miniature replicas of the adults—neat little blackcheek tonguefish, exotic sea robins, young speckled trout and redfish, and everyone's favorite—baby puffer fish inflated and bobbing like little balls on the surface of the water in the collecting pail.

Kids go wild at the catch. "Put only a few of each kind into the buckets. We don't want twenty thousand anchovies. They'll die." They hear, but they cannot resist. I do not press the point. After all, they are here for hands-on discovery. I will pour 19,975 anchovies back into the water as soon as I can. The rest we handle, discuss, and release.

One of the most abundant, most important, and in many ways the most remarkable fish in the shallows around Matagorda Island is fast enough to avoid most seines, although it falls ready prey to a cast net. The striped mullet (*Mugil cephalus*) definitely ranks as a keystone species in the barrier ecosystem. As the mullet goes, so goes everything from clumps of submarine algae to great blue herons.

The really remarkable thing about the striped mullet is its food and feeding strategy. I once asked Norman, my resident Matagorda philosopher and naturalist, what mullet eat. "Well," he said, "yew know I think they jest eat mud. Yew gut one, that's all that's in there. Yew can't hardly get one to take a hook except on accident." As usual, he was close to the truth.

Schools of striped mullet spend most of their time near the bottom with their heads down and their backs inclined about thirty degrees, their lips gently brushing the surface of the substrate. Thus positioned, they swim slowly forward, moving their bodies rhythmically from side to side as they vacuum up fine sediment. You can detect a school of working mullet at a distance by the mud plume they raise in the shallows and by the flock of Forster's terns hovering just above it. When a fish encounters a submerged object, it pauses in its routine to probe and suck over its entire surface. If a school enters a backwater where the wind has accumulated foam and scum on the surface, the fish rise and suck noisily at the surface film. They do eat great quantities of mud and debris, but what they are really after is the organic content— the detritus, the thick growths of algae, and the seething colonies of protozoans, microbes, nematodes, and whatnot that live in the sediment. So, mullet are piscine equivalents of foraging avocets.

A fish needs special anatomy to live off mud. The striped mullet has thick lips equipped with special valves, along with a muscular tongue and pliant gill covers to create the vacuum that draws in the sediment.

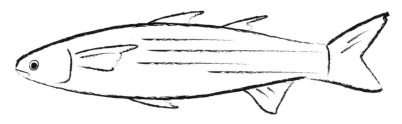

Striped mullet

The slurry passes through a battery of increasingly fine filters in the gill chambers, the last set of near-microscopic caliber. This apparatus screens most larger inedibles, which are spit out or pass through the gill slits. The remainder, the goodies still mixed with much silt, sand, and clay, is sucked through the slitlike gullet into the stomach.

From the stomach the slush is pumped into a muscular gizzard, where it is wrung and scarified using the grit as a grinding paste until all the soft particles are pulverized. Finally, the mud-colored puree enters the exceptionally long intestine, which is loaded with helpful bacteria and provided with adequate surface contact to absorb the calorific material while letting the inedibles pass.

Despite its specialized feeding anatomy, a striped mullet gleans only about one part of foodstuff from every hundred parts of sediment it ingests. Therefore, the fish needs to forage almost continually to meet its needs. The countless schools of ravenous mullet scouring the shallows and eagerly invading the salt marsh on high tide merit their keystone status not only for their influence on the food web but for their impact on the texture and chemistry of the sediment and the recycling of its nutrients.

There is another characteristic of the striped mullet that visitors always notice and ask about, which ecologists always try to dodge because they do not know the answer. Mullet jump. Mullet leap clear of the water, shining like silver spears in the sun, sparkling out across the bay where most sweeps of the binoculars will catch one or more in the act. Caught up in the sport, a given fish might leap half a dozen times in quick succession, progressing like a flat rock skipping across the surface.

The begging question, of course, is why. Why do mullet jump? The two most common answers both sound lame to me. One is that the fish are trying to rid themselves of parasites, this despite the fact that no self-respecting external parasitic fish louse would ever lose either its hold or its determination during a brief aerial excursion. The other is that the fish are trying to escape submarine predators. This one is closer to the mark, at least for compact schools of small mullet that frequently break the surface as they scatter before the torpedo assault of a hungry speckled trout. But these skittering little fish do not really leap clear of the water; they are just frenetically trying to get out of harm's way. The larger solitary mullet that vault in such neat arcs do so with a leisurely demeanor, almost seeming to pause in midair to enjoy the spate of sunshine. (It is my impression that they do not jump as frequently on an overcast day.) When they jump repeatedly, they advance forward in a straight line, not in a skittish zigzag path as though a predator were on their tail.

So, why *do* striped mullet jump? (I never asked Norman. I wish I had.) I have a heretical answer that will cause professional biologists to shudder but that is immediately accepted by my visitors as a logical explanation that fits all the observable facts. Mullet *enjoy* jumping! Is an animal with a dim brain smaller than a pea and a stomach full of mud capable of an emotion traditionally reserved for higher, cognizant beings? I don't see why not. Although I do not need to justify my conclusion to most visitors, I add a bit of "science" by pointing out that striped mullet are related to flying fish and so are possessed of a body shape and positioned pectoral fins that lend themselves to aerial excursions.

Perhaps the urge to jump is in a mullet's genes, a surging atavism that sends the fish soaring for no better reason than to exalt itself. As we gather on the boardwalk and observe a foot-long silver streak exuberantly describe a series of perfect parabolas directly in front of us, it is not difficult to go a step further and believe that this splendid fish is deliberately showing off its stuff.

One of the most interesting life-forms of the grassy margin of the marsh is the grass itself. Here, in a zone that varies from a few yards to a half mile in width, smooth cordgrass (*Spartina alterniflora*) reigns in undisputed monoculture. When the tide is out, the grass stands tall on a glistening, soft substrate that is an inland extension of the open mudflat. When the tide comes in, only the upper portions of the grass blades and seed heads protrude above the surface. Of course, between tidal extremes the plants experience intermediate degrees of submergence.

There is more going on here than meets the eye. For one thing, the distribution of the grass is directly limited by the tidal range. Beyond the reach of high tide smooth cordgrass does not grow, and its cessation is abrupt and clear-cut. Obviously, the plant needs periodic tidal wash to survive. Although isolated clumps of cordgrass invade the mudflat, when the tide comes in, these outliers are totally inundated and scoured by the waves, so they do not persist. Smooth cordgrass needs water, but it is not a submarine plant.

Within its favored zone smooth cordgrass grows chest high in thick, green luxuriance, and to gaze upon it one would never know that this plant has claimed for its own one of the most difficult environments in the seemingly passive, incomprehensible world of green plants.

Smooth cordgrass faces a trio of knotty biological problems: too much salt, too little oxygen, and periodic near-total submergence. In addition, it occasionally must survive temporary dehydration, overheating, and battering by storm waves. Lacking the behavioral repertoire of an animal, the plant responds to these stresses with stoic anatomical and physiological adaptations.

One reward for its ingenuity is that smooth cordgrass has the immediate shoreline to itself. No other local grass or multicelled green plant of any kind can compete for sunshine and nutrients here because it cannot withstand the stressful conditions that plague the bailiwick of smooth cordgrass.

Take salt. All horticulturists know that even a little salt in the water causes their plants to wilt and die as a result of osmosis—too much salt around the roots draws water from the plant until it collapses from hydraulically imposed dehydration. (Drop a crisp lettuce leaf into a dish of weak salt water, and watch it sag into a soggy mess before your eyes.)

Enter the simple genius of smooth cordgrass. Its jillions of near-microscopic root hairs—the organs of absorption—are sheathed in a special membrane laced with enzymes that allow water to enter but keep out most of the salt. The pump that actually pulls the water inside against the osmotic grain is impressive but not unique. Thin water columns reach up the stem from root to leaf. Each of these water pipes terminates in a microscopic hole on the underside of a leaf.

Evaporation of water from the top of each pipe tugs on the entire attached water column. This upward pulling force is transmitted to the level of the root hairs, which obligingly draw in fresh water molecules from the substrate to replace those dragged aloft. The botanist speaks of *transpiration*.

This action of an upper-level evaporator pump allows all green vascular plants from trees the height of redwoods to greenery that does not clear shoe-top level to extract water from the ground and haul it up among their tissues. But think ahead about the special situation of smooth cordgrass. As the root hairs pull in water, the rejected salt inevitably accumulates in the muck immediately outside. Were this to continue, even the doughty membranes and straining pumps of smooth cordgrass would be overwhelmed by the rising, inexorable osmotic drawing power of the crust of salt building around the root hairs. Thus, the marriage between tide and smooth cordgrass. The grass relies on the tide to rinse away excess salt.

Now we can understand the sharp edge that defines the upper level of cordgrass on the shore: it marks the precise elevation reached by a routine high tide. In fact, as this upper limit is approached, the flushing service of the tide gradually diminishes, and salt stress progressively increases. You can see the effect on the cordgrass, which changes from chest high where the tidal flux is adequate to a stressed-out ankle height at its inland boundary.

No machine is perfect, and even the polished, osmotic system of smooth cordgrass is no exception. It leaks, so considerable salt does get inside. Special vacuoles within the plant cells store some of this salt away from the working cytoplasm, and the cells use it to maintain their individual osmotic balance and healthy turgid state. The excess gets routed to special glands in the leaves, which manage to secrete crystals of pure sodium chloride to the exterior. Once again to the rescue, the tide arrives to wash the salt encrustation away.

Although our bodies must also maintain osmotic balance, it is a less consuming effort than the one smooth cordgrass is forced to wage. The best I can do to bring this silent challenge home to students is to have them wade out to observe the sparkle on the cordgrass leaves. Then I have them grasp a leaf between thumb and index finger and gently slide their grip from base to tip. "Now, lick your fingers." They do so, puckering in dim appreciation of what it takes for this grass to survive.

The foliage of a vascular green plant gets most of its oxygen from the atmosphere and as a by-product of photosynthesis, but the vast root system is dependent upon air pockets between soil particles for its supply of this vital gas. Once again, the yeomen root hairs perform the critical task of absorption. For smooth cordgrass, however, the challenge is daunting. The black muck surrounding its root hairs is practically devoid of oxygen: first, because ooze is too soft to cradle air pockets and, second, because the seethe of microbes at the surface uses the gas in its own boiling metabolism before it can diffuse into the depths. So, the root hairs exist in an anaerobic substratum.

But smooth cordgrass has engineered a dodge that solves the problem. It has built a special set of pneumatic pipes that stretch from the same holes in the leaves that serve as evaporation ports for its water pipes. The air ducts plunge down the stem and ramify into the tissues of the roots. As the roots go about their metabolic business, they consume oxygen and produce carbon dioxide. This sets up two diffusion gradients in the air pipes, one drawing fresh oxygen from the atmosphere down to the roots and the other drafting carbon dioxide from roots to atmosphere. This passive contrivance handles the demands of the root system without the need for an auxiliary pump or breathing apparatus. For demonstration, I cut across a cordgrass stem and let students look down on the severed ends of its hundreds of air pipes.

"OK, say you're a cordgrass root cell buried in the muck hanging on to dear life by breathing through a soda straw stuck up into the air. What do you do when the tide rises and floods your straw?" In jest someone sings out, "You hold your breath." To the twitter of laughter I respond, "Right! How do you do that if you're nothing more than a piece of dumb grass?" Pause. "You hold your nostrils closed," chuckles another imaginative jokester. But when I call out "Right" again, they begin to wonder if I am toying with them or if in fact they have happened upon an animal-like response in a passive plant.

At least they are now attentive enough to grasp my explanation. A pair of special cells borders each of the holes in the leaves. When the tide begins to inundate a leaf, the guard cells rapidly absorb water, swell up, and join to seal the opening to the air duct, just as a person might pinch his nostrils closed before submerging. Whereas a swimmer might be able to hold her breath a minute or so, the more slowly metabolizing smooth cordgrass can hold its breath for several hours, until the tide falls.

Because the closed pores are also used to draw in carbon dioxide for photosynthesis, it would seem that a plant forced to hold its breath during the daytime would suffer a setback in food production. Not so for resourceful smooth cordgrass. It is what biologists call a "C_4 photosynthesizer"—it has a means of storing carbon dioxide for just such an exigency, so it proceeds with life as usual even with its nostrils closed.

As the group slogged to shore, I glanced back and noticed that one student had not moved. I turned and waded back out to join her. I saw that she was staring down into the turbid water, caught up in a muse. As I approached, she looked up and said with an apologetic smile, "Poor grass." I perceived that she was quite serious, and I responded reassuringly, "Well, remember this is one tough grass. It will do just fine. But I am proud of you for feeling compassion for it. Even a crusty survivor like smooth cordgrass needs a bit of TLC now and then." In that brief moment we had shared something meaningful. Smooth cordgrass was but a medium, of course; it was the aura of communication that counted. Here was one of those totally unplanned golden moments for a teacher, when he tries to pass along something he thinks is important and there is a receptive mind there waiting, and before he realizes it he has touched another life.

The list of creatures associated with the smooth cordgrass zone is complex enough to recognize a smooth cordgrass community. Snails such as marsh periwinkles and virgin nerites slide up and down the lower stems, scraping off attached algae. One reason these snails keep above the waterline when the tide rises is to avoid the reach of blue crabs or stone crabs, which are among their most insistent predators. If a snail eludes the crabs, it may still be picked off by a clapper rail or snatched up by a marsh rice rat.

Ribbed mussels, clam worms, marsh crabs, mud crabs, tube-building amphipods, grass shrimp, and several kinds of killifishes all live out their scuttling, wriggling, burrowing lives amid the rootstocks. A variety of predators hunts along the mud surface among the grass stalks, from raccoons and gulf saltmarsh snakes to tiger beetles (of four species, all different from the one that inhabits the beach), and shore bugs. Herons and egrets patrol the margins, clapper rails slink between the stems, seaside sparrows and sedge wrens forage through the foliage, barn owls by night and marsh hawks by day sail over the grass tops, red-winged blackbirds alight on the seed heads, and boat-tailed grackles scrounge wherever they can.

All summer long the cordgrass canopy rustles with activity and emits an array of sounds—a whispery click, a *tic-tic,* and *ssspt.* These are produced mostly by male saltmarsh katydids, rapier katydids, and saltmarsh grasshoppers, each intent on attracting their respective female consorts. All are some cryptic shade of cordgrass green. I think these are the insects most likely responsible for the scallops eaten into the margins of the grass blades. These herbivores must beware of Brunner's mantis, a stealthy ambush predator with its trademark triangular head set on a swivel neck, the penetrating gaze, and the lightning-swift jackknife forelegs.

The waving canopy is also home to an array of spiders. Some common kinds, such as jumping spiders, crab spiders, and climbing wolf spiders, do not build webs but stalk, pounce, and overcome their victims. Each night long-jawed orb weavers string their large webs among the grass blades. Next morning the battered remains of these nets are clotted with the bodies of crane flies and mosquitoes. At the other size extreme, the filigreed snares of meshweb weavers hardly span my thumbnail. They are positioned in the angle where a grass blade attaches to the stem and are designed to capture aphids, midges, and gnats.

The most common ants in the cordgrass jungle are what Martha and I call valentine ants (*Crematogaster laeviuscula*) after the shape of their shining black abdomens, which they hold aloft when they get excited. They cut a neat round entrance hole in a cordgrass stem, then line the hollow interior with a papier-mâché of chewed plant fibers, and set up shop. I am not sure what the staple in their diet is, but I have seen valentine ants tending aphids among the stalk tips and sipping sap exuding from lesions in the stalks.

Flies, flies—everywhere in the cordgrass canopy there are buzzing flies. Deerflies, with brown blotches on their wings, the females with the habit of alighting so slyly and deliberately between my shoulder blades that they have a chance to get a quick draft of blood before I can unlimber enough to swat them in that awkward spot. Long-legged flies, each one a living spark of gleaming metallic blue that somehow avoids getting tarnished even while sprinting over the surface of the ooze. Horseflies, with such enormous, glowing, emerald eyes that they are aptly called "green-heads." The females lay eggs on the lower reaches of cordgrass stalks, and their leathery-skinned, knobby maggots telescope through the muck feeding on polychaete worms, midge larvae, and microcrustaceans.

A horsefly on the wing is literally faster than the eye can follow, yet there is an aerial predator here that can snatch one in midair. I frequently see a sleek, spare robber fly perched atop a cordgrass stalk sucking the body fluids from a freshly caught horsefly. This fighter plane of the insect world uses its bristly legs as a basket to ensnare flying prey so it can be stabbed with the robber fly's daggerlike proboscis. I once saw a robber fly smash into a flying cicada, subdue it, and with a great buzzing of wings manage to reverse the fall of its heavy prey and gain a feeding perch atop the bend on a cordgrass leaf. This whole predaceous robber fly scenario is played out on a reduced scale by little look-alike dance flies that pull down flying gnats and midges.

Among my favorites are the picture-winged flies. They have brown-barred wings and bright metallic bodies and seem very aware of each other, for they spend their time swirling round the grass stalks chasing each other, all the while flitting their pretty wings. I am sure they are sending some sort of semaphore messages to each other. When I see a cordgrass stalk with a dead tip, I frequently find a fly maggot inside; I suspect it will pupate into a picture-winged fly.

There is more to the menagerie in the cordgrass. In late summer scorpionflies (they are of ancient lineage and are not true flies) join the cordgrass coterie. They have droll, drooping snouts, four weak wings, and a yellow-and-brown pattern that resembles that of a paper wasp. They do not seem to eat much of anything, although I have seen them sucking at fresh bird plops and pilfering prey from spiderwebs. Although scorpionflies are harmless, the males hold their abdomens with the tips upturned, reminiscent of a stubby scorpion's sting. Because a scorpionfly has the color of a wasp and a copulatory apparatus that looks like a stinger, I can never get a visitor very close to one.

As you would expect, cordgrass is infested with cordgrass bugs (*Ischnodemus falicus*). These elongate, straight-sided insects fit neatly into the slot between a leaf sheath and the stem, "Like they were made for each other," one perceptive young man exclaimed. When their cover is peeled back, the agile little bugs put on a comical show as they deftly squirrel around the stem. As they have sucking mouthparts, I presume that cordgrass bugs draw sap from their host plant.

Something would seem amiss if on any sunny day I could not look across the top of the cordgrass canopy and see a drift of saltmarsh dragonflies (*Erythrodiplax berenice*). The smoke blue males and brown, yellow-spotted females like to perch on the very tips of the grass stalks,

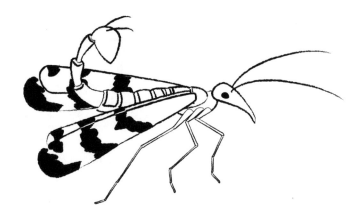

Scorpionfly

where they have a good view of each other and of small flying insects upon which they prey. On the entire continent, this is the only species of dragonfly with an aquatic larva adapted to tolerate brackish water.

AUGUST '96: *While slogging through the smooth cordgrass on the edge of Bray Cove, I noticed small, colorful beetles milling around on the flower heads. Later saw the same kind on flower heads of salt grass, so they are apparently important pollinators for these two salt marsh grasses. Many were paired up, the female dispassionately feeding on pollen and the male mounted rather precariously on top trying to get his mate in the mood for more serious business.*

Took a few back and identified them as soft-winged flower beetles (Collops sp., Melyridae). *They are pretty under the scope. Soft, hairy all over. The orange wing covers bear two pairs of squarish, gunmetal blue blotches. The orange pronotum has a single square blue mark. The third antennal segment in the males is greatly enlarged and bears a peculiar hook with bristles on the tip. Books say he might use the hook to hold the female during copulation, but in the pairs I saw, the male's antennae were simply waving in the air. Maybe male clashes with male, each trying to hook the other. In both sexes there is a series of soft, bright orange bags protruding from the sides of the body beneath the margin of the wings. Again the books speculate—the bags might secrete a defensive goo. Apparently no one really knows. I tried my acid test—I got Martha to sniff at my dead specimens— but she could not detect an odor. If she can't smell it, it's not there.*

In the summertime, with the tide out and the mud dried enough to hold my weight, I often hear a wave of soft rustling and clicking spreading ahead of me as I proceed through the smooth cordgrass, and I catch furtive movements retreating ahead of my feet. There in the dank shade is a veritable army of little turquoise-colored squarish bodies, each one scuttling sideways over the mud as it tries to keep its distance and to put several grass stems between us. When I come to a spot where the grass thins, I stand stock-still for several minutes, and gradually the low-slung horde either forgets me or decides that I am no menace. As the wave of agitation subsides among them, individuals begin to show themselves as they go about their business, scraping at the surface of the mud, gesturing to each other in subtle body language, and waving their periscope eyes while intently watching the movements of their nearest neighbors. I have happened upon a drove of mud fiddler crabs (*Uca pugnax*), one of the most important and certainly one of the cutest denizens of the smooth cordgrass community.

Mud fiddlers live in large colonies in the salt marsh. Each crab excavates its own burrow, which extends a foot or so into the muck, and this becomes the home base to which it routinely returns after a foray on the surface. The finger-sized entrance holes provide a convenient and fairly accurate means of estimating the size of the fiddler population. Here there is an average of 2.4 holes per square foot, which translates to over one hundred thousand fiddler crabs per acre of salt marsh, making fiddlers by far the most common medium-sized crustacean in the community.

Their abundance is only one reason that fiddlers are regarded as keystones in the marsh. They feed low on the food chain, are relished by every carnivore that haunts the marsh, and through their burrowing and feeding activities promote aeration, mixing, and recycling of nutrients in the sediment. Aside from their ecological significance, fiddlers are fun to watch.

The prime occupation of an active mud fiddler is to forage under cover of the cordgrass canopy while the surface of the muck is exposed on low tide. All the local crabs respond to the same opportunity, so for several hours hundreds mill about together. A crab will pick at any bit of vegetable or animal debris it comes across, but the animal spends most of its time rhythmically scraping up dollops of sediment and cramming them into its mouth. In this activity the females use their two equal-sized pincers in rapid alternate movements, while the males prop their characteristic fiddle pincer to one side and feed one-handed.

A mouthful of sediment is mixed with water and passed through a series of increasingly delicate mouthparts, the last several armed with fine featherlike hairs that sweep the diatoms and light particles of organic matter out of the heavier mineral mass. The foodstuff goes down the gullet. After a dozen or so gobs of sediment have been processed, the inedible material that has accumulated is packed into a little pellet, deftly spit onto the rim of a pincer and set aside on the mud. Like the striped mullet, fiddler crabs feed at the base of the food chain—they simply "eat mud"—and so transform a near limitless resource into tasty protoplasm available to an array of upper-level marsh animals. Of course, the crabs are not intent on sacrificing themselves to this ecological service, but they nonetheless play out their fate.

Aside from the entrances to their burrows, evidence of mud fiddler activity is easy to perceive even when the crabs themselves are not abroad. They leave telltale scratch marks and little scooped-out places where they have picked up sediment while feeding. Next to these gravings are neat little piles of mud pellets, often stacked like miniature cannonballs, the discarded material cleaned of its organic content. Each burrow is surrounded by a semicircular fringe of larger mud balls that have been brought up during excavation and maintenance of the tunnel. This ceaseless digging on a scale of a hundred thousand–fold per acre renders an earthwormlike benefit to the marsh by turning over tons of anaerobic ooze.

Finally, if you do not mind getting down on hands and knees to peer into natural depressions in the surface of the mud, you will discover where the tide has gathered together thousands of tiny dark cylinders of mud fiddler feces. Here, far below the level of your close scrutiny, the microbial decomposers are busily at work, reshaping and recycling microscopic bits of organic matter that even the gastric mills and proficient guts of the mud fiddlers let pass.

Mud fiddlers are quick to dodge for cover or to fold into the nearest burrow at the least suspicious movement in their vicinity. Even retreat into the burrow does not save unwary crabs that pause in the upper reaches of their tunnel, for the bills of long-billed curlews and white ibis are well designed to adroitly pluck their prey from such refuges.

Once extracted by an ibis, a fiddler is usually shaken and sometimes thrown rudely to the mud several times to incapacitate it before it is

Ibis with fiddler crab claw

crushed and finally swallowed. If the crab is a male, the birds deliberately try to shake the big pincer loose, perhaps to avoid having it clamp down on their sensitive bill tip. I once saw a white ibis glumly walking along shaking its head from side to side, a disarticulated fiddle firmly affixed to its bill. The cast off fiddles do not go ignored. Blue crabs feast on them, and I have seen box turtles crunching them up.

Other birds, including willets and all the egrets, herons, and gulls, will take fiddlers opportunistically, and I suspect seaside sparrows peck up freshly minted crabs. Of course, raccoons crunch up any fiddler crab they come across, and marsh rice rats are also adept at catching them. Mud fiddlers also fall prey to gulf saltmarsh snakes, cottonmouth moccasins, and young alligators, and those crabs that venture into the shallows run the risk of being attacked by a redfish or black drum. Once I saw a southern flounder rise and inhale a swimming fiddler. I have seen blue crabs suddenly charge out of the water and grab a mud fiddler in each pincer before the panicked company of smaller crabs could disperse. One afternoon I saw several tiger beetles skirting alertly around a cluster of tiny newly metamorphosed mud fiddlers that the beetles seem to have herded together. Unfortunately, my shadow spooked the lot before I could determine whether a beetle was going to launch an assault.

It is easy enough to get caught up in the quiet agony of the vascular plants and overlook one other green denizen of the salt marsh that seems oblivious to the struggles being waged on every side. Scattered across the low marsh, hunkered directly on the wet mud beneath the creeping canopy of vascular plants, are rumpled rags of blue-green slime. When I first learned of them in school, they were called blue-green algae and were regarded as nothing more than a ho-hum step up the ladder to greater things. These days their distinctive lifestyle is recognized, so they are now called cyanobacteria and are relegated among the bacteria. By whatever name, these lowly organisms can surely claim one of the oldest lineages of any creature on Matagorda Island. And although they may be a step toward higher plants, one need go no further than cyanobacteria themselves to find both marvel and ecological significance in life.

Cyanobacteria colonized mudflats over three billion years ago, long before there was any more organized greenery anywhere on land. So, they have had plenty of time to come to terms with the rigors of their habitat. Their genius lies in their primitive abstinence. Lacking leaves, stems, and roots they have no complicated, sensitive architecture to protect. Without flowers and pollen they produce no fruits, seeds, or tender sprouts. Their wad of filaments is built on cells that manage to function without chloroplasts to contain their chlorophyll or nuclei to house their genes. For these archaic strands the bare basics of photosynthesizing and dividing are enough.

Give a cyanobacterium a whiff of nitrogen and carbon dioxide from the air, a dash of minerals from the mud, a splash of water to wet its gelatinous cell walls, and a dole of sunshine to activate its blue-green stain, and it will ask for nothing more, ever. Deprived of one or more of these meager ingredients, the rubbery mass turns black, curls upon itself, and waits. In that quiescent state the creature can withstand prolonged submergence, a smothering overload of sediment, and days of baking heat. Let the adverse conditions ease ever so slightly and the suppressed colony begins to take on its living color, regain its spongy texture, and resurge to its dreamy ages-old level of metabolism. In the cyanobacterium the salt marsh has met a passive living obstinance to match the combined acrimony of the elements themselves.

Blue-green algae (I still prefer that name over the newer one) are among the relatively few organisms that can tap the abundant nitrogen gas in the air and fix it in a stable chemical form that then leaks into the sediment to become accessible to all surrounding plants and animals. Since available nitrogen is often in critically short supply in the salt marsh, blue-green algae make a significant contribution to the continued productivity of the community. And of course, as all green things do, the blue-greens exude bubbles of oxygen as a by-product of their metabolism.

A menagerie of small creatures lives in and around these quiet blue-green blobs, taking advantage of their moist, gelatinous cover, tunneling through their dank interiors, and grazing on their blue-green bounty. Bacterial colonies, diatoms, green algae, ciliate protozoans, acoel flatworms, nematode worms, polychaete worms, oligochaete worms, and a variety of amphipods and microcrustaceans wriggle and squirm through the microbial mass. A kind of brine fly with a brassy sheen and russet eyes settles on the surface and uses its sponging mouthparts to mop up moisture and nutrients. These flies remind me of fruit flies happily sopping up banana medium in our genetics lab at college. The females plug eggs into the interior. These hatch into little white maggots that feed voraciously and then form yellowish pupae just beneath the surface layer. Least and western sandpipers know how to probe the algal mats for both larvae and pupae, and these little birds, as well as saltmarsh tiger beetles, snatch up the adult flies.

SEPTEMBER '96: *Into the low marsh today, where the tide is finally coming back in. Found the shallow bottom entirely covered with a thin sheet of bright blue-green algae. How did it start up so quickly? Two days ago this site was dry and had been so for several weeks. The algal mats were then hard and black, looked like old cow pies, and had scorpions and field crickets hiding in the dust underneath. Amazing! This stuff is not only alive but perking, for it is effervescing with a jillion silvery bubbles of oxygen.*

Put a smidge into a vial and then onto a slide under the compound scope. If I needed verification of its vitality, I got it. The blue-green filaments are slowly writhing like a mass of torpid snakes! Lots of tiny red polychaetes are sliding among the algal strands—Mediomastus californiensis. I can see algal filaments wound up in their fecal pellets. The worms must be what the dunlin were probing for; saw lots of these birds dipping methodically where I got this sample.

If I tear a mat of algae and look at the edge under the binoc at 20x, its laminated structure is evident. Thin blue-green sheets separated by equally thin layers of sediment, as well as an occasional skein of purple bacteria. These strata must record the history of the particular algal mat—the bands of sediment represent intervals of submergence and deposition, while the green

bands reflect emergence and regrowth. Like annual rings in a tree, but these
tiers are keyed to tidal activity rather than the passing of the seasons. Even
within a millimeter-thick green layer there are definite zones: sun-loving cells
uppermost, followed by shade-tolerant ones and a basal plate of dark-adapted
creatures that contrive a living without sunlight. The whole is a stratified
record of indefatigable passive resistance, the surest route to endurance in the
salt marsh.

Now and then while I am walking on wet mud in the low marsh
or along the upper edge of the mudflat, my foot slips sideways. When
I regain my balance and glance back, I see my distorted track brightly
colored in livid purple violet. I have inadvertently exposed—and by
such simple exposure, consigned to death—a film of exotic bacteria
(*Halobacterium salinarium*) that spend their entire existence sealed just
beneath the surface of the mud.

If any denizen of this marsh is more hoary than the cyanobacteria,
it must be these purple bacteria. They came into being in a far-distant
age when there was no oxygen in the atmosphere, and to this day that
vital gas is alien and poisonous to them. Yet they need sunlight to nurture their wan metabolism. How to avoid oxygen yet bask in light—
that is their seemingly insoluble challenge. Yet, here they are. They live
in this marshy muck for the very reason that it becomes anaerobic almost immediately below its surface. In this oxygen-free niche the bacteria spread out in a film one cell thick directly beneath the topmost
particles of mud. Here they manage to absorb dim flickers of the infrared component of the solar spectrum, a weak but penetrating band
invisible to us but powerful enough to drive their simple photo-
synthetic machinery. So, they lie there, entombed and unheralded,
fixing nitrogen as diligently as the cyanobacteria, succoring on a cast-
off segment of sunshine in such a biochemically weird manner that
they do not even produce oxygen as a by-product, for in so doing they
would commit suicide. When I exposed them to the air with my foot-
step, I committed mass bactericide.

Kids are intrigued when we happen to uncover purple bacteria in
the marsh. They like to squat and wipe the velvet purple mat with a
fingertip and offer their most profound concomitant of personal discovery, "Gaah." I prattle about the biology and ecology of what they are
seeing, but I hold the *philosophy* of the experience for last. "Would you
believe that there is a common biochemical thread between these most

ancient of creatures and yourself? Look closely at them, and you can see it right before your eyes."

They look. "I don't see anything but purple stuff," one finally comments. The others agree, but they wait expectantly.

Now I have caught them. They are ready for the only revelation about purple bacteria that they will remember. "Well, that's it; that 'purple stuff.' And it's not only right before your eyes, it's *inside* your eyes."

Now their minds are wide open with momentary astonishment and confusion, and I ram it home. "You all know that the basis of your vision resides in a purple pigment called rhodopsin in your eyes." (Furtive glances and weak nods as a few call up vague recollections from biology class. The rest are willing to take my word for it.) "Rhodopsin is composed in part from retinal, a purple carotenoid pigment. These lowly bacteria make precisely the same pigment, mix it with a protein, and produce a light-sensitive substance called bacteriorhodopsin. So, while you are using your retinal to see these bacteria, they are using their retinal to 'look' at the sun. It is indeed a small, interconnected world, isn't it? Now, let's hear you say it, three times fast."

They do so with enthusiasm: "back-TEER-ee-oh-row-DOP-sin." Never in over several billion years, I presume, have these unassuming purple microbes received a more resounding accolade.

A variety of animals populates the low and high marshes. Mud fiddlers proceed as far as the muck goes; then they are replaced by sand fiddlers (*Uca panacea*) further inland. These two lead comparable lives indelibly separated by the microstructure of their mouthparts: mud fiddlers can sift food from muddy sand, and sand fiddlers can sift food from sandy mud, but not vice versa. So the line of distribution between the two is as sharp as that between plants.

Predatory tiger beetles of several species race over the open ground, plant hoppers with a tolerance for salty sap infest the low canopy, great southern white butterflies drift over the yellow sea ox-eye blossoms, while a fairy cloud of western pygmy blue butterflies flits around the golden pollen dust atop the glassworts. Marsh rice rats leave their dainty footprints inscribed all over the mud. Somewhere among the plant stalks clapper rails nest, producing eggs that can withstand occasional inundation by salt water and fuzzy black chicks that can swim as soon as they pip.

Where the mix of sand and mud is just right, piles of little round balls of substrate lie scattered about that suggest the existence of an extensive population of subterranean creatures. The pellets are smaller than those discarded by feeding fiddlers, and they are not associated with fiddler scratch marks. For some time Martha and I dismissed these spherules as the work of earthworms, until we realized that earthworms cannot tolerate the saline substrate of the salt marsh. What then?

Careful excavation provided the answer. By digging a hole to one side and then gently shaving one wall in the direction of a pile of sand pellets, we soon revealed a narrow tunnel about one-sixteenth inch wide descending to a series of horizontal galleries at a depth of six inches. Sound familiar? We were immediately reminded of our black beach beetles, so we were not totally surprised to uncover . . . beetles. They looked and behaved for all the world like enlarged editions of the beach beetles, and I eventually learned that in fact they belong to the same family (*Staphylinidae,* the rove beetles) and probably to the same far-flung genus (*Bledius,* spiny-legged rove beetles).

Aside from being larger (body length about three-eighths of an inch) and brown rather than black, these brown marsh beetles, as we came to call them, also differ from the beach beetles in their tunneling activity. Rather than dig shallow, horizontal runways, the marsh beetles excavate extensive, deep galleries. We presume, therefore, that they feed on microbes and detritus in the surrounding sediment rather than upon surface-living diatoms.

Once in the springtime I sliced into a beetle corridor that had dimples in the roof, each with a glistening white egg suspended at its center. Each summer we routinely encountered active beetle grubs and immobile pupae in the lower tunnels. So, it seems that the brown marsh beetles go through their entire life cycle hidden from the upper world. Well, not quite. Rain or a high tide forces them to the surface, gasping for air. At such times shorebirds are quick to take advantage of them. I saw a flock of western sandpipers glutting on flushed-out brown marsh beetle larvae. On another occasion hundreds of adult beetles had gotten trapped in the surface film of a tidal pool, and greater yellowlegs, black-necked stilts, and dunlin were pecking them up as fast as they could. Once we opened a beetle tunnel to find the occupant clutched in the jaws of a predaceous ground beetle. So, the brown marsh beetles are secretive but not totally divorced from the web of life that binds the salt marsh.

If the ecological health of a salt marsh can be judged by the abundance and vigor of its attendant swarms of mosquitoes, the Matagorda Island marsh deserves high marks. A week after exceptionally high tides, predictably near the spring and fall equinoxes, a multitude of mosquitoes erupts from the tidal pools bordering the salt marsh and spreads inland across the grassland into the sand dunes. Heavy rains stimulate those species of mosquitoes that hatch in freshwater. They emerge from pools among the dunes and grassland swales and spread toward the marsh. So, whether we are coming or going, we quickly stir up hungry mosquitoes. Because of the lack of vegetation and the occurrence of a steady onshore breeze, the only natural refuge is the beach itself, and if the wind fails, that, too, is subject to assault.

Only two species of mosquitoes are responsible for most of the seasonal torment on Matagorda Island, and two more join in after heavy rains. The black (*Aedes taeniorhynchus*) and the golden (*Aedes sollicitans*) saltmarsh mosquitoes are the main culprits. Both lay their eggs in low moist spots just above normal tide line, a clutch every other day, a dozen batches in a lifetime of a month or so. A high tide floods the eggs, which immediately hatch and proceed through the wiggler (larval) and tumbler (pupal) stages in little more than a week. Consequently, a week and a half after a high tide the marsh begins to vibrate with the drone of adult saltmarsh mosquitoes lifting off in numbers approximating several hundred thousand per day from each square yard of marsh. The females, which are the gender that seeks a blood meal to succor their developing eggs, lie in ambush among the marsh plants and in the interior grassland, ready to accost any hapless warm-blooded creature that passes their way. At sunset and through the early evening hours, the mosquitoes rise to actively seek out a blood host.

Rains bring out two freshwater species, the purple rain mosquito (*Psorophora cyanescens*) and the shaggy-legged mosquito (*P. ciliata*). Although they pass their peaks of abundance more quickly than the saltmarsh varieties, these large freshwater mosquitoes can dole out plenty of misery. They can, for instance, easily pierce the close weave of a heavy shirt with their proboscis; and they are suicidally insistent in their attack.

Of course, there are times—September is a likely month—when the island gets both high tides and rains, which bring on a double whammy of mosquitoes. During such intervals there is no recourse; both wildlife and people suffer and wait.

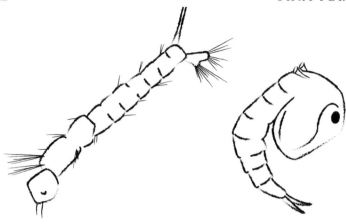

Wiggler and tumbler

I suppose that every naturalist comes upon enigmas of the sort that cannot be resolved by direct observation. For instance, I am counseled that only female mosquitoes bite and that the reason they do so is that they must have certain proteins vital to the development of their eggs and most conveniently found in the blood of a potential host.

Now, blood sucking would seem to be a chancy and rather hazardous undertaking, derived, perhaps, from opportunistic sipping at bloody wounds. The ravening female might not find her proper host, and even if she does so, she runs the risk of getting swatted while trying to purloin her vitamins. How much nicer for the parasite, and incidentally for the host, if she could subsist on plant sap as the male does and still manage to maturate her eggs. Assuredly, plant sap is little more than calorific sugar water, not protein, but what is to keep that resourceful combination of mutation and natural selection from working among the annual teeming swarms to quickly produce an emancipation from the vampire habit? Juggle a few genes and begin to manufacture endogenous isoleucine, the critical amino acid. No more difficult a biochemical trick, it would seem, than the ones already repeatedly performed to develop resistance to the pesticides with which we lace mosquito habitats.

As a matter of fact, a few kinds of mosquitoes have weaned themselves from the need for blood in their diet, but they have not enjoyed much advantage, for they remain a distinct minority in kind and abundance among the bloodthirsty clan. The awesome elephant mosquito

(*Toxorhynchites rutilis*), which I encounter occasionally on Matagorda Island, is one such nonbiting species. It gathers and stores the necessary proteins while still in the larval stage, by feeding on mosquito wigglers that share its stagnant pool. The adult is a truly magnificent animal covered with metallic blue green scales ornamented here and there with golden sequins and bearing a curious down-curved, dangling proboscis with which it sucks up flower nectar. Despite its size and colors, it is a slow-flying, rather vague, almost somnambulistic beast compared to its alert bloodsucking relatives.

Sometimes, when I have a group of visitors pestered to distraction, I cheerfully suggest that it would be nice if, by some shrewd magic, I could snap my fingers and eradicate all of the mosquitoes on the island. Of course, I get immediate and unanimous, even zealous approval to give it a try. But a few have second thoughts and hesitantly retract their sanctions, partly, I suspect, because they realize that I am deliberately leading them on. "Well, mosquitoes might have some ecological value," they say, although at the moment they will not admit to any that are up to counterbalancing their misery. In fact, there are quite a few positive ecological values to mosquitoes, and most of them have to do with the food web.

Take the millions of wigglers that animate every isolated tidal pool and rain puddle on the island each September. Their mouth brushes busily sweep up a vast cumulative load of diatoms, filamentous algae, nematode worms, rotifers, gastrotrichs, protozoa, bacteria, and suspended organic matter. Some aggressive species even accost newly hatched toad tadpoles. These they pack into black squirming tidbits of wiggler protoplasm that are not only accessible but absolutely irresistible to a variety of higher-order predators. For many minnow-sized fishes in the marsh, mosquito wigglers are seasonal staples. The triumvirate of sheepshead killifish, mosquito fish, and sailfin molly feed so voraciously on mosquito wigglers and tumblers that they can effectively prevent a local explosion of adult mosquitoes. To render this service, however, the fishes must gain access to the mosquito pools.

Female saltmarsh mosquitoes have a built-in shrewdness that prompts them to scatter their eggs in depressions along the upper fringes of the marsh, where they are likely to hatch in isolated, fish-free pockets of water. Prolonged high tides or a heavy rain allows the fish to reach most of these pools. I have seen determined little sheepshead killies turn sideways and flutter energetically over moistened muck in

their eagerness to be among the first to follow the lead edge of a rising tide toward bountiful feeding grounds. Tail drags made by alligators slogging across the marsh often provide a series of interconnect-
ing waterways that the venturesome fishes are quick to exploit.

Once in a wiggler pool on the upper marsh the fish glut and cavort,
seemingly oblivious to the fact that their paradise is temporary. Unless
they get a reprieve, the fish are likely to get trapped in a pool that rapidly dehydrates into a depression of soupy mud. Now the wiggler-
stoked fish protoplasm is moved up a notch, into wood storks, white
ibis, roseate spoonbills, snowy egrets, tricolored herons, laughing gulls,
boat-tailed grackles, gulf saltmarsh snakes, cottonmouth moccasins,
marsh rice rats, raccoons, and feral hogs.

Other marsh creatures do not need fish as intermediaries to get at
mosquito wigglers. Greater and lesser yellowlegs and black-necked
stilts wade out among the emergent vegetation, where they use their
sharp eyes and stiletto bills to snatch mosquito larvae one by one from
their refuge in the shadows. I think individuals average better than a
catch per second, and flocks of these birds keep at it for minutes on
end. I have seen shorebirds such as dunlin and western sandpipers get
in on the act, although they are less efficient at it.

Ducks are not usually thought of as insectivores, but in the mosquito
pools dabblers such as mottled ducks, gadwall, American widgeon, and
northern shovelers avidly slurp up the squirming fodder. The ducks
paddle along with necks stretched forward, the vibrations of their bills
creating a dense concentric pattern of radiating ripples that results
from their particular means of harvest. In a cycle that is repeated several times a second, the bill is gaped slightly to allow water and animal
prey (or seeds, algae, and suspended vegetable matter) to enter. As the
bill is closed, the tongue is raised to force the water out thin slits along
the edge of the bill, thus straining out the food. The retained organic
material is swallowed occasionally while the bill-clapping mechanism
continues to operate. It is an effective wiggler-catching machine.

Predaceous water bugs, aquatic beetles, and dragonfly larvae also
waylay their share of wigglers. Once I came upon a small mosquito
pool where a gulf coast ribbon snake was feeding on the trapped wigglers by swimming back and forth with its pink mouth wide open,
pausing now and then to raise its head and gulp convulsively. "Ever see
a snake eat a mosquito?" is a good lead-in to get a group to focus on
the subtleties of the food web in the salt marsh.

Legions of dragonflies of several species, dance flies, rough-winged swallows, barn swallows, cliff swallows, common nighthawks, and an occasional purple martin mop up adult mosquitoes in midair all summer long. I have even watched a spotted sandpiper, creeping as stealthily as its bobbing affliction would allow through the smooth cordgrass and with immense patience and concentration, pluck resting mosquitoes from the stems. Newly metamorphosed froglets and toadlets tongue-pop adult mosquitoes that settle in the wet grass or around freshwater pools. And each dawn finds thousands of tattered spiderwebs festooned with mosquito mummies. Yet the multitude is unperturbed, undaunted, and virtually undiminished—as enduring, it seems, as the salt marsh that succors it and is succored in return.

AUGUST '96: *Stopped at the mosquito ponds this afternoon. Spooked up a mixed flock of greater yellowlegs and black-necked stilts feeding there. Hot, the water must be nearly one hundred degrees Fahrenheit in the sunshine, so all critters are in the shade of emergent grass blades near the edge. I thought the "shade"' looked exceptionally dark, then realized that most of the blackness came from the mass of saltmarsh mosquito larvae concentrated there. Awesome, and an unsettling portent of things to come. For the moment, however they are no menace. I stirred through the grass with my foot and watched the seething cloud spill out like some dark immiscible liquid. I got grim satisfaction from putting them to panic, for they would soon enough make life miserable for me.*

AUGUST '96: *Visited the mosquito ponds to find them still clogged with wigglers and a rising proportion of tumblers. Used a hand net to swish through the grass blades and brought it up brim full. Pure writhing biomass! Had to support the sagging mesh with my hand. Later I determined that a netful of wigglers weighs 265 grams—over half a pound! I took a great glom of them back to the Center, doled them glistening and squirming into cookie tins, and froze them to use as food for the critters in the aquarium. Dribbled live ones into the aquarium and the killies—which had been leading drab lives on dried shrimp pellets—went into a piranha-like frenzy snatching them up. Despite my depredation, the population of larvae and pupae in the 250-by-15-foot pond seemed unfazed. Even more so than the arcane emergence of flies from carrion, this brackish cauldron verifies the spontaneous generation of life: warmed salt water congeals directly into twitching protoplasm. Nothing else can account for such profligacy. Can I convince students?*

AUGUST '96: *Sealed up against mosquitoes and doing pretty well until the little air conditioner failed in the workroom. It got stifling in no time, and we were worried about our computers and my color slides. I finally went out among the hungry cloud to see what I could do. Got the cover off the AC and the trouble was immediately evident—half a bushel of mosquito bodies jammed against the intake screen! Got that cleared, and the AC starting cooling again. Over the next two days I had to repeat the operation four times. When the plague finally lifted, I think I could have shoveled a wheelbarrow load of mosquito carcasses from beneath the poor air conditioner.*

SEPTEMBER '96: *Saltmarsh mosquitoes do not like wind, but they readily adjust to it. Today I watched them rise out of the grass as I passed, swing round and purposefully alight on my downwind side. There they nestled among the hairs on my arm and got right down to business, snug as could be. Others sought out the lee side of my head, then burrowed under the edge of my cap before starting to bite. Quite a few avoided the wind almost entirely by settling on my ankles, biting through my socks, and working their way up inside my pants legs. It is hard not to malign creatures with such insidious behavior. I swat, both for physical relief and for contrived revenge.*

SEPTEMBER '97: *Not only are we marooned on this island, but we are held hostage here. This is the thirteenth consecutive day of mosquito siege. We go outside only in an emergency, and then on the run. We have duct tape over every crevice in the trailer; even have to untape the doors to get in and out. I checked all the screens and plugged the slightest tears with hot glue. Still, we swat continually and sleep fitfully. I swear, I think the little black saltmarsh mosquitoes are coming right through the screens! At least this experience gives us a good appreciation for the fortitude of the pioneer ranching families that stuck it out on this island with nothing for protection but mosquito bars draped over their cots and smudge fires in the bedroom. The basis for their perseverance was much like that of the wildlife, I suppose—they never knew better, anticipated no relief until the plague lifted, and so did not founder in self-pity.*

SEPTEMBER '97: *Saltmarsh mosquitoes seem to have two behavior modes when I try to swat them. If one is merely perched, as inside the windshield of my pickup or on the ceiling in the trailer, I can hardly squash it with my hand. I think the puff of air ahead of my approaching palm alerts the* mosquito, causing it to lift off and then be passively swept aside at the last moment. A quick series of swats merely leads to a train of successful evasions, which, in turn, leads to frustration on the part of the swatter. However, once a saltmarsh mosquito alights and begins to bite, it seems to devote all its attention to the business of drawing blood, and it is then pathetically easy to annihilate. I use my middle finger, bringing it down from directly above. Immediately on contact I press and shear slightly so as to bruise the mosquito while rolling it aside.

SEPTEMBER '97: *Purple rain mosquitoes are well named; skewered on a pin and viewed in good light at 20x they are absolute jewels. Every part that is dark—the proboscis, the terminal halves of the tapered legs, most of the upper side of the abdomen—gives off an opalescent blue purple luster when turned in the light beam. The back is covered with a scruffy pavement of reflective golden scales, and there are bold golden yellow splashes ornamenting six of the seven abdominal segments. Underneath, the body scales are crafted in silver rather than gold. The clear wings bear veins shagged with thin brown scales, and their trailing borders are fringed with a flexible comb of hairlike scales. Like any jewel, much of this animal's beauty resides in its form and symmetry. Take a fly and meticulously trim its every body part for persistent flight, stealthy approach, and bloodsucking habit. Endow the whole with a demeanor and an unwavering perseverance to achieve the single mission for which it was crafted. You have a mosquito; a fly like no other.*

OCTOBER '97: *Sitting at my desk today, drowsy. Saw a golden saltmarsh mosquito alight on the back of my hand. Rather than swat her, I felt moved to watch her.*

For a moment she sat cocked back on her middle and hind legs while she held her front legs aloft, twiddling them together briefly as though antici-pating her feast. She really was a disarmingly handsome beast, sporting a golden velvet mantle, her sides sparkling with silver scales, her thin legs finished out in alternating bands of black and white and a solitary white ring around the middle of her black proboscis. Abruptly she straightened up and got down to business. She planted her front legs and arched down to position the tip of her proboscis on my hand between her legs. I could see the sheath of her proboscis elbow backward as the rodlike stylets emerged and sank painlessly into my skin. She must have hit a vessel right away, perhaps not entirely by accident. I would not be surprised if she had a heat sensor to guide her probe directly to a warm conduit. At any rate, she seemed content

*to hold to her position, and directly I saw her thin abdomen beginning to
swell and take on a warm pink glow. It could not have been more than ten or
twelve seconds before she raised her head to back her stylets out. The sheath
drew smartly down around her needle-jaws, and she rubbed her proboscis
with her front legs.*

*The mosquito had gone from svelte to ugly. Her abdomen was huge, tight,
and a dirty red. She looked more like an engorged tick than a streamlined fly.
She waddled as she took a few steps across my hand. Then with great effort
and an off-key hum, she lifted off and seemed headed for the windowsill, but
her load dragged her down, and she landed heavily against the wall instead.
There she clung, rendered immobile by her gluttony.*

*I felt a sudden urge to squash her while she was so vulnerable, but just as
quickly the feeling drained away. This island has given me so much; it is
satisfying to give in return. Through the intermediary of this mosquito bits of
my body will be dissembled, reworked, and scattered across the salt marsh.
The feeling is not too different from the thought of having my cremation dust
sprinkled over land I love. It may do little for the land, but the contemplation
of it does much for the psyche.*

During the first half of September 1996, Matagorda Island was
socked in by a three-week siege of mosquitoes. Our interior walls were
decked with their swatted black bodies and bloody splats, and at night
the window screens vibrated with their rapacious drone. It was hard
enough on humans, and finally the unrelenting assault even began to
affect the wildlife. The wild turkeys refused to forage; instead, they
perched in a glum row along the top of the hangar, their naked heads
pulled in among their ruffled feathers. Jackrabbits hopped about aim-
lessly, shaking their heads and letting their long ears droop. Meadow-
larks had rings of mosquitoes crusting the skin around their eyes. Then
the deer began to die.

In September the bucks are still in velvet. Their developing racks
are soft and pulpy with blood. This year the defenseless animals were
driven to distraction by the layer of voracious mosquitoes that continually coated their growing antlers. There was no respite, day or night.
They raked their tender racks through the grass, flapped their ears,
slammed their heads against their sides, twisted to flail ineffectually at
their tormentors with a hind hoof. In desperation, an animal would
occasionally just take off, bounding across the grassland in a vain attempt to find relief.

In the second week we began to find bucks dead in the surf. It took awhile for us to realize what was going on. Harassed beyond endurance, at night the deer sought the beach for deliverance. Slack winds allowed the mosquitoes to follow. As a last resort, some of the maddened animals finally entered the surf. Whether they stood in the battering waves or tried swimming to liberation across the open Gulf, I do not know. Perhaps the brine soothed the constant throb in their lacerated racks even as it protected them from further assault. I like to think that the creatures experienced some sort of release from their torment before they went into their final tremors.

Weakened by overworked spleens, drained bone marrows, and plummeting blood pressure, the deer succumbed to stress and drowned. We counted seven stranded bodies in three days and later found skeletons scattered across the grassland. Most were bucks. Of course, the scourge lifted, the wildlife perked up, the deer herd recovered fully, and only the people held on to a memory of this grim side of Matagorda Island.

CHAPTER 4

UNSEEN FAUNA

Sea breeze hurries past
Sea oats talk and signify
Dunes shrug smooth shoulders.

MOST PEOPLE, including biology instructors and even professional biologists, accept marine plankton on faith. The existence of a myriad of tiny floating organisms is so logically necessary to an understanding of the marine ecosystem that there is little need to perceive them directly. For life in the sea there must be a starting point, a crucial connection with sunshine, minuscule green things being eaten by tiny nongreen things. These, in turn, are eaten by larger things until the feeding frenzy coalesces into jerking flecks that we can just see, and it progresses up the size scale, with lesser fury and in lower numbers, into familiar creatures like killifishes, razor clams, raccoons, and tricolored herons.

Most of the living things on this island, aquatic or not, owe their existence, one way or another, to the activity of phytoplankton floating in the surface waters. Even humans. Much of the oxygen we breath bubbles into the atmosphere from the film of plankton.

When I mention plankton, visitors all nod knowingly, as though they can follow my gesture toward the water and actually see what I am talking about. Yet, not a one of them has ever had a firsthand encounter with this subliminal world.

I went through my entire college career as a biology major with only one uninspired look at a spiritless jumble of dead marine plankton. In all fairness, an inland school cannot do justice to plankton from the sea. The seething community of drifting creatures is too delicate to withstand handling and transporting, to say nothing of being manipulated by well-meaning but bumbling undergraduates. One of my great disappointments as a new instructor at Victoria College was my attempt to collect plankton fresh from San Antonio Bay, keep it in an aerated container overnight, and show it to students the next afternoon. We saw zilch. It was gone as though it had never been, disintegrated, settled into a hazy, swirling sludge on the bottom of the container. I did not try that again.

That failed exercise should have destroyed the students' faith in marine plankton, but it did not. They were pretrained to absorb, dutifully disgorge, and devoutly believe almost anything that I told them. After all, I was their WGA. Too bad. They miss the essence of science, of Nature, of living. They seldom get a chance to know what it means to be there, to stumble onto things, to discover, to tinker, to fail and try again, to question, to wonder.

In later years I did the next best thing. I showed them a good video of marine plankters. The presentation was certainly better than anything they would have observed through their own microscopes, but at the same time it was a vicarious cheat. It was too removed from real life, too divorced from real time, too predictable, too clean, too easy. I resolved that if I could figure out how to do it, I would have students *experience* plankton. When I moved to Matagorda Island, I got my chance to fill my own personal gap and to share the fun with others.

All you need to collect a sample of plankton is a funnel-shaped, fine-mesh net provided with a hoop to keep the mouth open and a bridle and cord to pull it just beneath the surface of the water. Have a few clear plastic peanut butter jars filled with water to retain your catch.

You also need to pick your time and place. The zealous comment that every drop of seawater is teeming with an interesting menagerie of Lilliputian creatures just begging to strut their stuff beneath a lens is, in my experience, an exaggerated boast. Given a choice, I plan a plankton excursion during the spring or fall, in the bay rather than the surf, and always after full dark. Daytime samples are disappointingly anemic; summer and winter catches show little diversity; a net in the surf brings in more sand than critters. So, I rev up the troops with a preliminary discussion, have supper while dark gathers, then load up and head for the pier at the bay on our great plankton adventure. If Jacques Cousteau's *Calypso* herself were awaiting us, we couldn't have a more merry and expectant bunch.

On the dock, with flashlight beams stabbing in every direction, including directly into my eyes, I demonstrate how to cast a plankton net: lob a gentle arc out over the water, perform a slow hand-over-hand retrieval with the cord, and execute a quick dapple into a jar of water to harvest the catch. Easy enough.

Then I let the kids take turns. I just need to be *sure* the cord is securely tied to their wrist before they give the net a heave! They will miss the water now and then, get the cord tangled around their ankles, and occasionally slam a friend behind the head with a wet net, but despite their ineptness, they do get things into the jars.

Once they learn that they can set a jar directly into the vertical beam of a flashlight to reveal a haze of jerking, whirling motes and an occasional sparkle of bioluminescence, the level of excitement and impatience begins to rise. Exclamations and questions come in an unending stream. "Wait until we get back to the Center; then we'll see what we've got," I respond for the umpteenth time. The delay gives them time to foment and speculate. Such fervor is only slightly more restrained with a group of adults.

Back at the lab, we pour all the samples into a large, clear plastic vat set on a black table. Lights arranged around the sides with their beams directed crosswise through the water highlight the living specks. Here is revealed a startling world of living creatures that we, by dint of our own labor, have just brought in from the sea. There are slender things and round things, fast things and things that just sit, silvery things and things so clear you can see their insides throbbing, hordes of things aggregating beside the lights, and a few things stalking and eating others right before our eyes! For a while I just stand aside and let discovery and bedlam reign.

Brightly side-lit against the black background, shapes and behavioral differences can be picked out without magnification: pudgy baby crabs, delicate shrimps with long-stalked eyes and whisking antennae, pulsing jellyfishes with dangling tentacles, clouds of jerking copepods, scooting barnacle nauplii, whirling snail veligers, comb jellies flickering with iridescence, and a variety of juvenile fishes; all these surrounded by a myriad of spinning, writhing, enigmatic specks. Does plankton really exist? You bet it does!

No matter how good the naked eye viewing, full appreciation of plankton demands magnification, ideally under a high-powered microscope. But that takes expensive equipment and considerable practice. Here on the island, with an enthusiastic but inept one-time audience, I opted to revert to video but with a hands-on twist: a microvideo camera attached to a microscope that feeds live images at 60x magnification to a television screen. I have the kids take turns fishing in the plankton tank with an eyedropper until all have caught the critter of their choice. I put each specimen on a slide, and everyone exclaims in unison as the huge exotic image dances across the screen.

Now I can point out specific structures and identify almost everything we see. Even when I honestly proclaim in a rapturous voice, "I don't know. I've never seen anything like that before. What does it look like to you?" they are entranced.

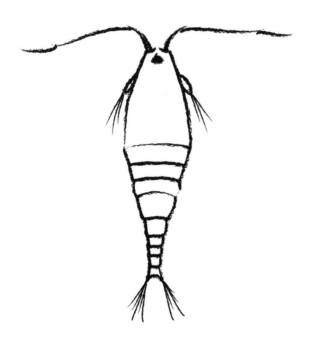

Copepod

By the time we are done all the kids can recognize a copepod at a glance, can pronounce its name correctly, knows it is a crustacean, has learned how it swims and feeds and carries its eggs, can tell you about the important copepod/diatom connection and, as often as you can bear to listen to the tale, will tell you how one night they helped catch copepods by the jillion. They pick up lots more that even I do not realize at the time. So do we turn "plankton" from token to reality.

Sometimes, when no one is here and the bay is right, the kid comes out in me. I go heave the plankton net and then sit for hours over my microscope, fascinated by the sheer wonderfulness of this silent, drifting world of elfin creatures. I can in one night identify representatives of all the major animal phyla and many of the minor ones and see forms so odd I cannot even guess their affinity; perhaps they still await scientific description. Some of them develop, grow, feed, exult, reproduce, and die while afloat in a dimensionless world that for them lasts but a day or two. Others are temporary denizens, larvae riding the currents until their instincts tell them to settle out.

When I extrapolate from a teeming droplet to the miles of bay shallows along the margin of Matagorda Island, I am staggered. Diversity aside, cumulative mass is incomprehensible! On a good night, with just a few throws of the plankton net I can bring in a bulge of throbbing protoplasm. What if I could effectively sieve a square mile on a spring evening? Nothing but the kids' "Gaah" can come close to covering the enormity of the result.

My diary is sprinkled with planktonic delights.

SEPTEMBER '93: *Up until the wee hours peering through the microscope and poring over the drawings in Smith. What a menagerie of textbook creatures comes to life! Barnacle nauplii, polychaete trochophores, snail veligers, crab zoeae, echinoderm bipinnaria, sea cucumber auricularia, hydromedusae, copepods, ostracods, nematodes, and a dozen critters that I cannot even get to phylum. Plus filaments, chains, and isolated cells of marine algae. Diatoms really are as exquisite as their drawings!*

SEPTEMBER '93: *I identified* Nitzschia, *which I have named the accordion alga. Its spindle-shaped cells lie side by side in clusters of eight or so. Now and then the cells jackknife apart, like an unfolding carpenter's rule. The colony sidles along with a ratcheting, accordion motion. Why look for exotic life on Mars with creatures like* Nitzschia *on this planet?*

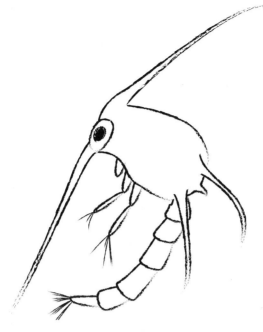

Crab zoeae

OCTOBER '93: *Copepods are in every sample, usually far outnumbering everything else. They cluster in the light beam, as though queuing to be sucked up by my eyedropper. All copepods look much alike to me, but I have identified* Acartia tonsa *as our locally dominant species. Typical in anatomy and behavior: solitary red eye and repeated jerks of its antennules to remain afloat. Most are visibly stuffed with diatoms. They nibble right at the base of the marine food chain: sunshine to diatom to copepod. Figure 120,000 diatoms/copepod/day; 50,000 copepods/killifish/day; 50 killifish/snowy egret/ day. Unplug the copepod circuit, and you might as well put out the sun.*

NOVEMBER '93: *Sample tonight crammed with veligers! All of snails, I think; no clams. This is how slow-crawling snails manage to get everywhere. Jillions, each with its velum extended, its cilia beating like mad, its body motoring around in circles. The chance of any one of them settling into a snail's existence is incalculably small. Most will get sucked up by a feeding siphon, zapped by a nematocyst, clogged in a strand of mucus, snagged by a gill arch, or simply drift off in the wrong direction. At the moment, however, every last one of them seems convinced that it is the ordained one.*

NOVEMBER '93: *In college we learned about "foraminiferan ooze," as though the creatures themselves were all extinct, leaving only shells to inform geologists about the age of the sea floor. Well, these distinctive little coiled shells are still very much around, filled with oozing protoplasm, ready to inform any interested biologist about the current status of the surface of the sea.*

SEPTEMBER '94: *Tonight I got hundreds of grass shrimp* (Palaemonetes pugio) *in my plankton net. A step up the food pyramid from copepods, these little crustaceans are the krill of this bay—universal prey. Many are carrying mats of eggs or clusters of bulbous-eyed embryos tucked beneath their abdomens.*

Hardly larger than baby grass shrimp are slender, clear, opossum shrimp (Mysidopsis almyra *and* Bowmaniella sp.). *When I focus on a resting female, I can see her multiple pairs of broomlike feet, constantly fluttering, her namesake brood pouch where she tends her clutch, and on her tail fan, the trademark nodular balancing organ. Sergestid shrimp* (Acetes americanus) *are another member of the clan, their long-stalked eyes giving them an extraterrestrial appearance.*

Each of these trembling creatures is exquisitely made, every part perfectly fitted, beady eyes on the alert, long antennae keening for the next assault. I

Accordion alga

Snail veliger

can see the whir of its racing heart, peer into its knobby brain, look right into the depths of its persecuted soul.

APRIL '94: *Spent an hour watching tiny creatures getting scarfed up by a small comb jelly* (Beroe ovata). *Among the motes, this eyeless, rust-colored bladder took on the proportions of an immense, slow-witted blimp. It lumbered forward, reversed its motors to back up, turned by pivoting on its rear end while slowly twirling on its axis. All this by coordinating the beat of its eight tracts of eyelash-cilia. Its movements created a turbulence that scattered and tumbled small bodies in every direction. With rhythmical precision, the flattened front end yawned open, drawing in a gulp of water along with all the plankters in the vicinity, like the maw of a whale shark in a Jacques Cousteau video. I could see legions of copepods and sergestid shrimp tangled in mucous strands inside the creature's gullet, victims of prior ingurgitations. Meanwhile, those that were destined to be slurped up next were mindlessly frittering away their last few seconds of life directly in harm's way. It makes me feel immune and immortal to peer down at the foibles and tragedies in this frenzied nether world.*

MAY '94: *Made a grand entrance to a plankton session tonight. With the lights off, while the kids sat twittering in the darkness, I held up a jar and poked the contained comb jelly with a glass rod. It obligingly lit up in all its bioluminescent glory to the refrain of multiple exclamations from the kids. Great sport!*

MAY '94: *Arrowworms! So clear that I didn't notice them until they moved, zipping along like feathered torpedoes. In place of an explosive warhead they have a set of ice-tong bristles around their mouth with which they snatch up copepods. Arrowworms are so different from other types of creatures that they are put into a phylum all their own (Chaetognatha, "bristle-jawed"). Some taxonomists suggest they deserve their own kingdom of life. To me arrowworms look like they would fit right in with that Ediacaran fauna that haunted the primordial seas three-quarters of a billion years ago.*

FEBRUARY '95: *I was surprised to get two kinds of burrowing creatures in the plankton net. Lots of minuscule burrowing sea cucumbers; I dig up the adults on the mudflats. These must be recently metamorphosed larvae, just finishing their planktonic phase and on their critical mission of dispersal before they settle to the bottom for the rest of their lives.*

    And my first cumaceans! No need for pictures here. I had long since memorized their distinctive shape: fat body with a pointy rostrum; long, narrow tail-like abdomen held arched out behind, tipped with a pair of spiky uropods. Nothing else they could be. I identified them as Oxyurostylis salinoi. *These all have a pair of long antennae marking them as males. On certain nights they rise en masse for a mutually stimulatory "social orgasm" that prepares them for mating. By chance, I have hit their prenuptial frenzy.*

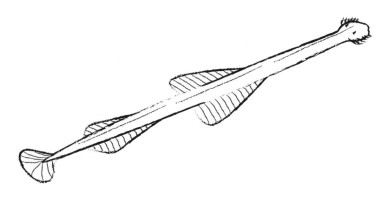

Arrowworm

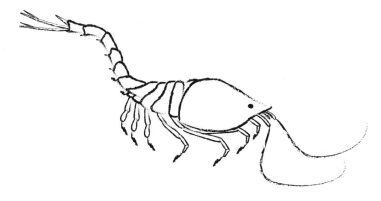

Cumacean

FEBRUARY '96: *One of those rare nights at the pier when everything came together perfectly—a great batch of kids, an inky sky, pleasantly cool, no mosquitoes. When we stirred the water with a stick, every radiating ripple ignited with bioluminescence! The urban kids were flabbergasted. In an instant they were on their bellies reaching down to create their own flaming scribbles. Moments before they had feared everything in the dark, from being engulfed by sharks to getting mugged. Matagorda Island was opening a crack in their confined world. Back at the Center we got a few of the sparkles under the microvideo camera and saw the little lily pad cells, complete with stubby stalks.*

Even before they demanded a name, several kids asked: "Where's its light?" So I held an impromptu and rather lame discussion of the difference between light bulbs and chemical light and how stress can throw the switch. It is not easy to simplify and stay accurate, but they seemed satisfied. I did much better with "What is it anyway? It's a kind of off-beat algae, a dinoflagellate. A one-celled thing. And it's got a name as pretty as its light, so I want you to learn it. Ready? Noctiluca scintillans—*shining light of the night. All together now: nock-tee-LOO-ka SIN-tee-lans. Three times now, here we go."*

The walls resounded! They won't forget; neither will I.

FEBRUARY '97: *I may have reached the pinnacle of plankton watching tonight. I scooped up what I thought was a hydromedusa or a worm egg case, and suddenly, under the microvideo there it was in all its glory—gossamer delicate, exquisite, stunning, absolutely unexpected—a larvacean!*

I sat there marveling in disbelief, watching the wispy bubble pirouette in its fluid universe like an embryo in its womb. If there are spirits, they must look and behave like this! The creature itself was nothing more than a squiggle in the center of its filmy, ephemeral bubble house. With its multiple sets of fine-meshed sieves for snaring and sorting the tiniest of plankters, this fairy globe is one of the most beautiful delights in its Lilliputian universe. The creature lives suspended perennially through the generations, exempt from gravity, never touching a solid surface, dissolving and respinning its remarkable balloon every few hours.

Oikopleura—an extravagant offshoot from mainline tunicates, but in this instance taxonomy and phylogeny are of no consequence. This one is for pure admiration and enjoyment. Larvaceans are not rare, but the opportunity to see one is. Because this one showed itself to me, I am tonight admitted into the ranks of the confidential elite, witness to choice insular secrets, blessed.

When I look across the white-capped surface of Mesquite Bay, I tend not to think about its plankton component because I cannot see it. Likewise, when I gaze over the rippling canopy of the central grassland, I tend to forget the sequestered world of little creatures that live out their lives amid the tangle of roots, jungle of stems, and perpetual gloom that grip the midrib of Matagorda Island.

If I try to walk through this thigh-deep sward, my feet get tangled and I am forced to seek out a game trail. To see the ground at all,

Noctiluca

I must pause and shoulder my way down through the wall of foliage and scratch aside several inches of vegetable debris. The pungent odor of mold assails my nostrils, and my pupils have to adjust from the surface glare to the sudden darkness. Rustles and scritches radiate away from the rude intrusion where I have let the outer world of light and breeze stream into this dank, buffered universe. I am immediately aware that there is adventure to be had here, if I can just contrive to observe without spooking or destroying the shy things that haunt this place.

Just lying on my belly in the grass will not do; the fauna is too tiny and too retreating to scrutinize. Besides, if I get too intimate, some members invade my clothing and proceed to dim my concentration. Nor is an insect net of much use; it sweeps the canopy but not the interior.

I have found the best solution is a compromise between the desire to watch and the practicality of seeing. It is an apparatus called a Berlese funnel. Through its use I can collect the creatures of the soil surface for viewing through my microscope. The downside is that all these organisms are dead and preserved in alcohol. I must use my imagination and books to animate the pile of small corpses, and I need to justify their sacrifice by passing on the knowledge thus gained to visitors.

The rig is easily set up. I use a large plastic funnel fixed upright on a stand with its small end set into a bottle half-filled with alcohol. A square of quarter-inch mesh hardware cloth is fitted inside the neck of the funnel. A double handful of litter and a half inch of soil from a suitable grassland site are poured in. The hardware cloth keeps stuff from falling right through. Then I switch on a hundred-watt light bulb positioned four inches above the funnel and leave the outfit to perk for several days.

The animalcules in the sample respond predictably: to escape light, heat, and dehydration, they scrabble downward. They easily pass through the quarter-inch mesh and—before they know what they are about—they have plunked into the waiting vat of alcohol. When I return, I have an assortment of interesting bodies ready for examination.

This sampling is actually selective. The microbiota—bacteria, fungi, protozoa, nematode worms, and such—if they move at all, do not move fast enough to reach the bottom of the funnel before they die, and so are not represented. The macrobiota, such as ground skinks and large ground spiders, are active enough to avoid field sampling and must be collected in a different manner. What is left are the mesobiota,

creepy-crawly things of small (but not microscopic) to intermediate
size. All are invertebrates (lack backbones), and most are arthropods
(enclosed in a jointed exoskeleton). There is a nifty name for the lot of
them: *cryptozoa,* "hidden animals."

The results from a typical sample will cover the bottom of a three-
and-one-half-inch dish with a tangle of legs, wings, antennae, and
bodies. It is staggering to consider the mass of living things on an acre
of barrier grassland; and there are nineteen thousand acres of grass on
Matagorda Island. The numbers of cryptozoa must approach planktonic proportions!

Life in the sod is mostly monotonously regular. This dark, partly
subterranean world lacks sunrise and sunset, wind, seasons, or rapid
temperature change. Only extreme shifts in moisture disturb the pace
of life. Rainwater percolating through the sand brings the danger of
drowning and the hazard of an enveloping surface film that can trap
and bind tiny bodies to the sand grains. Drought is less abrupt but
equally devastating for animalcules with proportionally large surface
areas and thin cuticles acclimated to moist cubbyholes. To avoid dehydration, they tunnel downward or hastily encapsulate in some resistant
form. When the season turns cool, the grasses send their nutrients into
subterranean rhizomes. Then jackrabbits, sandhill cranes, and feral
hogs grub for the concentrated foodstuff, abruptly turning the
cryptozoic habitat upside down.

Mostly, however, life in the sod simply rocks on. Conventional herbivores are absent because there is no greenery in the dark, but there
are miles of roots and rhizomes and banks of ascending stems all filled
with sugary sap waiting to be tapped by those with a piercing and
sucking proboscis. And so there are cryptozoic versions of sucking
mites, plant bugs, burrower bugs, leafhoppers, scale insects, and aphids.
The only traditional members of this fauna that are poorly represented
are earthworms, which do not proliferate in dry sand with its low organic content.

While colonies of termites process bits of fiber and wood, the ubiquitous bacteria and fungi exude cellulase, the enzyme that promotes the
deterioration of bulk vegetable debris into detritus. Hungry detritivores are ready and waiting: legions of wingless insects called springtails and hordes of soil mites are joined by lesser numbers of harvestmen, minuscule rove beetles, earwigs, bristletails, barklice, moth larvae,
fly maggots, and teeny ants.

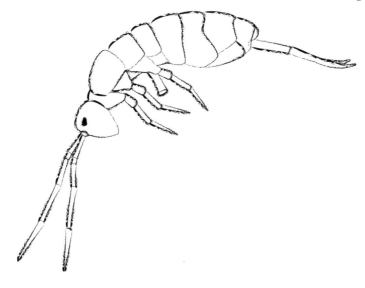

Springtail

The welter of passively munching bodies attracts the attention of diminutive carnivores: predatory mites, dwarf spiders, pseudoscorpions, assassin bugs, predaceous thrips, even aggressive species of fungi that garrote and absorb their prey.

I frequently get excited enough to swivel round directly from my microscope to my word processor to enter a cryptozoic note in my diary before the fervor cools.

MAY '94: *What copepods are to plankton, springtails* (Collembola) *are to cryptozoa. They are everywhere, succulent and plump. Long ones, round ones, smooth ones, bumpy ones, naked ones, fuzzy ones; munching machines, made to convert detritus into tidbits of flesh. Each has a forked hickey folded under its belly, the built-in spring that catapults it out of harm's way. Springtails hardly have room to hop in their confined habitat, and jump or not, they must serve as every soil carnivore's fodder.*

JUNE '95: *Mites! The most numerous and diverse microarthropods in this sheltered habitat. At first I took the seed mites* (Oribatei) *for specks of mineral matter until I saw legs attached. Every sample is sprinkled with them. The hairy, long-legged spider mites* (Tetranychidae) *are more colorful and more evident. There must be a few parasitic species of mites in this assemblage, but*

*most seem to lead independent lives. One of the real wonders of Matagorda
Island is that in all my rambles through its luxuriant, pesticide-free grassland,
I have never gotten a chigger (the parasitic larva of harvest mites). Maybe its
complement of mosquitoes is scourge enough for one barrier island.*

SEPTEMBER '96: *Got two pseudoscorpions in the sample today! For plucking
up springtails and mites, you could not engineer a neater little ambush
predator.*

NOVEMBER '96: *I knew fungus gnats* (Mycetophilidae) *by name only. Books
say the adults flit weakly over damp moldering sites where their maggots feed
on fungi. Now I know them on sight—long-legged, fragile mosquito-like
flies with slender, beaded antennae and wings with few cross veins. The
compost heap beneath the grass canopy on this island must be fungus gnat
heaven. It seems that everywhere I look out here I find a paradise.*

DECEMBER '96: *Sound the trumpet! Today I saw my first dipluran! All one-
eighth inch of him, from threaded antennae to the pair of little forceps on his
tail end. He is remotely centipede-like, eyeless, and ghostly white. Because of
his rear appendage, he is a "forcipate dipluran"* (Japygidae). *His lineage goes
right back to the base of the insect class. Insect wings had not been invented
when he came along. He is an "apterygote," wingless from the beginning.
Springtails and silverfish are his cousins. Now if I can find a proturan, I will
have a grand-slam of the apterygote clan, all from Matagorda Island.*

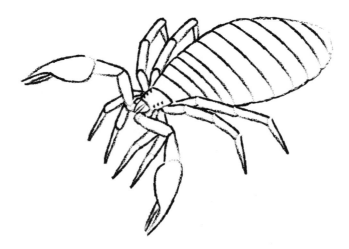

Pseudoscorpion

Dipluran

FEBRUARY '97: *While working through a Berlese sample, I made a discovery—for me—a brand-new order of insects, Embioptera, a web spinner! A short-legged little bug no more than a quarter-inch long, but I can clearly see its trademark—the enlarged basal segment of the front tarsus where its silk gland is housed. It uses special hollow hairs to spin a shining wall inside its gallery in the soil. They are colonial critters, but only this one individual was unfortunate enough to plop into my alcohol bottle. Only ten species of these tropical insects occur in all of North America, and we have one on Matagorda Island:* Oligembia *sp.*

To canvass the larger invertebrates and ground-hugging vertebrates on Matagorda Island, I use a drift-fence-and-pitfall apparatus. The drift fence is cross shaped, with each of its twenty-five-foot arms made of a shin-high strip of galvanized metal set on edge in the ground. At the central intersection and at the end of each arm, I sunk a five-gallon plastic bucket flush with the ground. Any smallish, nonflying creature that encounters the metal barrier will tend to follow it (to "drift") until it falls into a pit.

This outfit is permanently laid out in the field, but most of the time I inactivate it by covering the pits and opening gaps in the fence. I set the trap for one week each month. During this week, I go out each morning to inspect and catalog the catch. To add breadth to the endeavor, I installed four identical devices in sand dunes, grassland, salt marsh, and oyster-shell ridge. With these I can find out what sorts of small creatures scuttle around unseen on Matagorda Island, and I can also tell which of the major habitats they prefer and during which seasons they are most active.

As expected, after several years of collecting data, I have verified the existence of a rich and diverse fauna of ground-living creatures on the island. I have counted thousands of individuals of over three hundred kinds. The number of species would be larger if my ability to identify minuscule insects and arachnids were better. Taxonomic restraints notwithstanding, the endeavor has been both revealing and fun.

It was clear early on that in terms of both biodiversity (number of kinds) and biomass (number of individuals), the oyster-shell ridge and salt marsh were about equally productive; the grassland ranked next, and the sand dunes lagged well behind. No surprise. The ridge and marsh each have lots of environmental "edges" with a profusion of microhabitats that can shelter and nourish an array of small creatures. The surface of the ridge is littered with bleached oyster shells on a substantial layer of dark soil developed atop the sand. A dense stand of woody shrubs casts shade, gives protection from the wind, and provides a rare opportunity for arboreal animals on this nearly treeless barrier island. The drift fence in the salt marsh crosses the transition from low to high marsh and lies in a zone of episodic flooding as well as seasonal drying. The substrate is rich in detritus. When wet, it supports luxuriant growths of blue-green algae, and when dry, deep cracks rend its surface. So, there are lots of places for little creatures to find food and shelter, and their species composition shifts with the tides and the seasons.

The grassland and the dunes each present a more monotonous aspect. Because of the buffering effect of the grass canopy, the interior of the sward supports a significant fauna; but the open, windswept sand dunes are a grudging environment.

Regardless of habitat type, catches in the pitfalls were most varied and most numerous during Matagorda Island's most amenable seasons for wildlife—following the spring and fall rainy months. The take dropped during winter and reached its low point in summer.

A real menagerie of creatures bumbled into the pitfalls: spiders, beetles, roaches, crickets, ants, scorpions, centipedes, millipedes, snails, harvestmen, true bugs, flies, cicadas, silverfish, caterpillars, sow bugs, crabs, frogs, toads, lizards, turtles, snakes, rodents, and even one bird and several fish. Certain kinds of creatures made up the bulk of the catch, and their proportions were about what you would expect—over half were insects; nearly a quarter were arachnids; there were quite a few crustaceans; all the rest appeared only occasionally.

No naturalist would be surprised to learn that beetles accounted for three-quarters of the kinds of insects, most belonging to the common ground-dwelling families: ground beetles (Carabidae), darkling beetles (Tenebrionidae), rove beetles (Staphylinidae), snout beetles (Curculionidae), scarab beetles (Scarabeidae), click beetles (Elateridae). There was also a welter of lesser groups, many that I could not identify. Clearly, all over this island, mostly at night, there are legions of beetles scurrying around. The very abundant ground beetles, predators armed with fierce grasping mandibles, must constantly ravage the host of weaker creatures in this world of nooks and crannies. Meanwhile, darkling and rove beetles grind up fresh or decaying vegetable matter, and dung beetles and sexton beetles process fecal matter and animal carcasses. All these beetles are eaten by other creatures. I have dissected feces from box turtles and horned lizards and regurgitation pellets from American kestrels and burrowing owls, all full of bits of ground-up beetle exoskeleton. Coyote dung is similarly packed. The collective ecological impact of the beetle fauna on the island ecosystem must be significant, though largely unappreciated.

The orthopterans are noteworthy insects because several kinds are large and abundant. Herbivores or detritivores, they are food items in the diets of predaceous insects and arachnids as well as amphibians, lizards and snakes, birds, and mammals. Field crickets (*Gryllus pennsylvanicus*) and wood roaches (*Parcoblatta fulvescens*) range through all habitats except the sand dunes and low marsh. I have found their remains beneath the webs of funnelweb spiders, in regurgitation pellets of black terns, and crammed into coyote feces. In the dunes, field crickets are replaced by ground crickets (*Nemobius* sp.), and wood roaches give way to sand roaches (*Arenivaga bolliana*).

A female sand roach is wingless, hairy, flat, and nearly round. Dropped onto a dune, she instantly slices beneath the sand and leaves only the merest trace of sliding sand grains as she swims beneath the surface. She is a detritivore, but I wonder how she finds enough to eat in these barren dunes. How does she maintain her body fluids or nurture her brood? What predators must she elude? A neat little animal! Just one more of the fascinating life-forms on this island; one more reason that I can spend a lifetime of rapture here.

Two prominent grasshoppers manage to avoid the pitfalls. The large bird grasshoppers (*Schistocerca americana*) erupt from the grass canopy in long, soaring flights, while the dunes grasshoppers (*Heliastus subroseus*) hold their ground. I sometimes discover these sand-colored dunes grasshoppers only by following their distinctive track of parallel rows of dots across the sand to a nearly imperceptible bump. It takes a finger-poke or a shadow-pass to provoke the bump into flight. While in the air, the dunes hopper catches the eye with its red hind tibiae. Then, as it drops back to the sand, it flexes its legs, hiding the color and leaving the observer confused and blinking, and the hopper safely hidden.

I have found thirty kinds of ants on Matagorda Island. They are as ubiquitous as beetles and individually far more numerous. Native fire ants (*Solenopsis xyloni* and *S. geminata*) commonly invade pitfalls to attack and haul off trapped animals. Valentine ants (*Crematogaster lineolata*), named for the shape of their shiny black abdomen, live in large colonies beneath surface debris, while their look-alike relatives (*C. laeviuscula*) excavate galleries in plant stems throughout the grassland and into the smooth cordgrass in the salt marsh. Both species sip liquids from animals that die in the pitfalls, and they tend aphids for honeydew. Several times I have found herds of aphids tended by valentine ants inside smooth pods of papier-mâché on grass stems. Pyramid ants (*Conomyrma flavus*) are the only species easily able to maintain tunnels in the dry sand. Their characteristic piles of excavated sand occur throughout the dunes and in openings in the grassland, and their spindly-legged workers with long, fluttering antennae frequently visit the pitfalls.

There are at least three kinds of fungus-growing ants on the island. None is common. Occasionally I find a cleared area in the grassland where the large red Texas leaf-cutter ants (*Atta texana*) have established a bustling city. Under the watchful eyes of big-headed soldiers, the workers toil tirelessly through the night hauling green clippings to nourish their fungus gardens deep in the sand. Another species of fungus gardener (*Trachymyrmex turrifex*) leads a more hidden life in dark soil on the oyster-shell ridge. The locations of its isolated colonies of only a dozen or so individuals are marked by inch-tall earthen chimneys, and the little ants suspend their fungus beds from rootlets in the ceilings of their subterranean galleries. These ants, covered with spines and prickly bumps, crouch and feign death when disturbed. A third very similar species (*T. septentrionalis*) leads a buried existence in the grassland. On rare occasions, I see their nest holes opened and surrounded by fans of excavated soil pellets in the grass near our house trailer.

In addition to finding a few army ants in my pitfalls, I occasionally see a sinuous trail of fluid movement coursing across the ground. Army ants on the move! These are not the aggressive types that ransack tropical forests of the New World, but they are more passive temperate cousins (*Eciton nigrescens*). I think they spend most of their time in subterranean chambers, but occasionally they feel the restless urge that characterizes their kind. Then the pale yellow ants emerge in their thousands to follow their leaders in fast-stepping single file. It is a silent, energetic, disciplined rally of the sort that only caste-bound ants can muster. All these workers are eyeless, but chemical trails and pattering antennae keep them precisely in line. These are not raiding columns, I think, but a colony, loaded with its brood, moving to new chambers.

Just as beetles dominate the catch of insects, so spiders make up the bulk of the arachnid harvest. And where ground beetles are most prevalent, so ground spiders outnumber orb weavers: wolf spiders (Lycosidae), ground spiders (Gnaphosidae), sac spiders (Clubionidae), funnelweb spiders (Agelenidae), dwarf spiders (Linyphiidae), jumping spiders (Salticidae), and a scattering of others. Unlike more diverse beetles, all spiders are carnivores. I am always amazed at the numbers of bulky and robust wolf spiders in the traps. I can confirm their abundance by using a flashlight at night to reveal the greenish-white sparkle of their eyes everywhere in all terrestrial habitats. Though seldom given consideration when one thinks of major predators, wolf spiders and their relatives must account for much of the killing that goes on each night on this barrier island.

I have discovered two species of tarantulas on Matagorda Island. The large brown females and black, long-legged males of *Dugesiella hentzi* are restricted to the oyster-shell ridge and are moderately common there. *Aphonopelma steindachneri* is a pretty tarantula, somewhat smaller, with a large, feltlike brown spot on the tip of its pale abdomen. It is either rare or seldom leaves its burrow, for I have seen only one specimen in the grassland.

I was surprised to find tarantulas on this sandy barrier and even more amazed to come across a species of trap-door spider (*Myrmekiophila fluviatilis*). Heavy rains force the trap-doors from their burrows, and that is when these beautiful velvety brown animals appear in my traps and wander over the ground in the grassland. A trap-door spider abroad, with shining mahogany carapace and enormous chelicerae, stalking deliberately with ponderous stride, is an animal that exudes dark intrigue. Elsewhere, these spiders have been excavated from within ants' nests, and it has been suggested that they feed on ants (thus the generic name *Myrmekiophila,* "ant lover"), but I doubt it. I rather think they take advantage of ground cleared by ants as convenient spots to construct their cleverly hidden burrow with a hinged lid and to practice their ambush predation on more plump-bodied invertebrate prey. I have never found a burrow on the island—something else to look forward to.

Black widow spiders (*Latrodectus mactans*) are common wherever there is surface debris. I think my trap records overestimate their abundance, however, because these spiders seek out the pitfalls as perfect places to string their ragged webs. The same is true for brown recluses (*Loxosceles devia*).

Most jumping spiders can scale the smooth interior of my pitfalls, but I occasionally discover the colorful little ant-mimic (*Peckhamia picata*) and the large, hairy, emerald-jawed jumping spider (*Phidippus audax*), which jockeys itself to watch my every move with a riveting stare. Rounding out the arachnids are several common kinds of harvestmen (relatives of the more familiar daddy longlegs) and the island's one species of scorpion (*Centruroides vittatus*).

Judging by my pitfall results, myriapods ("thousand-leggers") are not abundant on Matagorda Island. The sandy substrate and drying atmosphere are unfavorable for them. Still, representatives of five families of centipedes have fallen into the traps. The commonest are small brown centipedes (*Lithobius* sp.), but certainly the most spectacular is the four-inch-long, brightly varnished, blue-and-yellow *Scolopendra* sp., armed with a wicked pair of fangs folded beneath its head. As with scorpions, I use forceps to lift these large centipedes out of the trap. I have collected only one kind of millipede belonging to the family Polydesmida.

I expected crustaceans to be important in aquatic habitats, but I was unprepared for the variety and abundance of them in the inland pit-falls. It was clear that at night and during wet weather, gill-breathing crustaceans are scuttling around well into the interior of the island and that a few even lead semiterrestrial lives.

Each night, so long as the substrate is moist, a dither of saltmarsh beach hoppers (*Orchestia grillus*) emerges to course across the low and high marsh. These three-quarter-inch-long, flattened, shrimplike amphipods eat detritus and tiny carcasses, and I get them by the dozens in my pits. If I am late in running the traps, the delicate animals wither up and die wholesale in the dry air of midmorning. Saltmarsh beach hoppers are a good example of the value of the trap—I seldom see them in the marsh by day and certainly would never suspect their teeming numbers. What else goes undetected right under my nose?

Sow bugs (*Porcellio laevis*) are abundant beneath surface debris in all island habitats except the open beach. Sow bugs are isopods, pillbuglike (but do not roll into a pill) and flattened from top to bottom. They are among the most land adapted of the crustaceans, for they carry their brood in a special pouch beneath their bodies and do not need to return to the sea to release their offspring. Visitors are always charmed when I turn a mama sowbug upside down and point out her marsupium bulging with squiggling babies. Sow bugs need moist air to breathe, but they are more tolerant than saltmarsh beach hoppers to dehydration, so they range right across the island in protected sites. I have seen wolf spiders and carabid beetles with sow bugs in their clutches.

I anticipated getting ghost crabs and great land crabs, but these were not the end of the crab harvest. Both sand fiddlers and mud fiddlers routinely appeared in the traps in the marsh and well away from the water's edge on the oyster-shell ridge. They apparently travel widely at night. So do wharf crabs (*Sesarma cinerea*). Though known for adaptability and durability, the blue crab (*Callinectes sapidus*) is basically an aquatic crustacean. Yet, even during nonrainy periods, I routinely caught half-grown blue crabs several hundred yards from water on the

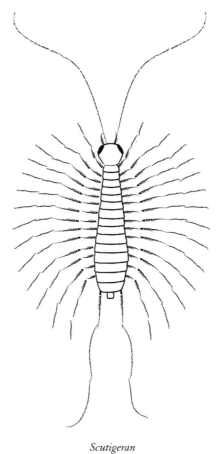

Scutigeran

oyster-shell ridge. In air dry enough to curdle the gills of sow bugs, these crabs were circling the bottom of the plastic buckets, as alert and as pugnacious as only blue crabs can be.

The traps revealed that each of the four habitats harbored at least a few distinctive invertebrates. The sand dunes stand out in this respect, perhaps because they are so demanding. Here the pitfalls collected wispy, fast-moving, long-legged centipedes (*Scutigera coleoptrata*); primitive and heavily scaled firebrats (*Thermobia domestica*); dark, hard-backed harvestmen (*Mesosoma nigrum*); beautifully camouflaged and incredibly quick sand wolf spiders (*Arctosa littoralis*); brightly colored and grotesquely sculptured dwarf spiders (*Erigone autumnalis* and *Ceratinopsis interpres*); the larvae of owl flies (Ascalaphidae), which look like robust, bizarre versions of doodlebugs; minuscule yellow ants, among the smallest of their kind in all of North America (*Brachymyrmex depilis*); and, of course, lots of ghost crabs.

The grassland yielded funnelweb spiders (*Agelenopsis naevia*), a huge variety of obscure beetles, and ants that build their nests beneath tussocks of cordgrass (*Aphaenogaster texana*). From the marsh came the saltmarsh beach hoppers and a seething mass of maggots from sundry sorts of flies, including especially soldier flies (Stratiomyiidae) and horseflies (Tabanidae).

The oyster-shell ridge quartered an interesting coterie of characteristic animals associated with its heavy soil and woody branches. To illustrate only from the ants: two kinds of semiarboreal carpenter ants (*Camponotus rasilis* and *C. abdominalis*); a peculiar ant of Mexican affinity that feeds almost exclusively on sow bugs (*Leptogenys elongata*); a large black ant that lives a secretive existence in small colonies in heavy soil (*Pachychondyla harpax*); the arboreal, alert, fast, and slinky *Pseudomyrma pallida* that squirrels around tree branches at my approach.

Although the traps were designed to catch invertebrates, they incidentally captured an assortment of small, ground-living vertebrates as well. Hardly as large as a field cricket, the plump and shiny eastern narrowmouth toad (*Gastrophryne carolinensis*) scurrying through the grassland jungle frequently tumbles into the pits. It is occasionally joined by big-eyed juvenile southern meadow frogs (*Rana sphenocephala*) and gulf coast toads (*Bufo valliceps*) dispersing from the nearest freshwater swale. Two other common hunters among the grass stalks, the little ground skink (*Scincella lateralis*) with scales of liquid copper and the legless slender glass lizard (*Ophisaurus attenuatus*), routinely show up in the traps. In the sand dunes I get lizards called prairie-lined race runners (*Cnemidophorus sexlineatus*). If large to medium-sized snakes get into the pitfalls, they must manage to get out again, for I have retrieved only one small massasauga rattlesnake (*Sistrurus catenatus*) and several juvenile gulf coast ribbon snakes (*Thamnophis proximus*).

It always bothers me to run my traplines on a winter morning and discover torpid little balls of fur in the pitfalls. These are fulvous harvest mice (*Reithrodontomys fulvescens*). I put them in my pocket to warm up awhile before I release them. I can tell from their abundant fecal pellets that both hispid cotton rats (*Sigmodon hispidus*) and marsh rice rats (*Oryzomys palustris*) have been in the buckets, and I suspect that

Narrow-mouthed toad

before they leap out, they feed on some of the invertebrate captives. In the springtime I catch quite a few newly weaned rats that cannot make the leap to freedom. Coyotes and raccoons also sometimes reach in and pilfer the pitfalls.

Once after high equinoctial tides I found sheepshead killifish swimming around in two flooded pitfalls in the salt marsh. The doughty little fish must have slithered on their sides to get there. I even managed to catch one bird—a sanderling, probably seeking a safe roost site in the sand dunes. It got into a bucket and did not survive the winter night.

There is other unseen fauna on Matagorda Island. If I sweep an insect net over the grass canopy, I might snare a toothpick grasshopper (*Leptysma marginicollis*) or a sachem skipper (*Atalopedes campestris*). The same net whisked over a blossom of beach evening primrose may capture a halictid bee (*Augochloropsis* sp.) with armor made of hammered green metal or a squatty flower spider (*Misumenops asperatus*) precisely colored to match the soft yellow petals. If I turn my compound microscope on the water film caught between sand grains on the beach, I enter the confined but busy world of whipping nematode worms and gliding gastrotrichs. A hand net drawn through clear brown rainwater puddled in a swale in the grassland occasionally brings up clam shrimp (*Eulimnadia texana*); or a shaft of sunlight might pierce the knee-deep water to ignite a sparkling, drifting cloud of perfect spheres—colonial rotifers (*Conochilus* sp.). It is obvious that the hidden worlds on this island are not limited by Nature, but by my ability to perceive them.

CHAPTER 5

COMPARATIVE ANATOMY

Waves smooth beach sand
Each grain sorted just so
Only wind finds fault.

WHEN I WENT THROUGH the University of Texas over forty years ago (no need to specify "UT, Austin"; there were no satellite campuses) with several hundred other aspiring zoology majors, I took Zoology 414, comparative vertebrate anatomy. It was a mandatory course, diabolically designed to make or break, a rite of passage, like boot camp. Everyone complained about the mountain of facts, extra hours in the laboratory, and the pitiless professors. And as in boot camp, those who passed developed the lasting camaraderie of those who survive a life-threatening experience together. When we "passed comparative," we were on our way.

The lectures in comparative were interesting enough but tedious. We took reams of class notes, memorized our underlined copy of Romer, learned everything the student grapevine had to say about our prof's favorite quiz questions, and prepared ourselves for an exam wherein we might have twenty minutes to discuss the major steps in the evolution of the vertebrate ear or to compare the aortic arches of a frog with those of an elephant. Everyone agreed, however, that it was the comparative lab that was the backbreaker.

Lab met once a week for four grueling hours. The room was appropriately morguelike—huge, open, with long, slate-topped tables, leaning stacks of wax-bottomed dissecting pans, and deep sinks where we could rinse an entire carcass. One wall was lined with barrels containing the study specimens pickled in a mix of formaldehyde and methanol. The whole room exuded the breath-snatching odor of the pickling brine, and for the entire semester we carried the aura with us wherever we went. Even now, when I open my lab manual, the reek still rises to sharpen my memory. These days such exposure is recognized as being mutagenic, a fact of which we were blissfully ignorant.

We began our comparative laboratory experience by using huge tongs to reach through a grease film into the vile yellow murk in one of the barrels. There we groped blindly among the unseen rigor-hardened lumps until we got a grip. Then we heaved up the specimen whose every anatomical detail we were about to intellectually consume.

First came the lamprey, autochthon of the backboned lineage. It looked like a length of rubbery gray hose, flattened tail at one end and flared oral hood lined with rings of horny teeth at the other. The thing looked positively evil.

The dogfish shark was next. We spent several weeks delving its every anatomical nuance. These were injected sharks, so we reasonably could be required to trace every branch of their latex-impregnated blood vessels and, far more difficult, to recognize them as blue and red dots on sharks cut in cross section.

We spent only a week on the mud puppy, an ugly, foot-long salamander made more loathsome by the ravages of the formalin.

Then came the pigeon, hands down the most repulsive specimen on the agenda. Plucking its soggy plumage also removed clots of skin. Even before actual cutting began, the carcass looked as if it had been chewed up and spit out.

For the last third of the semester we were engrossed with the cat. Even the cat lovers among us were not too distressed, for the wet, board-stiff cadavers with foggy eyes, matted hair, and fixed, toothy grimaces did not look any more like kitty cats than the pigeons looked like birds.

After completion of each specimen, there was a dreaded lab quiz. We filed in grim silence past lines of pans with chunks of embalmed meat impaled with numbered pins signaling anatomical details to be identified on sight. It was designed to force a sleep-deprived, minutiae-crammed mind to draw an utter blank. But after the initial shock, most of us rallied, filled in the blanks on our answer sheets, and staggered out to the nearest bed or pub.

What has all this to do with Matagorda Island? Backboned creatures are relegated to the major category Phylum Chordata—creatures that possess a unique combination of three anatomical traits: a notochord, pharyngeal clefts, and a dorsal, hollow nerve cord. Note that a backbone is not one of the basic features. True, most of the animals under consideration do have one and so are called *vertebrates;* thus comparative vertebrate anatomy. However, there are several small and reclusive organisms that lay at least ephemeral claim to the Three Sacred Traits but lack a backbone. These creatures, called *protochordates* ("first chordates"), are positioned at the base of the vertebrate genealogical tree, for encapsulated within their soft bodies lie the heritage and hope of the vertebrate lineage. So, they are given nodding acquaintance in Zoo 414 as a preamble to greater issues. Patience; we have not yet come to the island connection.

In our first laboratory session we got a hasty look at these protochordate curiosities. The acorn worm specimen lay, as it must have for decades, in sediment-covered fragments on the bottom of a jar of milky formalin. I stared soberly at what resembled a long-forgotten container from the back shelf of a refrigerator, harboring the dregs of something now unrecognizable and certainly inedible, past ready to be heaved.

The sea squirt was an intact but formless brown blob about the size of a walnut. The bolus had absorbed preservative until it had the same specific gravity as the fluid, so it was buoyant. Movement of the container set the blob into a prolonged ghostly twirl, giving it a surreal animation beyond anything the creature had experienced in life.

The lancelet was something else. Being fishlike in appearance, this inch-and-a-quarter-long creature was definitely the most credible of the protochordates for being conjured as a forebear of the backboned clan. It had a head, tail, muscles, fin-folds. We got a specimen mounted in a block of clear plastic so it could be handled and viewed under a binocular microscope. There, once they were brightly illuminated and stained a vivid red, we got our first look at the Three Sacred Traits. From there we went on to work out the cluster of buccal cirri, the band of myomeres, the atriopore, the endostyle, and all the rest.

Everyone agreed that the lancelet was by far the most appealing of the protochordates, and the name of this particular variety, amphioxus, rolled easily off our tongues and into our growing lexicon. Then someone ran across the catchy chorus from a Tom Laher ditty set to the tune of "Its a Long Way to Tipperary": "It's a long way from amphioxus; it's a long way to us . . . ."

So there you have the three protochordates according to Zoo 414. All as dead as rocks; as if they were all extinct, and we had only these few jaded reliquiae to show they ever existed. Stepping stones to ourselves, but so utterly alien and stiffened with formalin that no amount of quiet study ever could pluck a filial heartstring. After the first lab quiz we never saw the specimens again. Out of sight, out of mind. Surely I still would be vague about protochordates today if I had not moved to Matagorda Island.

One of our delights is to work along the shallows near the tidal passes with a shovel, sieve box, and collecting pail, digging and sifting at any interesting hole, bump, or squiggle that we find in the substrate. When the tide is out, the exposed sandy flats are punctuated with low, biscuit-sized mounds made of sagging coils of sand squeezed up from below, as though from a toothpaste tube. Excited digs with the shovel yielded only the cloying odor of iodine. Then we learned to look for a coil being actively extruded and to quickly lunge at it with the shovel.

At last, as the ooze drained out of the sieve, there was a limp, cream-colored worm fragment weakly writhing on the screen. We washed it, dropped it into a jar of water, got a waft of its antiseptic breath. Although it was nothing more than the severed rear end of the creature, the bit was enough to verify what we had hoped for—acorn worms, alive and well right here on Matagorda Island!

We have learned more about acorn worms. They like black, anaerobic, sandy-silty muck in shallows subject to tide but shielded from the turbulence of the surf. They are most numerous just inside the tidal passes.

The worms make poorly defined U tubes in the ooze. At the tip of one leg of the U is the conspicuous pile of fecal casts. A funnel-like depression is at the other end. The worm pulls in sediment, causing the loose surface material to slump, forming a basin into which more nutrient-rich stuff slides. The animal slurps up the food concentrated in the bottom of its feeding funnel until the local supply is exhausted. Then it swings aside and begins anew. If the site is productive, a single fecal mound might be associated with one active and several abandoned feeding basins within a radius of a couple of feet.

The trick for the collector is to guess (with no clue that we could detect) which feeding funnel is being used. A lucky plunge of the shovel between that depression and the mound will get a piece of acorn worm, and the fragment will likely include the head and forebody.

The front third of the body is relatively durable. Beyond that the flabby tube readily snaps into squirming pieces. Eventually, I got proficient enough to score about one out of ten attempts, but I have never even come close to extracting an intact acorn worm. There is no second chance. The worms retract into the soupy depths immediately when disturbed.

What have you got when you have a piece of acorn worm in a pan of water? Certainly more *perception* than substance. Here is the shadowy creature in whose top-shaped larva and vermiform adult body lie many of the secrets to the kinship between the spineless animals and those with backbones. But you can hardly fathom that just by looking.

An acorn worm is an unimaginably dim being that passes its entire existence in a monotonous universe of fluid sand devoid of dimension, direction, time, season, light, irregularity. Driven solely by appetite, the brute lacks even the satisfaction of locating food; it has but to open its mouth and engulf the omnipresent black gruel in which it is immersed. The intestinal lining manages to extract nutriment before the grit is extruded at the far end, so the animal itself is reduced to little more than a vaguely animated tube of dark sand.

Even sex in acorn worms is a languid, incorporeal affair devoid of courtship or orgasm, the sperm meeting the egg almost by happenstance. Little wonder that students are more aroused by my display of excitement than by the worm itself. One day, if they study comparative vertebrate anatomy, they may recall and appreciate the thrill.

The most common species of acorn worm around Matagorda Island is the golden acorn worm (*Balanoglossus aurantiacus*). Its front end is a typical fleshy, mucus-coated proboscis, in this case cream colored and fingertip sized. Filled with seawater, it is rigid enough to plow through the substrate, while the sticky mucus collects food particles. The proboscis projects from a cylindrical, creamy yellow collar that contains the mouth. To some imaginative early anatomist the proboscis and collar called to mind an acorn in its cup; thus the common name. (Students more readily see a phallic resemblance.)

Just behind the collar is a pair of golden winglike flaps that house the reproductive organs. If the worm lies quietly, a 10x magnifier reveals, under the flaps, the infamous pharyngeal slits where tiny gills extract oxygen from the water. Behind the flaps is a cluster of little greenish bags that contain digestive enzymes. The rest of the body is a flaccid, off-white tube about a quarter inch across, through which the dark intestine can be seen. Books say the animal may be three feet long, but we have never extracted more than eight inches at a time.

One memorable day I discovered a second, smaller species of acorn worm among the golden ones on the sandy tidal flat beside our boathouse. This one, the helical acorn worm (*Saccoglossus kowalevskii*) corkscrews as it digs and stays in a coil even when extracted and laid in a pan of water. This species has a relatively long, tapered proboscis that it pokes up onto the surface to drag detritus back into its burrow. This activity leaves a distinctive rosette of grooves, and a quick dig at that spot usually uncovers the creature.

Acorn worms shore up their flimsy burrows with mucus that is laced with bromophenol. The smell we recognize as iodine is actually bromine, a closely related element. Perhaps it wards off some potential predators, pathogenic microbes, or the invasion of unwanted tunnelmates. I bet the Karankawas, incessantly trying whatever came to hand, discovered the antiseptic value centuries before iodine was used in Europe.

A net pulled through widgeon grass brings up a variety of shrimps, crabs, jellies, snails, amphipods, and small fishes. Occasionally, the list includes rubbery spherical objects that one perceptive student dubbed "eyeballs." When a volunteer musters the courage to gather a few eyeballs for the collecting pail, there will likely be a squeal as a specimen suddenly shoots a thin jet of water up the would-be collector's arm.

We have two common kinds of sea squirts around Matagorda Island. The more abundant one, called a sea grape rather than an eyeball (*Molgula manhattensis*), looks not too different from the pickled specimen I saw in Zoo 414. The brownish exterior of the globose body is cluttered with growths of sundry hydroids, bryozoans, and algae as well as a dusting of fine sediment. This animal—for animal it is, despite its appearance—attaches to any hard substrate but is most frequently found among the stems in sea grass beds. There it sits, sucking water in one of its two small turrets, harvesting the load of organic matter with mucus in its gill basket, and squirting the water out the other turret. Its internal reservoir feeds the stream jetted out when the creature is disturbed.

The rough sea squirt (*Styela plicata*) is more rubbery and elongated and often lives in lumpy clusters. These and other kinds of sea squirts share some features that are so peculiar that even old comparative students can usually recall some of them: their skin is made largely of cellulose (a substance ordinarily associated with plants); they periodically reverse the direction of blood flow through their vessels; and they concentrate the rare element vanadium in their tissues (for what reason, no one knows).

Yet, the most remarkable aspect of sea squirts is that they are included among the protochordates. With only one of the Three Sacred Traits (the gill apparatus), how do they qualify? This, like so many paradoxes in anatomy, is resolved by looking to the microscopic, planktonic larva. The tadpole shape is clear enough, but staining is needed to reveal the notochord and dorsal nerve cord down the tail and the gill basket in the plump body. The basket is used strictly for breathing, not filtering; the larva does not eat. The larval sea squirt soon settles on some hard substrate and undergoes a metamorphosis during which it loses its tail (and along with it, two of the Three Sacred Traits), enlarges its gill basket for feeding as well as respiring, and takes up the passive form and mode of the adult.

APRIL '98: *Down to the boathouse at sunset with the plankton net. Put the sample under the microvideo. Only copepods and an occasional small comb jelly. Just before heaving the sample I noticed one, then several, tiny critters swimming in fitful bursts. They were only about a quarter the size of a copepod and looked like sperm. I lost two trying to get them into an eyedropper. Finally sucked up a third. Got it into a drop of water on a depression slide and jacked it up to 100x with the compound scope. Still looked like a sperm, or maybe a tadpole. Tadpole, a tiny tadpole! This must be a larval tunicate, very likely from the sea grapes that live out in the widgeon grass bed. I checked in Smith; it fits his figure to a T. This specimen is zooming around the perimeter of its droplet, whipping its elastic notochord like mad, making good use of its claim to fame before losing it. Right out of a page of Romer, but here with vim and vigor. I never thought I would be so lucky. Rather than pour the sample down the drain, I took it back to the bay. Small hope there, I know, for these few unique tadpoles, but good for my psyche.*

Amphioxus (*Branchiostoma caribaeum*) really looks its part as a connecting link between creatures with backbones and those without. Someone with the right background would note its close resemblance both to a larval sea squirt (an invertebrate) and a larval lamprey (a vertebrate). The inch-and-a-half-long animal has a tapered nose and pointed tail (thus, the common name, lancelet) and is trimmed with low folds rather than fins. It has no eyes, no scales, no bones—but it does clearly display all of the Three Sacred Traits. The prominent notochord extends right out into the snout to stiffen it for plowing through the sand.

Lancelets squiggle into the sand and come to rest, propped at an angle on their metapleural folds with only the head end protruding so they can pump plankton-laden water through their pharyngeal basket. If disturbed, an amphioxus swims in frantic bursts; the bands of muscles switch the supple notochord from side to side, propelling the body either fore or aft with equal ease. But a swimming amphioxus is a vulnerable amphioxus. All sorts of fish, crabs, mantis shrimp, ribbon worms, and even predaceous polychaete worms will quickly snatch up this tempting, opalescent wriggle of naked flesh.

Amphioxus

Amphioxus is the only protochordate that I had seen alive before moving to Matagorda Island. We sifted our first specimen from a current-swept bar a few miles south of the island. Later we discovered them in the passes at each end of Matagorda. They seemed relatively uncommon, at least where we worked, and the ones we found were always incidental to the worms and clams in our sieve. This seeming scarcity is probably misleading. I suspect that some animals escaped unseen through the mesh of our sieve and many others probably lay concealed beyond our reach. Nonetheless, I am reminded of a statement always appended to textbook accounts of lancelets. It relates that in a seaside village in southern China, fishermen go out each day and grub up over a ton of amphioxus, which they cook and eat. Frankly, I don't believe it.

No doubt about one thing, however. Matagorda Island has made the obscure protochordates from 414 come alive for us.

CHAPTER 6

CARDISOMA

*Blowing thistle down
One puff bounces out of step
Darling kildeer chick!*

RUMMAGING AROUND in the back of a storage shed, I found a skeleton that verified hearsay. Not skull and backbone with dangling arm and leg bones. Rather, it was an *exoskeleton,* a hollow suit of armor forged of heavy duty chitin, every detail intact, even its eyes staring at me. It seemed the creature it once contained might at any moment shuffle off into a corner. I propped it in a windowsill at the trailer, and we contemplate one another as I write.

Imagine a crab blown up to intimidating proportions: four inches across its broad back, stout walking legs sprawling a foot from tip to tip. The pincers are massive, the larger one a heavy-duty snipper three and one half inches long with a huge base to house a powerful muscle.

Bleached now, the shell was once sky blue with flushes of purple across the back, fading to blue white on the tips of the legs and pincers. Even the match-stem eyestalks were blue in life and topped with black eye bulbs. On each side of the rectangular mouth frame there is a large, squarish, orange brown patch, a pad of curled velvety hairs. Handsome, menacing, misanthropic, just as a crab should be. Indubitable proof of the existence of one of the most intriguing and enigmatic creatures on Matagorda Island—the great land crab (*Cardisoma guanhumi*).

My suspicions about these creatures were first aroused years ago. The Aransas National Wildlife Refuge called to ask me to come look at a strange and unknown crab. An employee had spotted it chasing her baby chicks and had caught it in a bucket.

I was on my way within hours. In the bucket I beheld my first great land crab: a large male, belligerent from too much poking. He circled the bottom of his bucket, raising his huge pincer in a threatening gesture when anyone peered over the rim.

"Look at this," Adela said in an excited tone. "This is what he can do. What do you think he would have done to my chickens if he had caught one?"

She handed me a battered aluminum soft-drink can with several slits cut through the side. It was easy to see why Adela was wide-eyed and why the crab was in a bad humor.

After double-checking its identity, I took the beast out to the shore for photographs and then reluctantly released it. It sidled into the fringe of smooth cordgrass and quickly disappeared.

I was sure that was the end of the great land crab caper. This happened not long after Hurricane Gilbert; the recent storm must have swept this crab up from the south. Although there are a few records of local sightings of isolated individuals, the species is basically tropical. It is established in south Florida, and there is an occasional beachhead population in extreme south Texas; but great land crabs are permanent and common residents of Atlantic shorelines only from Mexico to Brazil and throughout the islands of the Caribbean. A routine winter along the central Texas coast, I reasoned, would likely wipe out any venturesome or storm-pushed immigrants.

But the very next summer we found a curious hole beside the boat dock on the Aransas Refuge. We could not decide what might have made a three-inch-wide hole decked with a thick platform of freshly excavated mud, so I staked down a poultry-netting trap over the hole. Next day we were a little appalled to find the trap pushed partly off its moorings and lying, crumpled, to one side. At the time we figured a raccoon would do that. In hindsight, I am not so sure.

Months later we found a similar hole on an oyster-shell islet in San Antonio Bay. I tried to excavate it, but after half an hour of sweat and toil, I lost the tunnel in the muck and shell. "We're going to have to leave this for intrigue," our standard declaration for any outdoors puzzle we lacked either time or means to pursue. Five years later the skeleton in the storage shed would put us back on the trail.

Soon after we moved to the island, in early September 1993, Martha came back in high excitement from the beach with a great land crab she had discovered wandering near the waterline. As far as I know, it was the first live specimen ever documented from Matagorda. I showed it to Norman and to Joe who together represented daily scrutiny of the south end of the island for the past thirty-five years. Neither had seen the likes before.

This crab was an adult male and not enamored of our attention. When poured out onto the beach, he swiveled to face the source of provocation, reared back on his legs, and raised his pincers high in an intimidating display of bad temper and finger-snipping force. All of his kind that we later handled showed the same response to threat. We came to refer to this posture as their "universal stance."

Martha tried to keep the crab in place with a bamboo switch while I jockeyed for photos. He crunched the tip of the bamboo when he had the chance and even hung on to be suspended in the air several times before his photo session was done. When we finally let him be, he eased sideways down the beach, his four pairs of walking legs moving in robotic cadence. Even at twenty yards away, a wave of my hand sent him into his universal stance, almost as if he were waving back at me. Obviously, he could see my movement quite well and was still ready to defend himself.

He left us with more questions than answers. Where had he come from? There had been no recent storms. Did he hark to Hurricane Gilbert five years ago? Great land crabs are supposed to live in mangrove thickets and dig tunnels in muddy banks. What was this one doing on a sandy beach? Were there others hereabouts? Again, we had to leave the matter to intrigue.

By the next summer I began to get answers. Tromping through

muck and knee-high vegetation in the high marsh bordering Mesquite Bay, I found an abundance of the distinctive large burrows. Even in areas where the holes were common, the openings were hidden unless seen from close range. I had been walking right past them when I skirted the marsh.

My first tactic was to watch. From a vantage where I could see several holes, I stood as quietly as the salt marsh mosquitoes would allow for half an hour at a time. I tried morning and afternoon and after dark with a flashlight and never saw a thing. That left the ultimate alternative of invasive force.

On a morning in late August, we arrived on the high marsh armed with a shovel, a posthole digger, a plastic bucket, a thermos of coffee, and fortitude. We needed them all before we were done.

We selected a likely hole about three inches across, much larger than the finger-sized burrows of fiddler crabs. A few clods were scattered outside the entrance, but most of the excavated mud had been mashed into a thick pedestal on the front rim of the hole. The face of this platform was slightly concave and tracked with scratch marks etched by the passage of the occupant. On the opposite edge of the rim was a curved, two-inch-high wall of fused mud pellets that leaned partway over the entrance like an awning. The wall could hardly have deflected rain from the burrow, but it did shade the opening and camouflage the entrance. Within a foot there was a second, unadorned opening that looked less used but perhaps connected underground.

I set to work with the posthole digger, sinking a shaft beside the burrow and then carving sideways with the shovel to reveal its trace. It began at a slight decline, then turned almost straight down. At about five inches I encountered the junction leading to the secondary entrance. The burrow went down through sandy mud and into a stratum of black, anaerobic muck. After each gouge, I had to scrape the sticky goo off the blades. Tough going. Then at two and a half feet I hit clay; even worse. Time for a coffee break.

By thirty inches, with the passage still headed for China, I was having trouble cleaning out the hole and had to enlarge the shaft to make room to work. By this time I was covered with muck and sweat and was wondering if we had brought enough fortitude for the project.

Then at thirty-four inches I struck blue clay and a seep of groundwater. The channel enlarged slightly and leveled out atop the clay. In the dim light I saw something move down there! I had to lie on my

belly over the edge of the manhole-sized excavation to get down with
my pocketknife for the last delicate bit of scrabbling. It was easier than
I expected. I had hardly opened the final recess before a great land crab
popped into view and assumed its universal stance in the bottom of the
hole. Its retreat was a dead-end cavity just large enough to contain its
huddled body. In time I excavated quite a few more burrows and
found that this one was typical.

Fired with this success, I was out among the crab burrows in the
high marsh at first light next morning. Instead of digging, I got down
on hands and knees for a close inspection of the burrow entrances and
quickly found evidence of recent surface activity. Most of the entrance
pedestals had a thin veneer of wet mud with fresh scratch marks, and
there were new mud pellets scattered about—evidence of maintenance
of the burrow. Just off the edge of the pedestals I noticed a sprinkle of
fecal pellets. These were tightly packed cylinders, one-eighth inch wide
by three-eighths inch long, rounded on each end, brown with a greenish cast. I was reminded of deposits left by fiddler crabs, but these were
several times larger.

After softening them in water and viewing them under the microscope, I found the pellets to consist of indigestible plant fibers and
finely minced bits of greenery. I had also found fresh snippets of plants
just inside the burrow entrances and scattered around the pedestals,
and I could make out vague "runs" about a foot long radiating from
the burrows into the surrounding marsh.

Soon I had compiled a list of what our vegetarian great land crabs
were feeding on: sea ox-eye (*Borrichia frutescens*), perennial glasswort
(*Salicornia virginica*), seepweed (*Suaeda linearis*), maritime saltwort
(*Batis maritima*), camphor daisy (*Machaeranthera phyllocephala*), seaside
gerardia (*Agalinis maritima*), and sea-lavender (*Limonium carolinianum*). The crabs were simply harvesting what was available in the
high marsh. The only nearby plants they seemed to ignore were shore
grass (*Monanthochloe littoralis*) and salt grass (*Distichlis spicata*). From
the location of the fecal pellets and bits of greens, I judged the crabs
spent most of their surface time munching on the mud platforms,
where they could drop into their hideaways if disturbed.

Over the years I have kept several great land crabs in terraria. After a week or so in captivity they become, if not tractable, at least tolerant of being gently handled. They spend most of their time huddled
in a corner, but always taking the universal stance when disturbed.

True to their tropical affinity, the crabs are quite cold sensitive and succumb to temperatures ten degrees above freezing.

After a day or two captive crabs accept a variety of grocery store produce. Among their favorites are purple seedless grapes, fresh carrots, and apple slices. Surprisingly, they care for neither cantaloupe nor watermelon, and they will not touch lettuce. They do eat natural greens of the sorts that I found them harvesting in the salt marsh. When I dropped shield-backed katydids into the terrarium, the crabs took them with gusto. Although it bothered my conscience, I once dropped in a mud fiddler. Within the hour the fiddler was no more.

Now that I know the crabs better, I doubt that the one in Adela's yard actually was chasing her chickens. Perhaps the curious chicks were getting close enough to elicit the universal stance response, and Adela misinterpreted what was going on. Still, I would not be surprised if the young of low-nesting marsh birds like clapper rails were taken by a land crab. I am not inclined to experiment to find out.

Eventually, I did catch glimpses of land crabs on their mud pedestals, but invariably they saw me at nearly the same time and dropped out of sight into their tunnel. I found that if I walked gingerly on a warm rainy day, I could find a crab or two clinging just inside the entrance to their burrows where they seemed to be wrapped in daydream. Rarely, near sunset, I have spotted a land crab hustling for its burrow from a few feet away, where it had apparently been snipping food plants. I suspect that with a low metabolic rate and little activity, these crabs have a very low calorie intake and need to make only brief feeding forays.

Once secure in the depths of its lair, a land crab must be immune to inclement winter, storms, and predators. I have found their burrows filled to the brim after heavy rains or high tides; yet, when the water subsides days later, these same tunnels show evidence of being reamed out and put back in use. The inhabitants must have sat out their submersion, gills providing a waft of oxygen, thinking nothing at all.

The great land crab comes across as a recluse, miser, and stoic; it needs little, asks little, does little, and seems quite content to crouch in total vacuity at the bottom of its dark, damp tomb. Still, it is amazing that so large an animal can live in such abundance on my doorstep and go so long undetected.

There is one time of the year when great land crabs do show themselves boldly aboveground. However, their appearance is not predictable. In our first year on the island, we saw none abroad. In August and September of the next year, we saw half a dozen in the yard around our trailer, several more at night on the road to the beach, and occasional broken exoskeletons on the airstrips.

But the third year they really put on a show. We began seeing individuals here and there in late July and early August. Soon, we could reliably find several adults on the airstrip about sundown, methodically sidling east toward the Gulf.

In mid-August, we began a systematic survey. From sundown until 10 P.M. we drove an ATV along all four arms of the airstrip, down local roads, and along a two-mile stretch of beach, using a spotlight to scan the terrain. When we found a crab, we noted its location, marked it with an identifying number, recorded its sex, took a few measurements, and released it. That may all sound simple and scientific, but it was an adventure because the great land crabs were not anxious to cooperate with our investigation into their comings and goings.

In the first place, it is not all that easy to catch a land crab. Before it was dark, we could see them and they could see us. They would stiffen and go into a universal stance when we were at least thirty yards away. As we approached, about half these animals dropped their pincers and hunkered on the asphalt; the other half agilely scampered for the grassy margin. We had to keep our eyes on them. Even so, I am sure we missed a few. An occasional individual suddenly vanished while I was getting out to catch it. Only after I ran over a couple did I learn to look under the fender on top of a tire, where the crab had sought refuge.

After dark we could approach more easily. Land crabs' eyes do not shine in the light, but their pale undersides are reflective enough to stand out boldly. When caught in the light beam, all individuals merely stopped and did a universal stance.

However, a crab approached is not necessarily a crab caught. First, I tried an insect net. This resulted in a tangle of pincers, legs, and netting that could hardly be unscrambled. My cap worked little better; once it was grasped by a pincer, I had to tear it loose. A bucket over a crab left us as bad off as before—how to get the angered beast in hand.

I finally hit upon a plastic tumbler. Coming down smartly from above, the tumbler covered the creature's body while leaving its flailing appendages exposed. After painful trial and error, with cuts on every finger, I perfected a deft movement to grasp the bases of the pincers and hold the struggling crab for processing. While I held the obstinate animal, Martha numbered its back with a felt-tip pen. We noted sex (determined by the shape of the abdomen) and size and released the critter. The entire operation took about two minutes.

Through the rest of August and September we marked and released 327 great land crabs. By the end of September their occurrence had dwindled to make further effort unrewarding.

What did we find out? As in any such pursuit, we learned some things and realized how much more we did not know.

While handling the land crabs, we learned more of their defensive tactics. Each stout walking leg is tipped with a bone-hard spine, and the crab, in pushing against my wrists to pull free from my grip, delivered smarting puncture wounds; it was like being poked with an ice pick. Many a crab momentarily escaped my grasp as a result of such spearing, and I guess the same would happen with a tender-nosed predator.

About once in twenty encounters, a crab squirted strong jets of water from both corners of its mouth. These spurted out about five inches and lasted about a second. An unsuspecting predator would certainly pause to reconsider, and that might be the edge the crab needs to make its escape.

Despite the crabs' repertory for self-protection, we did find disassembled exoskeletons frequently, and we saw several crabs hobbling along with only two or three intact appendages. I think coyotes and raccoons account for most of this predation, and I once saw a coyote chomping up a freshly killed land crab. Coyotes approach large ghost crabs from behind, tap them down with a forepaw, and deliver a disabling nip. They can probably catch a land crab in the same manner. Along the margin of the bay, raccoons routinely kill stone crabs that sport a pair of powerful pincers, so coons can probably handle land crabs as well. Considering the temperament and jaw strength of a feral hog, it could take a land crab with little trouble, though it would likely consume a crab exoskeleton without leaving the remains that we observed.

Crab movement began just before sundown and tapered off by midnight. Surveys in the wee hours yielded only an occasional individual.

We apparently got in on the seasonal start of the migration, for all crabs were moving toward the Gulf. On the first night, we found many on the airstrips and roads but none on the beach. The next night two animals appeared on the beach, and then they got numerous there on succeeding nights.

Despite marking 327 crabs, we had only six recoveries, each one within a stone's throw of where it had been marked, usually only a few hours before. What we really wanted we never got—recovery of a crab on the beach that had been marked on the airstrip, or vice versa.

Where did all our marked crabs go? Marked individuals in captivity kept their numbers for weeks, so those in the field probably did not simply lose their marks. We made runs along the beach outside the usual two-mile stretch but never found a marked crab, so they were not just spreading out and missing our target beach. We could not easily scan the dense grassy interior of the island, but we suspect that most crabs took advantage of the airstrips and roads as easy avenues between marsh and Gulf, so marked crabs should have followed a straight path to the adjacent beach. We are still mystified.

Was this a one-way, one-time pilgrimage to the sea or a circuit from the burrows in the salt marsh and back? We never saw a crab heading inland, and our marking data are no help. At the peak of crab movement I found the burrows in the marsh occupied, so not all crabs were migrating. We estimated the trip from bay to Gulf might take a land crab two nights, but without recapture data we could not verify this. Certainly, they are capable of the distance; land crabs in Florida have been recorded making an eight-mile journey to the sea.

Midway through August we discovered large holes in the back sides of the dunes. I dug up several of these and invariably found, three feet deep at groundwater level, a great land crab. The holes in the dunes definitely had not been there before the migration, and over the next months, they disappeared. So we suspect a one-way journey. Crabs reaching the beach dug into that unnatural, hostile environment and eventually died there. Perhaps our newly established population has not synchronized its life cycle with the environment of Matagorda Island.

Migrant crabs, 161 males and 166 females, were all adult. At first, males outnumbered females three to one. On the first two nights we found 71 crabs, only one female. As the survey continued, the two sexes evened out. Then, in the two weeks around the full moon on September 8, the proportion of females rose to exceed males by nearly three to one. During this time we found nearly half the females carrying eggs. Either all these berried females (so-called for the berrylike cluster of eggs carried beneath the abdomen) were on the surf line or we dug them from burrows in the dunes.

The female crabs must have been going to the sea to release their eggs. We found two females at water's edge with only a few eggs clinging to their swimmerets, as though they had just released the main egg mass. What were the males doing? Other observers, in other places, have found that mating occurs in the male's burrow in the marsh. Yet, mixed-sex swarms have been recorded on the move in Florida. Perhaps the males are simply caught up in the spirit of the move.

Studies in Florida document spawning from June through early December with peaks in September and October on the nights before and after a full moon. Our observations suggest that on Matagorda Island, the animals begin to get restless in August and spawn in September during the entire week before and after the full moon. Although no crabs were marked in the Florida study, the investigators suggested a reverse migration after spawning. We believe our crabs stayed on the beach, digging in and eventually dying there.

We have seen an occasional land crab on the beach during every month of the year. Most seemed to be wetting their gills at the waterline. Some were so cold they could hardly move. I think these were the stragglers from the year's migration, wandering around disoriented but still trying to make a go of it in the dunes—tropical animals outside their normal geographic range and out of synchrony with the Texas seasons. Creatures still wreathed in enigma.

We saw very few land crabs moving in September 1996 and found only one berried female on the night of the harvest moon. There was no noticeable migration at all from 1997 to 1999.

I had about decided that our island population had indeed been swept in on Hurricane Gilbert and that it was gradually dwindling. Then, early in 1998, while trekking the high marsh, I noticed some odd crab holes—too big for fiddlers but too small for adult land crabs. We made a dig—all the way down to blue clay again—and there uncovered a belligerent juvenile great land crab doing a grown-up universal stance in the bottom of the hole! It was just under an inch across the back and, just as the books described, it was pale purple brown with numerous tiny purple dots. Its discovery raised more questions. How and when did it get here? Did it emerge from Mesquite Bay a quarter mile away, or did it come in from the surf over a mile to the east? Is our insular population of great land crabs stable and reproducing? We look forward to keeping an eye on our enigmatic crustacean neighbors.

CHAPTER 7

PREDATION

Mouse tracks in dune sand
Perpetual or fleeting?
How long shall we wait?

SPECIFIC INSTANCES of predation are more interesting than any discourse on the topic, so I will let my diary get right to it.

SEPTEMBER '93: *A surprise in a pit trap this morning. Tried to retrieve a small wood cockroach only to find it "attached" to a mat of dusty debris. Actually it was in the clutches of a camouflaged critter that had no intention of letting go its meal. By the time I got back to the microscope, the dry shell of the roach had been discarded, and the rubbish-covered predator was huddled in a corner.*
    What a malevolent-looking little bushwhacker! I could see the resemblance to an ant lion (doodlebug), but this was larger—about half an inch long—squattier and more robust. Its fat abdomen was rimmed with thin fleshy protrusions, each with a fringe of plumose hairs. The hairs caught the dust and chaff that so effectively hid the outline of its body. The broad, flat head bulged at the sides with muscles to work the pair of ice-tong jaws, held

wide open, ready to snap up the next victim. According to the books, first a paralyzing venom and then digestive enzymes are pumped down a tube in each jaw. The liquefied contents of the victim are sucked up through the same channel. That is what happened to the cockroach.

So, what was this critter? The larva of an owl fly. I have seen the adults flitting on weak, gauzy wings around our porch light like fuzzy, fat-bodied damselflies. With large, owlish eyes and long, thin antennae ending in delicate knobs, they are spectral creatures of the night. The larva is a carnivore; the adult, as far as I can determine, does not live long enough to bother with eating.

SEPTEMBER '97: *This morning, in the knee-deep trough inside the first bar in the surf, a "feeding frenzy" was in high gear, water and air alive with movement. A noisy, mixed flock of terns and gulls was dropping repeatedly into the shallows, and it seemed that every plunge was successful. Everywhere there were birds with silvery fishes writhing in their bills, gulping, climbing, diving again. Brown pelicans lazily rode the waves and dip-netted. We could see a mile up and down the beach, a cloud of birds the entire way. The collective impact—the numbers of prey and of predators, the furious level of activity, the unrelenting attacks and unadulterated gluttony—was staggering.*

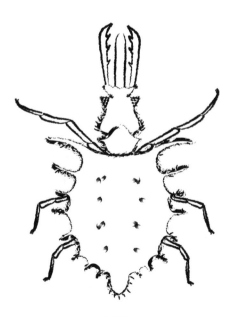

Owl fly larva

Not only were the beleaguered schools being bombed by birds from above, but they were being torpedoed by predatory fishes from below—speckled trout (Cynoscion nebulosus), *sand trout* (C. arenarius), *skipjacks* (Elops saurus), *and those piranhas of the Gulf, bluefish* (Pomatomus saltatrix), *were slashing through the multitude, while speckled crabs and blue crabs snatched up the disoriented, the maimed, and the dismembered parts.*

I waded out. The clear water was a turmoil of fluent brown streamers, rocking with the tempo of the waves, shot through with sudden flashes of silver—schools of small fishes, argentine sides glittering in the sun as they dodged for their lives. Halos of clear water developed around my legs as the swarms opened, steered around me, and zippered closed again, following some silent signal of spacing that kept all the teeming members aligned and simultaneous. Young striped anchovies (Anchoa hepsetus) *trying to grow up in a hostile world. Relying solely on the scant safety in huge numbers, no one of them with more than a vanishing chance of living out the day, the week, much less of maturing. If they comprehended their lot, they would give up. Mercifully, they are innocent, so they persevere. Somehow enough make it, and next autumn the hopeful horde will be back, ready to run the gauntlet that is their lot in life.*

I let the plankton net drift in the trough; the sample teemed with tintinnids, diatoms, dinoflagellates, crab zoeae, crab megalops, barnacle nauplii, and gastropod veligers. If an anchovy opened its gaping mouth and swam forward, its battery of fine gill rakers would be loaded with food in no time. Anchovy as predator, anchovy as prey. What a wonderful, flagrant world we live in!

JUNE '95: *Had the good fortune to see a large speckled king snake that had not noticed me. With its neck arched so the black tongue could flicker across the oyster shell as its head cast rhythmically from side to side, it was moving forward with the fore part of its body raised slightly off the ground. The serpent seemed totally fixed on the chemical cues transmitted from the whisker-fine tips of its tongue to the pair of sensory pores in the roof of its mouth. The books say the creature can tell the difference between the signals from left and right tips of the forked tongue, allowing it to follow a chemical trail. The casting movements kept it astride the scent.*

This king snake was obviously following fresh spoor. Then, before I was really prepared for a culmination, the serpent thrust forward slightly and engulfed a baby bird that had been crouching invisible and motionless among the shells. It was over in an instant. A brief kink in the neck sent the little

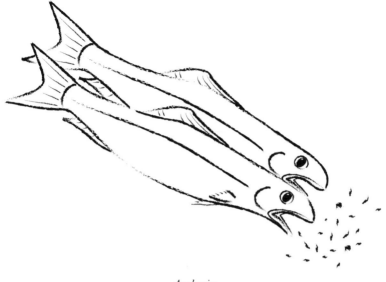

Anchovies

bolus back into the snake's belly where it did not even make a bulge. The snake gaped once to readjust its loose jaw sockets, and the tongue began to flutter again as the reptile slid off the shell into the saltwort.

When the snake was gone, I noticed movement down the levee. A Wilson's plover in distraction display—tail fanned, one wing dragging, twittering plaintively. Maybe she had more chicks in the vicinity, and her performance was for my benefit, but I think it was a forlorn attempt to divert the snake. Her scrape must have been nearby, the scant depression where she and her mate had huddled for three weeks over a small clutch of speckled eggs, beating the odds against the elements and passing predators. Judging from the size of the chick, today must have been its big day. It had wandered only a few feet along life's path before the king snake caught its fleeting odor. There was no defense. Generations of natural selection for near-perfect fuzzy camouflage coupled with the tendency to crouch unmoving when threatened, the while circled by Mom engaged in her frantic dance to the tune of piteous trills—all to no avail against a predator homing solely through its tongue.

Chance is always the great leveler, frustrating theories, confounding sensibilities, hornswoggling logic, holding the future hostage, ensuring that even the "fit" are not home free. Good luck for the king snake; bad luck for the plover chick. Luck of some sort that brought me to that place at that precise moment. A genuine event now irrecoverably past but some part of it caught and converted into a personal experience subject to tolerable recall; painful to witness, titillating to ponder. This is how the island and I converse.

JULY '94: *Saw a great blue heron skewer a striped mullet in the marsh. When the fish switched, the bird had trouble hanging on. It managed a labored flight to the dike, the heavy fish fighting all the while. The heron set its catch on the ground but caught sight of me and took off, leaving the fish flopping. I went over to inspect the mullet. It had a deep puncture wound above one pectoral fin where the bird's lower mandible had pierced it. The upper mandible had been clenched over the fish's back. The fish was sixteen inches long and weighed 1.1 pounds. Could the great blue have manipulated and swallowed such a large fish? Knowing the bird, I have no doubt.*

JUNE '95: *A great blue heron with the tail of a large fish—a mullet I think— hanging from the corner of its mouth. It was not trying to swallow; just standing there looking a bit uncomfortable. Most of the fish was jammed deep in the bird's gullet. I suspect that after digesting the head end awhile, this arch glutton would get the rest of its meal down.*

JULY '96: *Driving down the main road we saw, on the distant edge of a drying pond, a great blue heron swallowing something. Got binocs on him before he was done, and agreed that what we saw disappearing down his maw was a pair of long, thin, reddish pink legs. An adult black-necked stilt! I wish we had seen the initial encounter.*

MARCH '98: *Walking way out in the tidal flats, I saw two coyotes ahead. I had the wind, and they were busy at something. Then I saw a large, brown, mud-stained feral hog off to one side. At first I thought the coyotes were paired up to assault the hog. They restlessly sat and paced about, then hesitantly advanced together on the hog. That great beast responded by raising his hackles and charging forward briefly. After a tail-tucking retreat, the coyotes were soon back at a prudent distance, the hog returned to his spot, and the sequence began again.*

    Finally, I could see that the hog was feeding on something; the coyotes apparently were trying to snatch scraps of his meal. The hog was not having any of that. At last I stood up and walked directly toward the trio. First the coyotes and then the boar spotted me. All three did a surprised double take and then hied off on separate tracks through the cordgrass. I inspected the item of contention. Two freshly killed piglets, or what was left of them, lying within a

few feet of each other! The hindquarters gone from one carcass, the other
missing the head and one foreleg; entrails and blood clots strewn all around.

Did the coyotes make the kills and the boar charge out to run them off in
paternal defense? Hardly. The coyotes were passersby. Sows have been known
to devour their young in hard times, but these piglets were in good shape, and
I knew the hog on the scene was a boar (I could see his cods through the
binocs). What then?

There is a version of the theory of natural selection called kinship selec-
tion, itself an aspect of the notion of the selfish gene, that suggests often nasty
ways that social animals use to ensure that their genes and not someone else's
are passed along. One version has males (lions and bears are well-documented
examples) savagely killing offspring of their own species to eliminate the
genes of competitive males and to bring the idled female into heat. The male
then mounts her, ensuring that his offspring will have undivided parental care
and more resources to themselves.

I suspect the boar came across an unfamiliar-smelling sow in his territory
and she had a litter that he sensed he did not sire. He managed to cut down
these two piglets before the sow and the rest of her brood scattered. Eating the
young may have been an opportunistic afterthought or savage insurance of
accomplishment.

I moved on with ample food for thought. The boar was gone, having done
what his genes told him to do. When he settled down, he would probably pick
up the sow's spoor and complete his mission. Very likely the two coyotes
would circle round, check the wind, and come back to clean up what was left
before the vultures arrived. Strange how things fall out.

*J*ULY '95: *Predation goes on as doggedly at the nether end of the scale as*
anywhere above. The first sea nettles (Chrysaora quinquecirrha) *are*
appearing in the bay, gliding beneath the boardwalk, pulsing as reliably as
heartbeats, opalescent bells trailing marginal veils of thin tentacles and four
rippling ribbonlike oral streamers. Two layers of skin enclosing a formless
pulp, lacking vitals but possessed of all of life's basic urges and primal
delights. Beautiful, silent, ghostly; drifting along in a serene coelenterate daze
unfazed by the ages; their pumping ballet driven by a dim nerve net, guided
by gravity, light, obscure scents, and venerable instincts. The tentacles are
armed with microscopic harpoons, coiled and ready to evert explosively, to
pierce and stun any soft-bodied creature that brushes into them.

Some afternoons the current sweeps in squadrons of comb jellies (Mnemiopsis mccradyi). *Whether by luck or some dim sagacity, the sea nettles are*

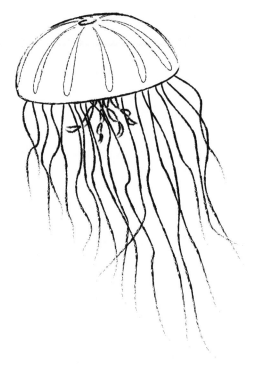

Sea nettle

waiting where the current slacks. They intercept tumbling comb jellies until their tentacles are heavy with weakly writhing transparent clots. It is hardly a slaughter, for there are no calculated leaps, no screams of distress and pain, no blood, no scattered entrails—merely jelly exchanging one shape for another. This is an archetypal rivalry, waged without limbs, teeth, eyes, or nerve cords. The soundless drama harks back through the ages to a time when all life was wet and soft, yet carried a gnawing appetite and the impulse to appease it. From such beginnings—endlessly played out, diversified, practiced, foiled, and counterfoiled by both predator and prey—come the multifarious cat-and-mouse matches that help knit the fabric of this island.

JUNE '97: *This afternoon I came upon a hog wallow knee deep in water, the scum-covered surface broken by bubblelike eruptions so that the puddle seemed to be simmering in the heat. At the instant each vesicle burst I got a glimpse of a glistening white body. Using my cap for a net, I determined that the stifling pool was full of large southern meadow frog tadpoles surfacing for gulps of air.*

I saw many tadpoles against the bank, some weakly moving and others belly up. At first I thought they were victims of the rank condition of the muck hole, until I discovered that each was in the clutches of an insect nearly as large as itself. It was easy to fish out specimens with my cap, for the tenacious predators were reluctant to let go their prey.

Predaceous diving beetles (Cybister fimbriolatus), *living up to their name, were ripping into the soft bellies of the tadpoles, feasting on their spilled vitals. The insect's inch-and-a-quarter-long body is oval, low-domed, hard, smooth, and so slick it is greasy feeling. It is as streamlined as a surfboard; even the eyes are inset to fit the contour. With creamy margined, bronze green wing covers, oarlike hind legs fringed with chestnut-colored hairs, and a pair of formidable, meat-tong mandibles, what a well-fashioned submarine predator the diving beetle is. Yet, despite its form and swimming ability, this creature lacks the finishing touch of gills. It compensates by popping to the surface and poking its rear end up so it can take on a load of air beneath its wing covers. When I watched for them, I could see dimples among the tadpole bursts, for the pool was at least as jammed with beetles as with pollywogs.*

So here in this fetid cauldron an ancient game is played out: prey at a disadvantage; a predator glutting on the windfall. But there is a quirk. Usually, the backboned creature does the glutting, and the spineless creature does the dying. Here the tables are turned: insect brings down amphibian. Just as there is no moral here, so there is no justice, no atonement for the ages of predation by frogs on bugs. Just life striving to live and death coming as it inevitably must.

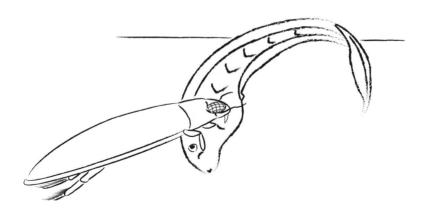

Diving beetle with tadpole

JULY '97: *Flushed an adult crested caracara from the road. The bird banked and settled down twenty yards further along, reluctant to leave the site. Where the bird had been, an ornate box turtle lay on its back. It was so freshly killed that its legs were still reflexing. The head had been snipped off at the neck and the lower jaw disjointed from the head, and both were lying near the shell, still seeping blood.*

Caracaras are stealthy. I surmise that the bird, seeing the turtle crossing the road, had come in low from the rear, landed behind its prey, and with a quick stride or two, reached over the shell and snipped through the spinal cord before the turtle could retract. Perhaps the jaw was wrenched loose during final decapitation. This probably explains the empty box turtle shells that I see occasionally along the roads. When I drove on, the caracara lifted and settled back on the road near the carcass.

AUGUST '97: *The water in tidal pools turns bad in the summer heat, and the fauna begins to die. Birds ravage it daily, raccoons and feral hogs pillage by night, and the survivors finally turn upon each other. Eventually, nothing is left but a jostling mass of large blue crabs—the crustiest and meanest of the lot—milling about in the muddy swill, constantly menacing each other, alert to the slightest show of weakness, and watchful for any edible scrap.*

Trapped in a fetid hole with the searing ooze turning to brick around them, blue crabs and sheepshead killifish are the last creatures to succumb, and before they expire the crab will likely eat the fish. I once came upon such a sun-baked inferno reeking with the fester of death. I had hardly paused at its edge before several blobs of mud heaved out and purposefully labored into the scant ephemeral protection cast by my shadow: blue crabs, foaming at the mouth in a last-ditch attempt to cool down but still baleful eyed and ready to raise their pincers when I moved. True grit.

I watched one crab that spotted a horsefly on the mud. The crustacean patiently stalked the fly and finally made a quick but unsuccessful grab for it. That slight commotion attracted a dozen other crabs eager to share in the potential catch. In the melee one individual grabbed another by the leg, snapped it off, and made away with it. Another crab managed to snatch a wasp that had unwisely settled on the surface film to take a sip. The crab sank with its prize, dogged by nearby crabs intent on wresting it away.

One afternoon I saw turmoil in a tidal pool. A blue crab had just grabbed a young willet that had naively wandered into the shallows. Even as I watched, the fresh carcass began to disintegrate before the ravenous onslaught of every crab in the pool. Within half an hour the willet was reduced to a few slivers of bone still being sucked and fought over; even the pulp-filled quills and vanes of its feathers had been gnawed away. A sobering, piranha-like spectacle.

NOVEMBER '94: *Joe came over to show me seven large "bots" that he had taken from the stomach of a big redfish. The things did look like huge versions of the barrel-shaped maggots that I recall extracting from blisters in the hide of cattle. But those maggots are the larvae of bot flies that lay their eggs on body hairs of grazing animals. The eggs, licked from the coat, hatch inside the host, feed on internal tissue (some do infest the stomach lining), and eventually escape the body, drop to the soil, pupate, and emerge as an adult fly. Hardly the sort of life cycle to involve a saltwater fish!*

On closer examination I found, instead of the grappling-hook mouthparts of an internal parasite, a set of ragged tentacles sprouting from one end. No eyes, no appendages, not even a head. The nearly featureless, cigar-shaped body, four inches long by one inch across was sheathed in a tough brown tunic studded with sticky papillae. These were not maggots but sea cucumbers (Sclerodactyla briareus), *sluggish denizens of the offshore shallows. They lie buried in the sand, bent so both ends are just exposed. At one extremity the sticky tentacles grope for detritus to stuff into the mouth, while at the other the anus sucks in water to aerate internal gills. With a dim but enduring lifestyle, sea cucumbers are related to starfish and urchins. I sometimes find the scarified bodies of sea cucumbers rolling in the swash after storms.*

Redfish are active predators that feed largely on fish (menhaden, anchovies, silversides, mullet), brown and white shrimp, and blue crabs. A study of over a thousand redfish stomachs revealed that the fish had eaten everything from squid to sea horses, but not a single sea cucumber. But these fish are opportunistic foragers and are known to grub soft bottoms. Here was evidence that redfish eat brown sea cucumbers, at least occasionally, in quantity.

Told Joe what he had, or I tried to. He listened, but apparently I did not get through to him. Late this afternoon he came back by all smiles. "You know them bots?" he said. "They don't stay on the hook too good, but while they last they make damn good bait. I got two butterfly drums and a keeper red off them seven bots." An interesting second harvest. I did not bother trying to correct his nomenclature. It made a better fish story his way.

FEBRUARY '97: *There are two predators that I know of on this island that are so good at their raptorial trade that they seem to take prey at will with minimal effort. Today I saw one of each of these fast and deadly superhunters working from the same snag on the beach.*

An arctic peregrine falcon was finishing up a kill when I spotted her with my glasses. Even as I watched, she humped forward slightly and darted fast and low on shallow wing beats toward a flock of sanderlings working the swash near where I was standing. Although they seemed preoccupied searching for coquina clams, the little shorebirds quickly perceived the feathered missile launched at them. They flushed but had hardly zigzagged out over the first breakers before the falcon was among them. She hurtled in from the side and slightly above, adroitly snatched a sanderling with her talons and rose in a graceful arc. Within moments she was back on the snag tugging feathers from her catch, and the flock of sanderlings, minus one, was busily pecking in the sand further down the beach.

It had all gone so flawlessly and passed so quickly that it was as though nothing had happened at all. When the peregrine had finished and disappeared over the dunes, I approached the snag. Beneath her perch I found four fresh sanderling carcasses in a loose pile, each with only the breast meat plucked out. Peregrines are so efficient and so confident that they can afford to dine on the choice cuts and drop the rest—a rare luxury in nature.

While pondering the deadly proficiency of peregrine falcons and the blissful innocence of sanderlings, I became aware of the same scheme being played within the shadow of the snag, with a different cast of characters and on a smaller but no less lethal scale. A robber fly (Asilidae) was perched on a fragment of bark at knee level. Like the falcon, it was trim, streamlined, keen eyed, a perfect killing machine. A fragment of a Portuguese man-of-war lay bleaching on the sand nearby, attended by a crowd of anthomyiid flies busily sopping from the festering mass of tentacles. Every thirty seconds, as if on cue, the robber fly disappeared, the swarm of flies exploded into the air, the robber-fly reappeared on its perch, and the anthomyiid flies settled back on their jellyfish. I watched through several cycles from close vantage but never caught any more detail. The action was literally faster than my eye could follow; it made the falcon/sanderling version seem like slow motion. But the result was the same.

Each time the robber fly regained its platform, it had a fly clutched in its mouth. It sucked at its prey for perhaps ten seconds. Then it dropped the carcass, polished its mouth bristles with its forelegs, peered about with awesome eyes, and vanished on another foray. The breeze had scattered the remains, but I retrieved the shriveled exoskeletons of seven anthomyiids from beneath the robber fly's perch. Under the microscope I could see that only the

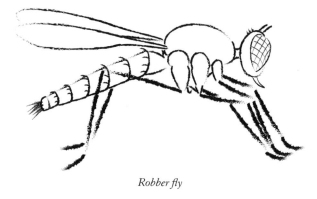

Robber fly

abdomens had been tapped. Like the falcon, the robber fly could afford to be an epicure.

July '97: *I was sitting on the porch this morning when I heard the querulous low whistle that inevitably warns of an impending explosion. Hardly had time to set my nerves before the detonation—a whir of stubby wings and a scatter of feathered shrapnel as a covey of baby bobwhite quail burst from the shade beneath the edge of the house and settled in puffs of dust in the yard. Mom had given the warning, and like mouse-sized clockwork toys, they zipped erratically, separating and coalescing as they made their way toward the tall grass at the edge of the yard. Cute little upright soldiers, each with its topknot raised. Then I saw what set off this burst—a large western coachwhip* (Masticophis flagellum) *slid into view from beneath the porch.*

What a magnificent serpent! Well-named, a pale tan, three-and-a-half-foot-long braid, right down to his finely tapered tail. Always nervous and alert, this one was especially keyed up. He flowed rapidly, without the slightest indication of muscular movement, into the middle of the yard while maintaining an ominous, erect cobra stance with the front eight inches of his body. There he paused for an instant in all his glory, small head swiveling atop its periscope vantage, menacing yellow eyes scanning the yard for movement, black tongue quivering, every muscle fiber taut, a hair-trigger trap on the verge of springing. But Mom had gotten her brood into the tangle of long grass and had given the soft signal to huddle and freeze. Abruptly, the coachwhip streaked into the grass and for about fifteen seconds I tracked the upright head and neck cleaving through the stems. But it failed to flush the quail and finally dropped from view.

JUNE '99: *Heard a commotion beside the old pirogue in the yard and looked up just in time to see a large coachwhip emerge from beneath the vessel with a young cotton rat in its jaws. The snake slid rapidly across the yard with the front eight inches of its body held upright, the little rat squirming and squealing in its mouth. But the amazing thing was that an adult cotton rat— surely Mom—was bouncing along behind nipping at the tip of the snake's tail! The coachwhip crossed the yard and went into the deep grass beyond, where I could follow its course by the protruding head-with-rat and by the weaving grass blades. Mom dogged the snake's tail right into the tangle. I quickly lost all movement. Perhaps twenty seconds later, Mom reappeared, humped to the pirogue, and disappeared underneath. She surfaced almost immediately with another baby clutched by the scruff of its neck. She scrambled up the side of the pirogue and carefully deposited the little one within the folds of a shrimp net that was draped nearby. Then she went back beneath the boat, and that was the last I saw of her.*

AUGUST '97: *Saw two does and a quarter-grown fawn. The adults were looking out across the grassland, ears flared and tails up, occasionally stabbing the ground with a front hoof—sure sign they had spotted trouble. Suddenly, both took off at a dead run. About seventy yards away they ran nearly into an adult coyote standing in the cordgrass. The coyote easily dodged aside, ran off a bit, and sat down. The does stopped, eyed the coyote balefully a moment, then put their ears down, stretched out their necks, and ran at him again. Again he gave ground. This was all repeated twice more. The coyote finally appeared to tire of the harassment; it turned and loped out of sight over a secondary dune. The does settled down, rejoined the fawn, and proceeded out of sight into a swale. This time at least, the coyote would not dine on tender venison.*

I have never seen a deer give birth, but I have noticed does that looked like they were on the verge. Aside from being so pregnant they seemed about to pop, they were off by themselves, walking with heavy stride and with a furtive air. On several of these occasions I have noticed two or three coyotes intently watching the doe from a nearby vantage. If my suspicions were aroused, how much more keenly must the perspicacious coyotes have gotten the same message? I think they recognize a doe about to calve, discreetly follow, and either waylay the doe while she is down and snatch the afterbirth or take the helpless fawn as soon as it beds and the mother wanders off to forage. So, an innocent, wet, wobbly-legged, wide-eyed fawn will be pulled down, and a cute, roly-poly, blue-eyed fuzz ball of a pup will gorge on *regurgitated venison. I will know that the deer herd and the coyote pack on Matagorda Island are doing well by each other.*

OCTOBER '94: *A northern harrier rose out of a clump of smooth cordgrass with something dark dangling from her talons. When the hawk saw me, she banked abruptly and was startled enough to drop her prey. A clapper rail, still warm. What a beautiful bird: a rich chestnut breast, smoke-barred flanks, soft gray cheeks, a stumpy tail, thin legs, big feet, and slender, gently down-curved bill. Now relaxed at last from its lifelong vigil. Many times near sunset I have seen these marsh sprites materialize on the edge of their cord-grass retreats, constantly alert, ever fearful of the outer world, always ready to dart back into the security of the maze of stems. Eventually, with stub tail pumping nervously, they venture out, one hesitant step at a time, to work the waterline and oyster fringe to supplement their staple diet of mud fiddlers, saltmarsh snails, and marsh insects. In the springtime I sometimes see a nervous hen with a scatter of black fuzzy chicks tripping in her wake. Mostly it is their staccato of dry kek-keks that confirms that the bowels of the salt marsh are haunted by clappers.*

OCTOBER '95: *A dozen laughing gulls flapping erratically and clucking continually as they rise several feet off the water, then plunge to peck at the surface and rise again, swallowing something. More gulls arriving as I watch. With binoculars I see ripples and an occasional splash in the water. Then a dark tail emerges, switches several times, and submerges. Nearby, a dorsal fin breaks the surface, along with a large bronze-red back. More tails, several protruding far enough to show a dark eyespot at the base, churning, staining the water with billows of fine brown silt. From the turbulence, a brief shower of bright sparkles erupts into the air, then falls back; and the gulls are ecstatic.*

What's going on? A school of big redfish (red drum; Scianops ocellata), a cluster of fifteen or so, is feeding in the shallows. They are grubbing up pods of brown shrimp and snagging as many of them as they can. Because the fish work head down and tail up, fishermen speak of this as "tailing." The sparkles are reflections off the bodies of the shrimp, which flick strongly backward out of harm's way, frequently into the air. In their effort to avoid the redfish, the shrimp expose themselves to the gulls.

SEPTEMBER '94: *A double-crested cormorant lolling on the bank at Long Pond, digesting a crop full of mullet. As I approached, it reluctantly waddled to the water and plunge-dived out of sight. I watched for the bird's head and neck to reappear unobtrusively somewhere along the far side. Instead, a dark wing suddenly extended into the air near the middle of the pond. That sank quickly and was replaced by a foot and leg awkwardly protruding from a boil of radiating ripples. What was the matter with the cormorant? Moments later the jaws of a large alligator hove into view, jerking spasmodically in an effort to juggle the limp body of the cormorant into swallowing position. The gator went under before it fully engulfed its prey. I watched awhile, but except for a train of muddy bubbles, the surface of the pond remained calm. The rest I had to imagine. Perhaps, blinded by the murkiness of the water, the swimming bird inadvertently passed within snapping distance of the submerged alligator, maybe even brushed against it. A fatal mistake. I wonder how often it happens.*

AUGUST '97: *After weeks of broiling August sun and hot winds, Hanger Pond was reduced to a tepid, shin-deep puddle surrounded by a broad band of evil-smelling ooze. The birds were having a field day: snowy, reddish, and great egrets; white ibises and roseate spoonbills; great blue and tricolored herons; a flock of wood storks; a constant barrage of Forster's terns; even a flight of black skimmers cutting the thick surface; laughing gulls, willets, killdeers, Wilson's plovers, black-necked stilts, and a few greater yellowlegs around the edge. All busy taking advantage—each in its own way—of the congestion of floundering, slime-covered, oxygen-deprived fishes, insects, and crustaceans that struggled hopelessly in the thickening muck.*

There was hardly enough water to cover the backs of the largest striped mullet, and their torment was compounded by the recurrent assaults of a large alligator that sprawled across their sanctuary. The gator did not chase the mullet; he just lay quietly until a fish tried to dash past. Then, in an explosion of mud and water and a clamor of rising birds, the alligator made a quick, wicked sidewise jerk of his head as he snapped at the nearest fish. While I watched, the gator got three large mullet in a row, missed twice, then got two more. Eventually, I was sure, he would get them all.

Each time he got a fish the great reptile threw back his head, convulsed several times to get its catch end on, and engulfed the fish, along with a mound of blood-splattered mud, in one tremendous gulp. He then fell heavily back into position, ready to go at it again. Awesome, savage, primeval, merciless, sinless, lurid, patently inhumane, poignantly thrilling. Shamelessly, I soaked it all up until my every fiber tingled.

The alligator was not done with his exhibition of carnage. The beast apparently felt something moving in the ooze beneath him, for he began to back up and grub with his snout. He made several lurching grabs and finally raised his jaws in triumph. As the water and muck drained away, I could see his mouth was propped open by a formless mass. Finally, a flailing leg and then a head emerged from the glob. The gator had shoveled up a large red-eared slider. Then, instead of the usual bolting maneuver, the alligator unaccountably lapsed into an antediluvian trance. While the turtle struggled weakly, its captor just lay there with his massive jaws wedged open, clutching but not killing, as though savoring the moment.

After fully ten minutes of stupor, the alligator stiffened, and all four of the turtle's legs stood out rigid and unmoving. Ever so slowly those formidable jaws were closing! A modern rendition of a conflict unchanged since its rivals first met in the swamps of the Triassic 200 million years ago. Determined assault pitted against stolid defense; prestressed armament strained to the limit; pea brains steeped in time-tested instinct. On the one side were the ponderous jaws, heavy palate, and powerful temporal muscles; on the other there were thick, flattened ribs and chunky vertebrae solidly fused into an impregnable armored vault. Everything locked in one-track reptilian obstinacy.

As the pounds per square inch steadily increased, the turtle, feeling the press of its impending fate, extended its neck in an upward curve with mouth wide open, as though in a final gasp for life. What did the slider sense? Certainly that something was terribly wrong and getting progressively worse. Pain, although sealed internally by the inability to scream, nonetheless acute. Perhaps it experienced a dim wave of stark chelonian terror. Near the end it ceased to struggle and merely looked out at its fading world with an air of relaxed resignation.

And what of the alligator? Through the roof of his mouth and the tension of his jaw muscles, the beast was surely aware of the mounting compression, of every slight change in resistance and shape as the slider's bones began to yield to the strain. Grant him crocodilian anticipation, a sense of impending triumph, all-consuming stomach juices already busy dissolving mullet now free flowing at the prospect of turtle.

The tension ended abruptly with a crunch as the turtle's shell collapsed and the great jaws closed. There was never any doubt about the outcome: the slider had been a crusty adult, but the gator was a big one. He would not be denied.

With his squashed prize still in his mouth, the alligator lay motionless in the mud. I watched, equally immobile, sweat streaming down my backbone, shoulders aching from the weight of raised binoculars. Long minutes passed. What was he waiting for? He seemed to have lapsed again into a reptilian daze, lost in a timeless, inscrutable realm beyond the comprehension and toleration of warm-blooded creatures. At last I yielded. Never try to outwait an alligator! I left him sprawled there and returned, pleasantly exhausted, to the security of my cognizant, quick-paced world.

JUNE '96: *Blew a circuit in the trailer tonight, and while fumbling in the breaker box by flashlight, I surprised one of the most unique predators on Matagorda Island in the midst of her meal. A spider, a scant half-inch long, with high-domed cephalothorax and spindly legs, her straw-colored body freckled with dusky smudges. She crouched amid the switches, startled by my light. Not much to look at, but it is not looks that make her interesting but how she brings down her prey.*

This spider had been feeding on a cockroach nymph, and I could see the telltale marks of its capture—zigzagged sticky fibers tacking the roach to the wall of the breaker box. This drama was done, but I have seen the spider's act. She waits till a silverfish-sized creature comes near, then creeps ever so slowly toward her prey with all the stealth and concentration of a cat watching a mouse. At three-quarters of an inch she is within range, but it takes good light and a quick eye to catch the action.

Once I put one of these spiders into a glass vial with a fruit fly and watched through the microscope. Even then, all I saw was a jerk of the spider's mouthparts and the sudden appearance of a lacework of shiny, mucilaginous strands that pinned the struggling fruit fly against the side of the vial. The spider's pressurized secretion from a pair of large glands in her bulging cephalothorax had jetted out through a hole in the tip of each of her two fangs.

*She lives up to her name, spitting spider (*Scytodes perfecta*). I presume that the spider oscillates her chelicerae rapidly during the expulsion to produce the crisscross pattern of strands. And there is more than stickum in that spray. It also contains a venom potent enough to subdue large prey and kill little things like the fruit fly outright. By the time the spider in my vial hesitantly approached her fly, it had quit moving, and she proceeded to suck its juices.*

SEPTEMBER '93: *A large flock of dunlin busy in a mere skim of sun-scorched water clotted with bubbling mats of blue-green algae. An unappetizing-looking mess! Working with shovel and sieve, I could not find a thing; no creature visible in the water or in the underlying crumbly clay. Finally, I discovered where the banquet was laid. In a thin stratum on the underside of*

Spitting spider

*the algal mats, I found a seethe of bloodworms (midge larvae; Chiron-
omidae). After half an hour's effort with sieve and forceps, I accumulated a
fingertip-sized pellet of red protoplasm, enough to fuel a dunlin for a few
hours, I suppose.*

JANUARY '94: *This morning on Shorebird Marsh lesser yellowlegs and western
sandpipers were busily stabbing in the shallows. Charting shorebird menus is
an exercise in the taxonomy of obscure invertebrates. Shallow digs revealed a
large population of Culver's sandworms, occasional bright orange orbiniid
worms* (Haploscoplos foliosus), *stretched and snapping strands of red
threadworms, and a squirming mass of teeny red annelid squiggles. All of
these within easy reach of a sandpiper's bill. I tried dragging a hand net
through the water while barely stirring the organic fluff off the bottom. Then
swished the net into a jar of water. Holding the jar up to the sun, I could see
sparkles of movement generated by a maze of barely visible tinies—just the
sorts of things that might catch the quick eye of a yellowlegs.*

*Back at the microscope I entered the secret world of pericaridan entomost-
racans—minute crustaceans that carry their young in a brood pouch tucked
between the bases of their numerous frilled legs. Mysids, looking for all the
world like miniaturized shrimp, zoomed through my microscope field.
Occasionally when one paused, I caught a glimpse of cream-colored babies
squirming in her blisterlike marsupium. So, a quick peck by a yellowlegs
might snare two generations of mysids at once.*

Less agile but no less active, more vaguely shrimplike tanaids (Hargeria
rapax) *motored about until their white, waxy bodies got stuck on the
underside of the surface film. When they were so immobilized, I could
distinguish the males by their disproportionately long pincers, which, at 60x,
gave them a menacing appearance. Disinterred from their tubes in the upper*

millimeters of silt, Hargeria seemed hopelessly confused in my brightly lit glass depression slide.

Here and there I found another inhabitant of the uppermost sediment, this one crouching in a daze. Cumaceans (Oxyurostylis smithi)*, with their plump bodies, distinctive "headless" front ends, and skinny upturned abdomens, are bizarre enough to be denizens from the nether world of the ancient Burgess shale. The tanaids and cumaceans were hardly three millimeters long, the mysids about twice that. This diminutive menagerie must feed on things yet smaller—diatoms, bacteria, protozoa, and suspended organic particles.*

This whole segment of the island food chain seems more fanciful than real—grotesque entomostracans sustained on nothing palpable and birds pecking avidly in seemingly sterile brine.

FEBRUARY '94: *Used the boathouse as an impromptu observation blind this afternoon, with a good scope trained on a long-billed curlew nearby working the tidal flat at low tide. The bird was plodding along as though half asleep, idly touching the sensitive tip of its ridiculously long bill into the puddle inside the mouth of each ghost shrimp burrow it came across. Suddenly, it seemed to detect some sign, through its bill I think, for it stiffened and paused. The curlew then probed rapidly into the burrow a dozen times, reaching half-a-bill deep and swiveling its head through a long arc, first clockwise and then counterclockwise as it bobbled. Then the bird stood stock-still for about three minutes—a significant quiescent interval for a foraging bird—the while cocking its head as it watched the burrow intently. All of a sudden, the curlew lunged forward, noodled to the hilt, and came up with a fine large ghost shrimp for its effort. How to get a struggling shrimp from the tip of an extraordinarily long bill back to the gullet? Tongue power; neat as a conveyor belt.*

I think the curlew methodically probed ghost shrimp burrows until its keenly sensitive bill tip detected slight vibrations set up in the water column by the movements of a shrimp. With the knowledge that the burrow was occupied and that the occupant was active and not very deep, the bird deliberately occluded the mouth of the tunnel with sediment gouged from its walls. Then it waited with an anticipation borne of prior experience. Within a few minutes the curlew was rewarded when a fountain of muddy water erupted from the hole as the ghost shrimp rose to clear its home of sediment. A quick stab with the 7.5-inch tweezer, and the prize was won. I don't know if all long-billed curlews know the ruse, but this one certainly did. And whether or not the curlew passes it on to others, it has inadvertently passed it on to me.

MARCH '94: *Watched a willet that had caught a blue crab too big to swallow whole. He took his prize to the water's edge, his sturdy bill giving him enough distance to ignore the waving pincers. The willet held the crab up by several walking legs and gave it a violent shake. The legs snapped off, and the willet gobbled these up while keeping an eye on the crab, which lay struggling on its back. Twice more the willet ate more crab legs, and the crab was reduced to a body armed with two weakly flailing pincers. The bird then grabbed the base of the larger pincer, popped the appendage loose, and cast it aside. At last the willet picked up the disabled body, mouthed it until the lateral spines were aligned with its bill and downed the whole in two eye-popping gulps. The entire scenario had taken one minute ten seconds. The willet left only tracks, scuffle marks, and one pincer on the mud. A Karankawa could hardly have been more thrifty.*

APRIL '96: *Cruising the beach at sunup during a late norther. The sanderlings are racing around with feathers puffed, their backs ruffling when they turn downwind, a discomfort that causes them to do a quick pivot. They seem to be working the strand rather than the swash. I got down on hands and knees to see what they were after. Anthomyiid flies, common scavengers of the wrack. They are usually too quick for the birds, but the sanderlings have discovered a weakness. The cold morning is keeping the flies grounded. When I prod them with my finger, they do little more than scuttle aside. Now, before the sun warms the flies, the sanderlings are having at them.*

FEBRUARY '97: *Sanderlings working the strand after a strong norther and a high tide. The debris is loaded with tiny terrestrial critters blown to sea and their bodies returned by the waves. A regular smorgasbord to cram ravening little avian guts: three kinds of rove beetles, five kinds of "other beetles," four kinds of flies, two kinds of hemipteran bugs, a few crab spiders, and a passel of wolf spiders. This morning the shorebirds are subsisting on grass-land fare.*

OCTOBER '97: *At the mouth of Cedar Bayou on a low tide. Scads of birds feeding. Brown pelicans, royal terns, Caspian terns, and Sandwich terns dive-bombing just offshore. Black skimmers cleaving along the edge of the channel. Bonaparte's gulls "water walking" across the current. Laughing gulls and ring-billed gulls working the waterline among the sanderlings and willets. Peeps all over the sand bar: snowy and piping plovers; western, semipalmated, and least sandpipers.*

The little birds were pecking so furiously that I could not resist shooing them aside to see what they were after. Even down on knees and elbows I could not see a thing moving among the sand grains and shell frit. Finally, the half-millimeter sieve revealed what the birds had detected—oodles of crab megalops scarcely a millimeter across; a scurry of sand-digger amphipods; a multitude of little dark squiggles I later identified as juvenile sand parchment tube worms; a few tiny mole crabs and lots of mustard seed–sized coquina clams. Everything in bountiful quantity, but nothing big enough to jostle the sand grains, at least not to my eye. But the peeps were having no problem gleaning a good harvest.

When I glanced up from my concentration on minutiae, I found the birds had returned and were busily pecking all around me, leaving me in a bird-free zone ten feet across. I rose and backed off the bar; peeps immediately scurried in from all sides to reclaim the gap.

OCTOBER '97: *White ibis are as opportunistic as any other bird on the island. Today I saw flocks exploiting three separate resources. This morning, on a low tide, a group of ibis was striding the tidal flat plucking mud fiddlers from the entrances to their burrows. Later, with the tide on the rise, another batch was wading among emergent cordgrass, swinging their partly opened bills from side to side, snapping and gobbling occasionally when they made a catch. I went out to see what they were getting: loads of young sheepshead killifish and juvenile brown shrimp and an occasional saltmarsh snail* (Melampus bidentattus).

This afternoon several hundred white ibis probing and pecking amid the fresh greenery in a recently burned stretch of grassland. I trudged out until I was surrounded by the birds' tracks in the soft ground and could not see a thing that they might have been feeding on! Almost decided they had been cropping greens when I discovered a bolus of food that an excited bird had regurgitated when I scared them off. It was loaded with caterpillars—fall armyworms (Laphygma frugiperda). *A few swipes of the insect net brought in the caterpillars, although I still could not spot them by eye. Also got meadow katydids* (Orchilium *and* Conocephalus) *that had escaped my notice. I am sure the ibis did not overlook them.*

MAY '98: *No rain at all this month. The freshwater ponds about gone. Birds flocking to tinies concentrated in the drying pools. I came across such a puddle no more than four inches deep bustling with lesser yellowlegs; Wilson's phalaropes; and semipalmated, pectoral, spotted, and least sand-*

pipers. The sandpipers were mostly along the bank, sniping at a thick mass of shore flies. The phalaropes were doing their thing—whirling energetically and pecking rapidly at what their spinning movements had stirred to the surface. The yellowlegs were taking advantage of the phalaropes' efforts.

I felt guilty interrupting the banquet, but I wanted to see what the phalaropes were stirring up. A couple of swipes with the hand net brought in a load of water boatmen (Trichocorixa); nothing else.

This puddle cannot last another week without a rain but is productive to the end. A bottom film of blue-green algae succors a population of water boatmen, while the algal slick exposed on the bank by the receding water nourishes a buzzing swarm of shore flies (Ephydridae). Not much to look at, but this tepid pool and others like it are important stopover sites along the Central Flyway. To keep on their grinding schedule, by tomorrow or the next day most of these birds need to be eight hundred miles north of here, feeding on bloodworms in the marshes of the Cheyenne Bottoms in Kansas. Calories from Matagorda insects will see them on their way.

MAY '96: *Out on an oyster-shell ridge late this afternoon with a group of Girl Scout leaders. The marsh was beautiful, every detail clear in the slanting sunlight. We stopped to focus our binoculars on a willet working the edge of the marsh hardly twenty feet away. The bird's eye, every feather, its reflection, and the ripples around its legs all stood out boldly. As we watched, there was a sudden splash, and the next instant the willet lay spread-eagled on its breast on the surface of the water, its legs extended, and its open wings quivering. I thought for a moment that a redfish might have made a lunge for the bird. But one of the women gasped, "My God, there's a snake!" I saw it then.*

A large diamondback rattlesnake had been coiled among the maritime saltwort near the waterline, perhaps for several days, immobile save for its flicking black tongue, watching and waiting for the right moment. At last the willet came into range. The snake struck, hitting the bird in the head. Rattlers strike and release rodents, then use their tongues to follow the dying animals' trails. But they try to hang onto birds that might flutter too far away and be lost. This rattlesnake never released its death grip on the willet, even though its head dropped underwater after the impact. The snake remained immobile for about a minute and a half, while the willet quivered through its final spasms. Then the snake slid backward with the willet in tow. It paused when the bird got tangled in the vegetation; then with a heave, both disappeared from view.

CHAPTER 8

DEATH

While northers still gust
messengers of cheer arrive
Barn swallow twitters.

PREDATORS ARE NOT the only cause of death. There are few places in this barrier island ecosystem where I can see birth and death more poignantly commingled and so often concomitant than in the bird rookeries. From late May into June, they foment on the oyster-shell reefs in Mesquite Bay. On narrow strips of sunburned shell with less surface area than an average lawn and mere inches of clearance above water, absolute pandemonium reigns as herons and egrets, gulls and terns, skimmers, and spoonbills perform their annual rituals. They gather on these forbidding outposts to avoid the predators that roam the mainland shores.

The purpose of these crowded aggregations is procreation; the means are nothing short of demonic. Because of haste and lack of materials, nests are ragged, insecure, the few precious sticks pilfered and repilfered. Nests are lodged in prickly pears, crouched amid sunflower stalks; some are mere basins scooped in the shell; few are shaded from the beating Texas sun by more than the parents' wings.

For a while there are eggs everywhere: intact eggs, cracked eggs, fresh eggs, rotten eggs, eggs baked hard by the sun, brooded eggs in neat clutches, abandoned eggs scattered among the oyster shells, eggs pipping, pipped eggs invaded by streams of fire ants, eggs deliberately smashed and their contents lapped up, sticky mustard-yellow smears where eggs once lay. Incredibly, a significant fraction of the eggs hatches.

Now most nests harbor several grotesquely ugly, big-headed blobs of wrinkled skin colored like a bad bruise. They develop rapidly into frowsy, demanding gullets ever anxious to appease ravening appetites by ramming themselves down a parental throat with nauseating gobbling sounds. The first hatched and strongest get the best service; the rest scrabble for the leavings and for parental notice. The smallest and weakest fall farther and farther behind, ignored by parents, stabbed by siblings, weakened and dehydrated, bloodied and blinded, until they can rise no more.

This is the time of maximum stench: from the ubiquitous, ammonial whitewash of guano, from bloated and decomposing bodies, from rotting fish, from every manner of heat-festered dying and death. The breath-catching miasma is exacerbated by a backdrop of droning flies, fluttering gular pouches, continual cacks, and muffled groans. The place has more the aspect of an abattoir than of a nursery.

Nearly half of the chicks that make the first cut are ill-fated. They are speared when they stray too close to a neighboring adult, snatched up by an alert gull, torn apart by a blue crab, or driven out of the nest to broil in the sun, wandering to final exhaustion amid the guano, festering fish parts, and blistering shells. The reef becomes littered with bodies and body parts in various stages of mummification. Yet, despite the carnage, many chicks manage to survive. For these, life gets easier and surer. Eventually, most of them lift off their infernal cradles to carry their purged bloodlines toward new challenges in an uncertain and uncaring world.

The overall result is marvelous—perfect new flying machines, strong sinewed, decked in fresh plumage, and metered in numbers to precisely fill the available habitat. Fewer in bad years, more in good ones; ebullient explosions countered by disastrous implosions; nature in balance. Throughout their lifetimes each pair of parents needs to launch only two successful offspring to hold the population steady. All the rest are expendable alternates, most of them doomed from the beginning; only in rare years of plenty do they become the feedstock for population expansion.

It is a pretty symmetry bought at the ugly price of abject misery and inordinate death worked deep into the fabric of this strategy for life— random variation, deliberate overproduction, ruthless culling. Is it strategy at all? If so, it must be a plan of evil connivance, for no divine scheme, no matter how shrouded in incomprehensible farsighted benevolent vision, could possibly sanction such blatantly wicked means to the pretty end. No god worth his salt would "take" in this cruel, pitiless way or, if so, deserves no respect from any sentient being. There are too many losers, too few winners, too much hurt.

More satisfying by far to take it all at face value. Accept misery and death as unfortunate but inevitable and vital parts of preterhuman life. Substitute uncomprehending, blameless amoral indifference for evil strategy, and thus appreciate how a mother can neglect a starving and bedeviled offspring. It is her advantage, and the salvation of her kind, that she is deprived of comprehension, feels no anguish or compassion. See foredoomed dying chicks as wrenching but absolutely necessary sacrifices for the survival of healthy and strong living chicks with adequate environmental space awaiting them. Consider dehydrated bodies as nutrients en route to new generations. Watch things fall out; see causes wreak effects and stimuli elicit responses; let chance, coincidence, luck, and fickle fate roll forth. Resist interfering. Refrain from pontificating. Reflect.

Grasp the enormous breadth of the gap that conscientious humans have opened between themselves and Nature. Our self-awareness, aspiration, compassion, virtue, hubris all set us completely apart, but not above. We cannot consider ourselves risen above Nature until we can achieve for ourselves a corresponding environmental harmony; until we contrive and enact the moral equivalent of misery and death, a conscionable means of holding our population numbers and individual demands to the sustainable carrying capacity of the planet. If we would mollify our own death, it must be by constraining our birth and curbing our glut. Otherwise, the ugliness of the real world will engulf us all.

When I look beyond the edge of my idyllic island universe, I perceive how low we have sunk, how far we must rise. Ten thousand human births each hour, every hour—an obscene, microbial rate of increase for so large and insistent an animal. Tens of millions of grasping, resentful, unsatisfied lives. Vanishing resources, disappearing grandeur, dwindling life-forms. All because we refuse to acknowledge the obvious. I would rather visit a reef rookery. There at least, the pain and suffering make sense.

In my diary I often encounter and ponder death on my ramblings.

APRIL '97: *This should be a joyous month of birth, not a time for death, but we witnessed a somber turnabout on the beach this morning. The strand was littered with pretty, broken, and tumbled bodies—songbirds that had run into some sort of trouble during their spring migration across the Gulf and gone down.*

Even under the best conditions it is a grim gauntlet they run. For days they frantically stoke reserves and build courage on the Yucatán Peninsula. When their livers are gorged with glycogen and their skin rippled with fat, their guts shrivel and the birds begin to fidget uncomfortably. Finally, the lengthening days warn them that their time is up. In the late afternoon, after the worst of daytime air turbulence subsides, excited flocks of doughty little birds succumb to a primeval urge and begin to launch out across the Gulf of Mexico. They set forth with no firm schedule, no concern for hazards, not even a cognizant goal. It just feels good to be on the way, feels right. For the birds, that is enough.

There is no turning back. Over the Campeche Banks the ultramarathoners go, across the tropic of Cancer, deep into the yawning pelagic environment— as alien a world as a furtive woodland bird can enter. Thousands strong, they fly on into the night, over the dark and featureless sea, reckoning by stars, sea breeze, specks of magnetite, instinct, and the sky-calls of fellow travelers, all following the ages-old celestial path worn smooth by the passage of genera- tions of their kinds. They pump rhythmically, breathe in perfect time, their bodies undulating slightly as they rest for a split second after each down- stroke. Eventually, they fall into a stupor, and half their brain dozes off while the other half attends the monotonous pace. The birds hold northwest at thirty miles per hour at an altitude of a scant hundred feet above the water, drawing steadily on their dwindling store of fat, sensing their progress through feedback from their smoothly undulating sinews, thinking nothing. The dim glow of predawn allows them to refine their alignment. If all goes well, by good light they will have sensed the proximity of Matagorda Island, the reliable haven where they will drop down to rest, rejoice, and rebuild their strength before pushing on.

But this time all did not go well. A late norther blew through last night, and the birds must have met it head-on not far offshore. They did the only thing they could do. They pressed on at reduced speed, under greater effort and increasing anxiety. So close, yet so far. For some the calories finally ran out, the seemingly indefatigable wing beat faltered, their confidence began to wane, they lost altitude, and—still fluttering gamely—they went down at sea. It is hard to imagine the survival of the fittest being more trenchantly played out than in this unseen and unrelenting trial of strength and determination.

We see the solemn aftermath this April morning—hundreds of sodden carcasses rocking silently at tidemark. However unpleasant to witness, it is a harshly effective way to expurgate the weak. We can do nothing except document this occurrence, tabulating the losers along four miles of beach: seventy-three yellow-breasted chats, twenty-one Baltimore orioles, eighteen orchard orioles, fifteen indigo buntings, fourteen blue grosbeaks, fourteen wood thrushes, twelve scarlet tanagers, ten summer tanagers, ten painted buntings, nine yellow warblers, eight rose-breasted grosbeaks, six Cassin's sparrows, five gray catbirds, four scissor-tailed flycatchers, four yellowthroats, three red-eyed vireos, three unidentified warblers, two warbling vireos, two Wilson's warblers, two hooded warblers, two yellow-billed cuckoos, and one each of black-throated green warbler, yellow-throated warbler, worm-eating warbler, American redstart, ovenbird, yellow-throated vireo, eastern wood pewee, great-crested flycatcher, western kingbird, eastern kingbird, and ladder-backed woodpecker. Even larger, stronger species were not spared: three cattle egrets, two blue-winged teal, and one each of white-winged dove, sora, common gallinule, and osprey.

Once I raise my eyes off the variegated strand and gaze out over the sunlit Gulf, it is hard to realize, harder yet to appreciate, that I am standing on the edge of an arena of death as well as of life.

SEPTEMBER '96: *Red tide! Last week the Coast Guard warned us of an extensive stretch of rusty red water offshore. We started getting dead fish on the beach this morning. By afternoon there was a solid windrow of bloating bodies. Made a census along one-tenth mile and counted 595 carcasses, forty-one kinds. That extrapolates to about 6,000 dead fish per mile. On the third day the big red drum began to strand. In a five-mile stretch we counted 1,511 individuals thirty inches or more in length; put nose to tail they would have extended almost a mile.*

AUGUST '97: *The Gulf has been in a quiet mood for a week, the water clear and only low swells to the horizon. Despite its eerie lifelessness, the sea had the energy to bring in a thick windrow of long-dead sargassum. Martha's well-honed beachcombing eye caught an unusual reflection in the mass of burnt-brown fibers. Little clams! Jillions and jillions of tiny little clams, all dead but still stuck tightly to the floating mat. We shook handfuls of sargassum, releasing a steady sprinkle of tiny shells onto the beach. We could have filled buckets, bushel baskets, a dump truck. Instead, we filled one instant-coffee jar, and it looked like a jar of coffee off the grocery shelf. Each pair of brown shells was just about the size of a granule of freeze-dried coffee; they averaged three millimeters—a shade under an eighth of an inch. Although the distinctive "wing" was not fully developed, these were baby Atlantic winged oysters* (Pteria colymbus), *an unusual bivalve mollusk occasionally found attached to whip corals or the rigging on floating buoys far offshore. We have picked up a few adults now and then. Jean Andrews lists them as "Southern two-thirds of coast. Uncommon." With this staggering show of profligacy, it boggles the mind to ponder the magnitude of death required to maintain even a relatively uncommon form of marine life. Richard Dawkins once wrote that a hen is but an egg's way of making another egg. Is life merely death's means of perpetuating dying?*

MARCH '97: *I came upon a small rain pool with a population of one of the most bizarre inhabitants of Matagorda Island—fairy shrimp* (Branchinecta)! *Not shrimp, but definitely shrimpy looking; half an inch long; nearly clear with an opalescent overcast; black, beady eyes; swimming horizontally, belly side up; drifting slowly forward on graceful waves of motion from the beat of multiple pairs of plumed feet. Delicate, silent, ephemeral, archaic, utterly enigmatic.*

How did they get here? How did these strictly freshwater creatures travel to this barrier island, and how did they appear in this puddle, which was nothing more than a sandy hollow before the rains began? What will they do when this water percolates into the sand, as it surely will in a few days?

The answer, according to the books, lies in "resting eggs," eggs with thick shells slathered with a special coating that allows them to lie dry for years and to be transported hither and yon in a muddy crust on the feet of birds and flying aquatic insects. The wraithlike adults hardly know life. When their transient microcosm dries up, they vanish along with it, having left their spawn sequestered in the bottom muck. There the resistant granules lie in a cryptobiotic somnolence verging on the inanimate, keepers of the spectral lineage until the rains return.

Among fairy shrimp, life and death engage in a subtle duel. The transient adults do not seem to die at all; they just disappear. The obdurate eggs do not wait; they just persist. The next generation does not hatch; it just incarnates. This cryptic wonder has been working without fail for 200 million years. Regardless of the logic of the texts, I take fairy shrimp for what they seem to be—miracles of life that toy with death.

MARCH '99: *Ah, the irony of death! This morning Martha discovered a ruby-throated hummingbird dead in the clutches of a bull thistle. Having just survived the perils of a nonstop pilgrimage across the Gulf of Mexico, this splendid traveler was brought low, its hypermetabolism stilled at last, when it stooped unwarily for recharge among the purple blossoms. Impaled on the plant's spines, the bird had evidently struggled valiantly but fruitlessly, and it finally died, ignobly, it seemed to us.*

Death, even as it stalks this island, paves the way for new life. Perhaps the most direct route is via the dissolution of a freshly killed body inside a predator. The soft anatomy of a Culver's sandworm yields before the digestive enzymes in the gut of a long-billed dowitcher, for instance. Within minutes, the major biochemicals of the worm have been disassociated, absorbed, transported, and reconstituted into dowitcher tissue or used to fuel dowitcher activity. This quick shift is a giant step up for worm macromolecules, a subtle transformation based on the commonality of life-stuff. They move from lowly, cold-blooded, and backboneless annelid to advanced, warm-blooded, and backboned avian with hardly time to "die" before they take on the stepped-up role of living again. Nonetheless, the worm is no more; the bird carries on. Death moves along the food chains like a peristaltic wave, pushing life to its fore.

Decomposition is the second major avenue leading from death to new life. It is a slower, more devious, and complex process of disintegration brought about mostly by echelons of bacteria. Decay is also, according to our sensibilities, a more revolting occurrence (decay of animals at least; we are unaffected by the composting of plants). We can watch a bird slurp up a worm with some amusement, but we hurriedly walk around a decomposing fish carcass. It is partly a matter of exposure. We smell the putrefying fish and perhaps see the movement of maggots, but we are spared the glutinous texture and retching odor of the caustic chyme in the bird's gut. Recall the loathsome taste and disgust of a bout of nausea to know the unpleasantness that goes on inside us all.

No matter, like the predator, the microbes are busy transforming the dead body into their own form of protoplasm and calories, but they work more roundabout. Lacking mouths and intestines, bacteria exude their digestive enzymes directly onto their food and then imbibe the resulting mush. No one kind of bacterium can handle all the types of tissues in a multicellular carcass. Most are specialists: some split peptide bonds to disassemble proteins, producing ammonia; others are attracted to sulfur-containing compounds and bubble off hydrogen sulfide; many attack the welter of hydrocarbons to yield carbon dioxide, hydrogen, and water. The whole is neatly choreographed into a (dis)assembly line, the by-products of one sort of degradation becoming the feedstock for the next. Ammonia is pounced upon and oxidized to nitrite and nitrate; hydrogen sulfide is reduced to elemental sulfur and hydrogen; some hydrocarbon metabolites are fermented to alcohols, organic acids, or methane gas.

The softer and more nutritious tissues go first, the more resistant ones linger, while inert ones like bones, hair, and scales may last until they crumble from chemical weathering. Eventually and inevitably, however, that part of the carcass not transformed into microbial protoplasm is mineralized—returned to dust, which can be moved by air and water and reenter the living world through microbes, plant roots, and sucking-and-sifting, multicelled detritivores.

The microorganisms of decay seldom have a carcass to themselves. Multicelled scavengers take their share, and by slicing large chunks into small pieces and ripping through tough outer coverings, they promote bacterial advance. On the beach in high summer, I have seen the whole biodegradation cycle of competition and cooperation transform the body of a four-hundred-pound bottle-nosed dolphin into a mass of bleaching bones, a scrap of black leathery skin, and a faint waft of tainted air, all within five days.

Events begin at sea when the dolphin dies. Sharks chop at the body; fishes and crabs tug at the dangling strands of flesh. Billions of bacteria assault the deteriorating tissues, producing gases to bloat and float the carcass, hastening its deposition onto the beach. Even before it is fully stranded, gulls will have plucked out the vitamin-rich eyeballs, and turkey vultures will venture just beyond waterline to tear at the shark bites.

Throughout the first day on the beach the great body festers in the sun, its once-vital fluids leaking into the sand, the plump curvature beginning to slump, the rank odors of decay wafting out as beacons to a host of sensitive antennae. Blowflies and flesh flies arrive within minutes. They find a hole—an eye socket perhaps—crawl in, take a quick sip of liquid nourishment, and lay a clutch of eggs. Beetles are not far behind: rove beetles, carrion beetles, burying beetles, darkling beetles, hairy fungus beetles, scarab beetles, and more. A varied array of thirsty species with sucking or sopping mouthparts arrives to drink the juices: daddy longlegs, leaf-footed bugs, soldier flies, hover flies, dung flies, scavenger flies, gnats. The steady drain of nutritious body humors stirs millions of nematode worms, protozoa, and bacteria living between the sand grains beneath the body.

Meanwhile, although they cannot slice through the tough skin, the vultures enlarge every opening and reach inside to the limits of their neck feathers to drag out whatever microbe-tenderized flesh they can tear loose. By this time a crested caracara or two lurks on the fringe to grab at scraps. During the first night, heavy-duty scavengers arrive. Coyotes and feral hogs worry the carcass farther up the beach, rip through its hide, and begin wholesale dismemberment and consumption. A nocturnal legion of ghost crabs arrives to wrench snippets, and beach hoppers aggregate on particles of flesh not already claimed by streams of native fire ants. Recognizing a prolonged feast, many crabs and hoppers dig burrows nearby so that they can conveniently emerge to gorge.

Because the carcass is now opened and softened, the second day is more frenzied than the first. The vultures and caracaras are joined by several species of gulls and a variety of opportunistic shorebirds. A signal event is the hatching of blowfly eggs into a rippling seethe of maggots. These produce powerful protein-splitting chemicals that cause the rapid disintegration of muscle tissue, which the larvae ravenously shred and engulf. As a consequence, the great dolphin begins its final collapse, and the countless hordes of bacteria go into high gear.

By the third day, with most of its sera drained away, dehydration is evident, driving out or inhibiting some of the early decomposers while luring in others. As the next days pass, the swarm of distended maggots spills out and squirms into the soaked sand to begin the process of turning dolphin tissue into bluebottle fly protoplasm in the secrecy of their pupal cases. Hister beetles, tiger beetles, assassin bugs, and predaceous ground beetles arrive to waylay the scrambling carrion insects, while robber flies zoom in to intercept rising flies in midair. When a night passes without a visit from a coyote, the banquet is about over.

By the fifth day only a few burrower bugs, fungus gnats, skin beetles, and dermestid beetles gnaw at dried scraps inside the hardened folds of skin. The bones lie in disarray, white, sandblasted, nearly sterile. The sand has lost its yellow stain. The air smells of nothing but the sea. The alchemy is done. The dolphin is gone, sifted into the sand, lifted on the sea breeze, sprinkled over the dunes, returned to the ocean, imbued deep in the vitals of dozens of different life-forms.

Is it any different with humans? I have read what others have thought, from the early Greeks through modern philosophers, and I have pondered on my own. And I have lived too long in Nature to come to any conclusion other than that expressed so bluntly and eloquently by Bertrand Russell: "I believe that when I die I shall rot, and nothing of my ego will survive."[1]

Everything I see and interpret on this island, all kinds of procreations, all manner of livelihoods, and all sorts of deaths and dissolutions follow the same fundamental pattern. I can divine nothing whatsoever about myself that might set me apart. Indeed, I would feel slighted to discover otherwise. My body is merely my medium of self-expression. When it ceases to function, the millions of neural synapses that have loyally maintained the electrochemical semblance of "me" will finally and irrevocably blink out. "I" will die. For me there will be no other life, no other existence, no posthumous retribution or reward, no resurrection, no hope; perdition; nothing. My soul? I do not entertain that desperate egoism. What is left behind, my "material remains," is nothing more than the several pounds of deanimated mineral stuff that happened to give me my last manifestation. Other pounds—tons, I suppose—that were once part of me are already scattered near and far. Now these last few can join the rest.

CHAPTER 9

CREATURES WE HAVE KNOWN

New moon, dark heavens
Yet, sand dunes twinkle with lights
Primroses wide awake.

A FAMILY OF WHOOPING CRANES on the marsh! A pair of adults with their gangly chick of the year. As always, the birds are no closer than spotting-scope distance. They demand their space, so I do not crowd them. After eyeing me awhile, they return to foraging in the shallows, but even at my remove I have made them uneasy. The adults look up frequently, standing tall and immobile. Then through the lens I see what is coming next: the male leans forward slightly, the female follows suit, and the chick stands bolt upright. The two adults lift off simultaneously in graceful diagonal trajectory, and the young bird flutters up in their wake. One of the parents gives a light toodle, and the other answers with a barely vocal susurration. Intimate crane talk. The trio flaps away with strong, measured cadence. The birds keep in close formation but do not gain altitude. They settle down again where they register as nothing more than white specks, even when I zoom to high power. At that distance they are still indubitably whoopers by size, color, stature, and sequestration, but they are too far off to study.

I slog out across the marsh to see what evidence the cranes have left of their foraging activity. I soon strike their trail of huge spread-toed prints in the shallows, each impression smeared when the birds slipped as they shifted their weight in the scarcely palpable ooze. The chick's smaller prints interweave those of the adults. It's following Mom.

What have the whoopers been up to? Bill marks and a scatter of dismembered legs show they were sweeping aside the organic floc and grabbing up small blue crabs hidden underneath. It is cold today. Likely the crabs were too torpid to offer any resistance. In favorable habitat, a hungry crane—I have never seen a satiated crane—can glean a young blue crab at the rate of one every two minutes, and the bird will keep at it as long as the fodder lasts. When the whoopers first arrive in fall, the chick has never seen a blue crab, but it knows to be right there when the adult female makes a strike. She shares with the chick; it flutters and squeals with excitement and in no time gets the idea. It will still beg as long as she puts up with it but soon weans into a proficient crab stalker.

Now and then I find a deep stab hole among the crane footprints. There are no telltale leftovers, but I know from watching with the scope what has occurred. Somehow a whooper has determined that there is a worthwhile morsel in the mud, and it has thrust bill-deep to secure it. If the bird is lucky—maybe every third attempt—it comes up with a razor clam (*Tagelus plebeius*), a thumb-sized blob of amorphous protoplasm housed in a pair of thin, easily crunched shells. The crane hardly breaks its foraging rhythm as it bolts its catch whole and searches for another. I can get an occasional razor clam with a shovel, but I cannot locate them with the cranes' accuracy. The clams leave barely discernible holes in the mud where they expose their siphons to draw in and expel water. Maybe the cranes can detect these cryptic clues. I rarely can, but I am not driven by a whooper appetite nor tutored by a whooper parent.

Whooping cranes are consummate scroungers, so my birds have doubtless taken some prey without leaving evidence that I can discern along their trail. On occasion I have seen them snatch striped mullet trapped in tidal pools and pick festered mullet carcasses off the bank, pluck saltmarsh periwinkles and marsh katydids from cordgrass stems, skewer a marsh rice rat swimming for cover, glom down a gulf saltmarsh snake, peck up skittering mud fiddler crabs at the rate of several per minute, pull most of a red-gilled worm from its burrow, dabble for brown shrimp, harvest jackknife clams forced to the surface by anaerobic muck, pick red-ripe wolfberries, and graze on the greenery of maritime saltwort and glasswort. For a scrounger this marsh is a brimming smorgasbord.

I envy the whooping cranes their perspicacity and intimate knowledge of the salt marsh. I suspect that much of that intelligence is acquired, learned from those experienced birds who know, picked up by example just as I saw the young crane being schooled by its mother. It is a vital wisdom of survival, a sense gained over the ages when glaciers dominated the land. Of going back and forth as the ice waxed and waned, and finally imbibing a pattern of annual migration that brought together the best of Canadian nesting and Texan wintering conditions. Young cranes must still learn the ancient route and the seasonal schedule, for it is not set in their genes. Likewise, my foraging whoopers must enjoy the benefit of a tedious culmination of antecedent trials and errors about what to eat and how to go about getting it. Hand-me-down crane culture, as vital as inherited crane DNA if wild cranes are to endure.

Remarkable. And to think that we almost lost it. In '41, all of the acquired expertise to direct the well-being of a wild and haughty whooping crane was housed in the memories of just fifteen birds. For those of us who love this coastal country, the demise of these last wild cranes would have been akin to the loss of the library at Alexandria. Such a waste, such an irrecoverable waste. We could live on after the tragedy, of course, but we would lead less full, more remorseful lives. Happily it did not come to that. The cranes' plight was discovered. Luck, concern, and unswerving commitment prevailed. Today the flock numbers over 180. From late October through April, fifty of these whoopers may grace the Matagorda marsh. There they continue to pass along their indispensable tradition among themselves. And in rare unguarded moments, when they let me get close enough, I pick up a nugget of crane acumen, and it allows me to see the salt marsh in a fresh light.

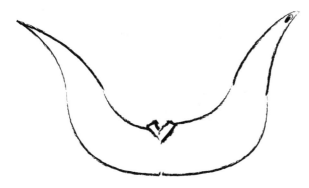

Bull's-horn acacia

On warm sunny days at our home on the Guadalupe River, two or three curious ants usually appeared, as if by magic, at our patio breakfast table. I finally spotted them popping in and out of chinks between the plies in the tabletop. Although they inspected everything, we never saw one take a crumb of food. They just raced in fits and starts around the table and up and down our sleeves. We fancied they came to see what we were up to, so we named them curious ants (*Pseudomyrmex gracilis mexicanus*), implying not "peculiar" but "inquisitive."

Handsome creatures, these three-eighths-inch ants are apricot streaked with black, with a black abdomen. They are slender and quick, with long legs, busy antennae, and large, cocoa brown eyes. Curious ants watch movement and look you in the eye with an unsettling gaze. Though they can deliver a sharp sting if cramped, these personable beasts are always welcome at our table.

I never expected to see curious ants on the barrier island, but they are here. I discovered them squirreling around mesquite branches, eyeing me cautiously and vanishing when I got too close. Their small colonies reside in hollow mesquite twigs and feed on small insects and honeydew. The thought of these sly ants slinking along their secret scent trails among the shadows is as enchanting as discovering the isolated copses are haunted by pixies.

In Mexico's dry scrubland grows a small tree called bull's-horn acacia (*Acacia cornigera*). Its twigs bear solidly fused pairs of woody thorns two to three inches long, inflated at the base and tapered to tips diverging like horns. So the name. Northbound longshore currents some-times deposit Mexican flood outwash on the Matagorda beach in which the thorns are frequent finds. They are especially desirable souvenirs for visitors whose alma mater is the University of Texas (mascot, the "hook 'em horns" Texas longhorn).

What has this to do with our curious ants? Despite their robust ap-pearance, the thorns are hollow. Most pairs have a small oval hole near one tip. A Mexican species of curious ant (*Pseudomyrmex ferrugineus*) has cut the hole and lived within the hollow thorn. A young queen ant chews into a thorn and removes the light pith, making a spacious and durable cavity for her brood. The workers need not forage far; the acacia provides wells of nectar and nodules of nutriment among its leaves. In return, the ants rid the tree of all sorts of herbivorous insects, and they prune back seedlings and branches that might shade out their benefactor.

Revealing their affinity to their Mexican cousins, our curious ants are known to occasionally take up residence in the thorns of mimosa trees in South Texas. I wonder if there is a colony inhabiting a mes-quite thorn on Matagorda Island.

A four-foot blacktip shark was pulled from the surf, the hook re-moved, and the animal rolled back into the breakers, when I noticed a small fish flopping in the wet sand. "Suckerfish off the shark," the fisherman commented casually kicking it toward the water. A remora! A creature I knew only from pictures. In no time I had this treasure in a milk jug of seawater on its way to our aquarium.

A member of the remora clan, this one was properly called a shark sucker (*Echeneis naucrates*). It was a juvenile only four inches long with a potential to be more than two feet long. Its distinctive feature was on top of its head—a flat, oval disc crossed by a series of plates. The disc can be pressed against a flat surface and the fleshy margin sucked down to make a tight seal. The fish can hitchhike with sharks, sundry bony fishes, sea turtles, and even boat hulls. When schools of small fishes or scraps from the host's meal appear, the sucker can detach and forage, then zip back to its perch. The fish presents a nifty example of evolu-tion: the peculiar attachment disc is a highly modified dorsal fin.

Even aside from its adhesive head shield, my shark sucker was an eye-catching animal. Long, thin, and streamlined, its gray color enliv-

Shark sucker

ened by a black stripe from snout to tail, outlined in silvery white. The winglike pectoral fins and pointed pelvic fins were jet black; the dorsal and anal fins and the tail were dark with silvery edges. Quite a handsome little beast!

The shark sucker took well to aquarium life. It could swim with ease and grace but preferred to idle just under the surface. It never attempted to use its sucker against the glass or on any of the larger fish in the tank. It readily ate bits of shrimp and small chunks of fish but seemed uninterested in small fish swimming nearby. Inside a week, it anticipated being fed, excitedly zipping around at its customary feeding station when I approached. Soon it was breaking the surface to snatch food from my fingers. Unfortunately, this healthy appetite fueled rapid growth. Our four-inch fish soon doubled in length and was getting too large for the aquarium. Reluctantly, we put our trusting little shark sucker into a bucket and hauled it back to the surf. I waded out and gently poured the fish into the sea. There was no hesitation, no confused swimming about in an aquarium-sized space, no gesture of goodbye. It was gone in an instant, back where it belonged.

The badger was nearly out of sight, headfirst down a hole on the beach, heaving sprays of sand over his shoulders. With the breeze in our favor, we got close enough to hear him scratching and wheezing. Suddenly, somehow sensing us, he paused, backed out of his dig, and looked up at us with small, watery black eyes. What a fascinating creature! Low-slung, broad, and flat with grizzled gray face, a black, doglike muzzle, wiry whiskers, and thick-rimmed, low-set ears. A bright white stripe arose between his eyes and ran over the top of his broad head.

The badger gave us a long look, sniffed the wind, and with an explosive woof made a break for the dunes. I managed to get in front of him, causing him to veer toward the surf. He went as far as the waterline where, with the breakers at his back and no cover on either flank, he wheeled and made his stand.

What a magnificent, thoroughly intimidating brute! Coarse pelage fanned out in ragged cowlicks, his lips set in a snarl, head and shoulders held low and hind quarters high, he swiveled himself to face our every move. If we wanted trouble, he was willing to accommodate. Of course, I had no intention of taking up the challenge. I got what I wanted, a baleful grimace that filled the frame of my telephoto lens. With that triumph, I stepped aside and gave the badger an avenue to the dunes. He took it instantly, streaking for safety like a ragged carpet rippling over the sand. To this day, our thirty seconds with this badger ranks among the most evocative experiences we have had on Matagorda Island.

Visitors to the coast generally know that the sharp-edged, turret-shaped shells stuck to pilings, boat hulls, jetties, and reefs are barnacles. Some have been patient enough to watch the live animals extend their feathery legs to sieve the water for plankton and detritus. A few even know that barnacles are closer kin to shrimp and crabs than to snails and clams. These atypical crustaceans have mobile larvae that scramble among the plankton before they settle and grow into adults immobilized within calcareous plates. But there are barnacles, and then there are barnacles. The common, abundant ones are acorn barnacles, but there are less common, more bizarre species.

A gooseneck barnacle (*Lepas anatifera*) is covered with a close-fitting mail of limy plates and holds its body well above the substrate on a flexible, fleshy tube up to two inches long. This species lives offshore on floating drift. Lumber seems particularly attractive, and floating planks often have dense aggregations. These barnacles sieve for plankton and are strong enough to snare even small fishes and jellyfishes. A plank comes fresh from the surf covered with a seething mass of gooseneck barnacles, but soon they begin to dehydrate, and their plump brown necks go limp. When the shells gape, ruddy turnstones, laughing gulls, and ghost crabs feast on them.

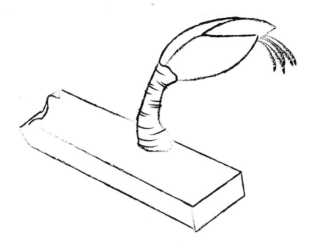

Gooseneck barnacle

Turtle barnacles (*Chelonibia testudinaria*) live only on the shells of sea turtles. Some of their heavyset, low-domed bony shells are usually stuck fast to the carapaces of any turtle that is more than a foot long. They are often clustered around the anus from which comes a regular gush of concentrated nutrients. The shell resembles a calcareous doughnut about the size of a silver dollar. The saw-toothed plates that secure the creature can be seen on the bottom of one that is pried loose with a knife. The shell makes a great "what is it?" to tantalize visitors.

Giant barnacles (*Megabalanus antillensis*) are the largest of their clan in the Gulf. These oversized acorn barnacles have ponderous, purplish shells nearly as large as a demitasse cup. This Caribbean species encrusts oil platforms and anchored buoys in warm, clear water offshore. When a storm brings a buoy onto the beach, we need a hammer and chisel to detach a few giant barnacles for show-and-tell.

Whale barnacles (*Xenobalanus globicipitis*) dangling limply from the flukes of a beached bottle-nosed dolphin look like parasitic worms, but they are commensal creatures. Having found this safe position, they have given up the armor of bony plates and are modified to hang on in the fierce currents generated by their host. Each individual is a vase-shaped, purplish, fleshy tube about two inches long capped by a stiff collar that protects the food-catching feet. The flat attachment disc has a starburst pattern of white plates that embed in the host's skin.

Occasionally we put fresh strands of bright yellow sea whip

(*Leptogorgia setacea*) into an aquarium to watch the delicate fur of coral tentacles appear. One day I noticed curved barnacle feet snapping in and out. Closer examination of a pore in a bulbous enlargement revealed a tiny barnacle enclosed in thin, brown, flakelike plates embedded in living coral tissue. And so we came to know the seawhip barnacle (*Conopea galeata*), a species found nowhere but cloistered in these animated filaments, and one more reason for our infatuation with this island.

One day in mid-June, I discovered a common nighthawk on eggs on an oyster-shell ridge. I piled a small cairn of shells nearby to mark the site. On July 7, two fuzzy chicks hatched. They both disappeared on July 26. Their time was up; I like to think that they took wing. The next year, exactly the same events occurred within a few days of the same dates and at the same spot. My oyster-shell cairn fixed the geography, and my diary confirmed the dates. The next year, the choreography was once more faithfully repeated.

Was this the repeated work of the same parent nighthawks? Without having banded the birds, I can only speculate. Possibly a member of each year's crop of youngsters was returning to carry on the family tradition. However, such precise and specific nest-site fidelity is characteristic of individual seasoned birds that have enjoyed successful nesting at a favorable spot. So, I believe the same adult nighthawks were returning to the same oyster-shell rendezvous on the same schedule for three years running.

These birds leave Matagorda in late September and fly to South America. In early April they return to Matagorda Island, and by June they are brooding their eggs on the same flakes of shell as before. What a remarkable feat of learning, navigating, timing, physical stamina, and sheer tenacity! Here are creatures with the freedom and ability to range over two continents, yet the exigency of survival constrains them into a far smaller world. Are they as severely regimented in all their life's endeavors? Probably so.

Rainbow dung beetles (*Phanaeus difformis*) are animated oxymorons—beautiful creatures with smelly habits. Adults are about three-quarters of an inch long, with black spiny legs for digging and a shovel-like snout for scooping earth and dung. The beauty is in their colors: emerald green wing covers shading to shiny chartreuse over the thorax and head, with a blush of rosy bronze on the top of the thorax. All with the resplendence of hammered metal. The male adds to his glamour and mating prowess with a long black horn curved high over his back.

Numbers of these beetles zoom over the sandy uplands of Matagorda Island almost year-round, but especially after rains. They are attracted to fresh excrement, on which they feed and lay their eggs. With the female doing most of the digging while the male pushes sand to the surface, they make a tunnel about a foot deep near the fecal pat. Then both carve out fragments of dung and form them into a round wad that they jockey toward the nest hole, moving not backward in typical "tumble bug" fashion, but forward, pushing the load with their broad snout.

At the bottom of the burrow, the female molds the dung into a sand-coated brood mass the size of a marble, in which she deposits a solitary egg. She then fills in the burrow and roars away, alert to the waft of another deposit of excrement. In about three months, a newly minted rainbow dung beetle scratches its way into the upper world and unfurls its antennae to sniff for wafts from dung.

Dung beetles do not lead carefree lives. Many females carry a restless bevy of tiny black flies clustered on their backs and circling around their heads. These stay aboard when the beetle takes wing, but when she goes underground, most flies get off and fidget around the tunnel entrance. It took me the better part of a day fiddling under 60x magnification to get to the family Sphaeroceridae (sometimes called Borboridae), a collage of winged, gnat-sized dipterans aptly called "small dung flies." However, beyond family, the trail dimmed. Harold Oldroyd, the final authority on flies in my library, says they are universal dung feeders and little more.[1]

I suspect the little flies can locate excrement without help, and once on fresh droppings they link up with dung beetles long enough to spike eggs into the fragments destined to be a beetle's brood ball. This gives to their offspring the beetle's protection as she guards her brood ball against dehydration. But now, which is the more efficient coprophage, the beetle grub or the several fly maggots? Which leans more to maiming or devouring its opponent? Which has the faster rate of development? What emerges from a given burrow may turn largely on a roll of the dice.

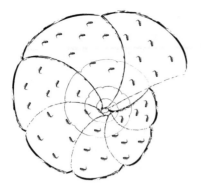

Forams

"At a rate of two feet per century, their pinhead-sized calcareous shells pile into layers of impalpable ooze thousands of feet thick across much of the ocean floor. Over eons, these layers may lithify into limestone. The massive chalk cliffs of Dover are upheaved strata built from an incalculable number of these tiny shells. They formed the stones of which the pyramids were built. We used to write on blackboards with them. Petroleum is located by following their distribution."

Every freshman biology student gets this brief introduction to foraminifera, an abundant but scarcely visible group of shelled marine protozoa. I was left with the vague impression that forams were ancient history, inanimate relics, empty shells, and passive stones. Certainly, I never expected to meet a live one.

But we got interested in the sandy debris lodged in dead olive shells. Viewed at 40x, this appeared as a sparkling, gem-studded jumble of mineral grains, shell fragments, and calcareous spines of sand dollars. And there was something else: flatly coiled, multichambered, snail-like shells and spindle-shaped forms that looked like seeds. An antiquated edition of Buchsbaum revealed that these were the shells of foraminifera. The "snails" I could not identify further; the "seeds" were from the family Miliolidae. And then a shell wiggled! I could make out wisps of clear protoplasm flickering around the margins of some of them. Live forams, solitary cells packed with all the wiles of long-term survival in an overwhelming world, precursors of the venerable ooze, trifling beginnings of great sedimentary beds, alive and well. Loads of them jostling below ordinary notice among the eddies inside spent snail shells right here on Matagorda Island! Who would have thought it?

• • •

Bioluminescence is magical. No matter the basics of luciferin and luciferase, nerve impulses that mix the two, oxidation and dephosphorylation reactions that produce the cool flash. The sudden, ephemeral glow in the dark still seems otherworldly. On any given night, Matagorda Island emits at least a few ghostly twinkles; on rare nights every breaking wave crest ignites in witch-fire; and on moist summer nights heavy blobs of phosphor rise and course erratically across the central grassland.

Noctiluca scintillans, the dinoflagellate protozoan that kindles flame in every water ripple, can soar to extraordinary concentration in either surf or lagoon. At these times, breaching dolphins leave fiery wakes, the base of our seawall is set ablaze, the breakers flicker as with sheet lightning, and our last steps along the wet beach are rimmed in fading glimmers of fox fire. This is "animal light" at its peak, in this case produced by a near animal, a single-celled protist.

Both of our common kinds of comb jellies are luminescent. Their eight rows of cilia that flicker with iridescence in daylight are even more spectacular at night, illuminated from within by underlying canals where the pyrotechnics are generated. When the bay water is cool, the sea walnut (*Beroe ovata*) lights up, while the phosphorus jelly

Comb jelly

(*Mnemiopsis mccradyi*) lights the way in the summertime. Sometimes the bay is so loaded with minuscule cydippid larvae of comb jellies that their combined glow resembles the homogeneous luster of *Noctiluca*.

In the springtime, oceanic purple jellyfish (*Pelagia noctiluca*) spin out of the Gulf Stream into the Gulf of Mexico and are stranded on the beach. The stiff, gristlelike bell is two to three inches across, its upper surface roughened by low papillae and its in-rolled margin bearing eight brownish tentacles. Four bright rose purple gonads show clearly through the bell, making for a pretty animal even in death and out of its element. Despite their specific name (*noctiluca*), I had to read to learn that they luminesce. On the next influx of purple jellies we visited the beach at night and sure enough, when we tapped a toe on a freshly stranded individual, it burst into bright posthumous glow, and the foot that stamped on it generated a splatter of sparkles on the wet sand.

A bottom-scouring surf brings in the velvety, liver-colored pats of sea pansies (*Renilla mulleri*), relatives of sea anemones, flattened for life on the surface of the sand in the offshore shallows. Fresh specimens soon evert their dozens of stalks topped by feeding tentacles. Intriguing enough by day, at night sea pansies reveal another trait. A touch sends sparkles of light dancing from stalk to stalk.

On warm, wet summer nights the grass canopy on the island comes alive with weaving and shimmering yellow green lights. Each light trail builds and then fades away, all in ghostly silence. These are the displays of male lightning bugs, or fireflies (neither bugs nor flies, but beetles). Almost everyone has seen such nocturnal displays on watered lawns.

I have found only one species of firefly (*Pyractonema angulata*) on Matagorda Island. It seems to glory in its position as sole "bearer of the light," for it is abundant and ignites an especially large globe. While the males put on their spectacular aerial light show, the flightless females and larvae (glowworms) creep among the grass blades emitting subdued steady pinpoints of light.

Lantern click beetles (*Pyrophorus* sp.) have three lights: one on each hind corner of the prothorax and one underneath the first abdominal segment. They do not flash like lightning bugs but light up all three bulbs slowly, glow steadily for ten seconds or longer, and then fade away. Their yellowish abdominal light outshines the glow of lightning bugs at peak flash. I have never learned how to induce a lantern click beetle to turn on its lights, nor do I know what use it makes of them.

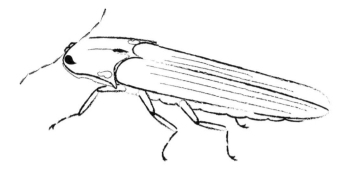

Lantern click beetle

Around Christmastime seedlings of black mangroves begin to strand on the beach. These are not seeds ready to germinate but budding little trees anxious to take root. The black mangrove (*Avicennia germinans*) is viviparous—its seeds begin to sprout while still attached to the tree.

Each waif has an inch-long pair of seed-leaves (cotyledons) from which it draws nourishment until it gets established. From between the green seed-leaves a root stock (hypocotyl) covered with a fuzz of root hairs pokes out and probes for a spot to anchor. Once this lifetime decision is made, it plunges in with total dedication. But the little mangrove's universe is ordinarily made up of gentle tidal oscillations

Black mangrove

and lagoonal mud, and only by accident of open ocean and sandy beaches. All signals on the beach are negative, and the throngs of mangrove seedlings that drift through tidal passes and land on the beach die of exposure.

One that founders in the lagoons on the back side of the island, where the substrate is soft and nourishing, fares much better. There in the shallow water it still feels the pulse of the tides but is protected by marsh and reefs. Having found what it is looking for, the sensitive hypocotyl elongates and produces rootlets.

At the University of Texas, the late Dr. Calvin McMillan demonstrated that black mangrove hypocotyls, while tolerant of some vicissitudes in their surroundings, are quite discriminating in several particulars.[2] Salinity of the water makes little difference; they can stand water with no salt or water with twice the salt of the sea. But they do not like to be jostled around. Put into tubes of seawater and bombarded with streams of air bubbles, the seedlings went into a stupor; with the air turned off, they immediately perked up with a spray of roots. So, seedlings set up shop only in quiet water. The rootstocks cannot reach the bottom to take hold in the substrate if the water is more than about two inches deep. So, little mangroves can get started in the shallows but not in deeper water.

Until they have sent up a stalk and grown their first true leaves, infant black mangroves are not hardened enough to withstand the cooking water temperatures of a Texas summer. Thus, their timing stratagem: plants bloom in midsummer, fruit in the fall, and cast their seedlings adrift in midwinter. If things go well, those plantlets that strike a promising site will have time to green up and build stamina before the lethal doldrums of high summer arrive.

Black mangrove is the only member of its tropical clan that has colonized the Texas coast. Occasional hard winters keep the Texas plants pruned into low, nondescript bushes with shiny green leaves. They lack the distinctive prop roots of the mangroves that line the coast of Florida and Caribbean shores, but a search in the shade of a clump of black mangroves is apt to reveal one exotic feature. To prevent asphyxiation in the airless muck, the roots send up vertical protrusions called pneumatophores that take in air through small pores. Especially when the tide is out, thickets and marching columns of these gray, pencil-thin woody spears are evident on the banks.

* * *

Shades of *Invasion of the Body Snatchers*! Hardly an hour ago I placed the rubbery white egg on a wet paper towel under an inverted glass jar. Now it had hatched, and even as I watched, the gnarled, clawlike orange fingers of an alien hand were emerging, expanding, reaching up inside the jar. It was an eerie spectacle. This was not an alien from outer space but an everyday inhabitant of Matagorda Island with an exotic life history.

For months, perhaps years, spiderwebby mycelium spreads unseen through the subterranean world of rhizomes and mulch beneath the carpet of grasses. In the wintertime, when the grasses are dormant and beaten down by several days of rain, the mycelium stirs. Nutrients stored away from the patient decay of vegetable matter are collected in nodules here and there in the maze of fibrils. A rapid uptake of water causes a nodule to swell into a turgid, white, egg-shaped mass about an inch in diameter. Its upper end erupts from the sand, and soon the egg hatches, cracking and peeling back, as its macabre orange fetus wakens. Growing quickly, the four spongy fingers remain joined at their tips as they expand to an obovate basket four inches tall, and the inner

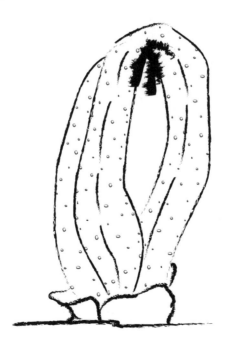

Columned stinkhorn

faces of the fingers begin to ooze a greenish brown slime. Attracted by the stomach-turning stench, bluebottle flies arrive to slurp at the sticky goo and fly away carrying flecks of spore-filled slime that can start another mycelium. Next day, its fleeting magic exhausted, the orange basket collapses into a faded and odorless lattice on the grass.

Such is the life of the columned stinkhorn (*Clathrus columnatus*), one of a group of fungi noted for sudden eruption, bizarre appearance, and malodor. The aptly named phallic stinkhorn (*Mutinus caninus*) sends up its solitary, slightly tapered orange pink stalk at about the same time and in the same grassy dunes. A dark slime on its apex attracts flies and even fools dung beetles into hauling it off. A third kind most clearly merits its generic designation (*Phallus*) with a solitary, slightly arced white stalk capped by a greenish "prepuce" complete with a gaping pore at the tip. This suggestive reproductive body seems designed not only to attract flies but to evoke stunned embarrassment in all humans who encounter it.

Little bugs called water boatmen (Corixidae) compose a significant fraction of the biomass in brackish water, especially in ephemeral "mosquito pools" at the upper edge of the salt marsh. A week after flooding by a high tide or runoff from heavy rain, the bottoms of these shallow spots are covered with a bubble-studded carpet of green and blue-green algae, aswarm with a dozen kinds of diatoms and seething with unseen clouds and films of bacteria. Protozoans, rotifers, worms, tiny crustaceans, and insect larvae, including saltmarsh mosquito wigglers, all appear as if by magic and all hurrying to do their thing before the water evaporates or the salinity rises beyond their threshold.

Water boatmen first appear as wingless nymphs hatched from eggs stuck into the algal mat during a previous inundation. These soon transform into quarter-inch-long adults that, because of their frenetic mobility, outclass even the scads of wigglers for dominance of the pool. When a pool is at its peak of productivity, a few swishes of a hand net over the algal mat will bring in a quarter pound of water boatmen.

Viewed at 10x power, water boatmen (*Trichocorixa verticalis*) are pretty, with a brassy green body, large apricot-colored compound eyes, front wings with an intricate dark reticulum, and prothorax with fine dark crossbars. They have an oval, streamlined body, minute antennae tucked out of harm's way, and oarlike hind legs with paddle ends enhanced by a fringe of hairs. These paddles also serve as grooming brushes with which the boatmen repeatedly wipe their eyes and tidy the margins of their wings, the while wiggling with apparent satisfaction. These versatile bugs can fly, walk, and swim but spend most of their time on frenzied business underwater, spurting ahead with backward snaps of their oars. Each individual must make an occasional dash to the surface where, in the blink of an eye, it captures a fresh bubble of air beneath its wings and dives back to the bottom.

The first pair of legs are bristle-studded scoops with which the bugs rake the floc of blue-green algal filaments into their mouths. Every boatman's intestine is swelled and discolored by a load of algae, and they produce a continual stream of fecal paste. Feeding *ad libitum,* boatmen have little else to do except reproduce. This they do with orgiastic abandon. Most females carry a male on their backs and are constantly pestered by more suitors trying to climb aboard. Eggs hatch and nymphs appear in all but the coldest months. No wonder the water boatman population rides a continual high.

When we moved to the island, I began individually marking the box turtles that live around headquarters by filing small notches in the edge of their shells. I weighed each one, measured its shell length, sexed it, and recorded where and when it had been found before releasing it at the capture site.

To date I have marked sixty-seven ornate box turtles, thirty-eight males and twenty-nine females, in the acres surrounding headquarters. All but six were adults (shell length 100 millimeters or more). The males averaged 110 millimeters in shell length and 285 grams in weight; the females, 111 millimeters and 316 grams. A long-term investigation of box turtles conducted near Austin by my mentor professor at the University of Texas, Dr. W. Frank Blair, determined that a specimen with a shell 100 millimeters long is about eight years old; one 110 millimeters long is some fifteen years old; and turtles 114 millimeters and larger are probably thirty years or older.[3] Judging by the Austin data, twenty-three (34 percent) of my Matagorda turtles were at least thirty years old. One crusty old male with a shell 130 millimeters long might have reached the half-century mark.

Among my turtles were only eleven recaptures: one was recaught three times, one was recaught twice, and six were each found once after their initial encounter. Although the data are scanty, the results are consistent. All recaptures were within three hundred feet of the spot where the animal was originally marked, even when captures were several years apart. So, my box turtles proved to be homebodies just as did Dr. Blair's turtles in Austin. Based on many sightings, he calculated that a typical adult box turtle occupies a roughly circular home range about 330 feet in diameter; an area of about two acres. My observations and intuition suggest that turtles on Matagorda Island approximate this pattern.

Turtles are first seen abroad in March. Most sightings are in spring and early summer and in the fall, the seasons most likely to have rain showers, bountiful plant growth, surging insect populations, and pleasant temperatures. The last turtles are seen in November. Through our cool months box turtles apparently do not wander about, even during occasional warm intervals; and I have never seen a box turtle on the move in August, our most severe summer month. So, the box turtle's passive response to inclement weather is to close shop and wait for better times. For a creature that can tolerate the catalepsy, it is a survival tactic that can hardly fail.

Clumps of Texas prickly pear (*Opuntia engelmanii*) on the oyster-shell ridges host a variety of tenants. In late summer many pads are decked with cottony white patches around the bases of the spines. The tip of a knife blade picks apart the waxy fibers to reveal a colony of slow-moving scale insects. Juveniles and winged males are mere specks; the plump one-eighth-inch-long females look like glutted ticks. Disturbing the protective covering generally injures some of the females, leaving the white fibrils blotched red, like a blood-stained bandage. An inquisitive fingertip is tinted deep crimson. It must have taken the color-starved aborigines no time at all to discover they could brighten their textiles and rouge their skins with this dyestuff. They quickly learned to brush off the insects and dry them for later use.

Bags of this cochineal (*Dacylopius confusus*) were among the treasures shipped home by Spanish conquistadors when they sacked the Aztec empire. Spanish padres in the cactus-studded country around San Antonio convinced their neophytes that it was good for their souls to tediously tap the local cochineal resource to enliven decorations on the whitewashed walls of their missions. Texian colonists quickly added the dye to their repertoire of homespun crafts. British redcoats and Canadian Mounties owed the color of their tunics to cochineal. Until the development of coal-tar dyes in 1856, there were times when the demand made cochineal worth more than its weight in gold.

The waxy mantle secreted by the colony seals it in a protected microclimate and conceals it from predators, while the red pigment seems to make the insects distasteful, but not to all. At least two creatures eat cochineals. I have seen fat moth larvae squiggling among the scale insects, each one eliminating a string of crimson fecal pellets. This is one of the few predaceous lepidopteran larvae, the caterpillar of an undistinguished pyralid moth (*Laetilia coccidivora*). It favors unarmored scale insects of several species. Both adult and larval ladybird beetles (Coccinellidae) are also well-known predators on aphids, scale insects, and other small, soft delicacies. I have caught these little carnivores with bleeding cochineals in their jaws.

Some prickly pear pads bear blisterlike swellings. Fresh blisters have a glutinous plug of pale yellow green exudate produced by the cactus in an attempt to close a central pore in the wall of its bulging wound. A slice through a fresh vesicle reveals a fat caterpillar marked with rings of cream and chocolate, its metronomic feeding undeterred. All of the creature's body cavity not taken up by the gut is filled with a blue, multilobed hepatopancreas. In young caterpillars this is visible through the skin, for which it is named "blue cactus borer." Full-term

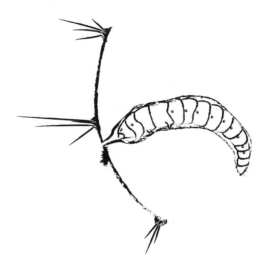

Blue borer

borers, an inch and a half long, drop from the pads, pupate in the soil, and emerge as gray brown pyralid moths (*Melitara junctolineella*) related to the moths whose larvae eat cochineals. After mating, the short-lived female moth sticks a row of flattened eggs along a cactus spine. Hatchlings descend to a pad and bore in.

When the caterpillar is done, the inner walls of the vesicle crust over, and the dry cavity with its convenient opening is occupied by somebody else: it may be crammed with an entire colony of red-and-black carpenter ants (*Camponotus rasilis*). Or a gentle nudge may cause a little ghost spider (*Aysha gracilis*) to erupt from a silken tube attached to the inner wall.

The waxy bloom of some cactus pads is embellished with pale scribbles, trails made by a little grub feeding on the layer of green parenchyma tissue just beneath the epidermis. This larva works with rhythmic, energy-efficient feeding movements characteristic of caterpillars, but all its parts are mashed flat. The dark jaws slide crosswise, like a pair of hedge shears, pruning the cactus tissue in a channel sized to fit the sideways sweep of the forepart of its body. Here is a true Flatlander, its every anatomical part and movement confined to a two-dimensional universe. It is the leaf-mining larva of yet another small, nondescript moth (*Marmara opuntiella*).

On this windswept island the tumbleweed habit seems inevitable. Fall witchgrass (*Leptoloma cognatum*), a common member of the upland sward, is inconspicuous until October and November when its brooms of purple seed heads shoot up and unfurl into thin, stiffly branched panicles nearly a foot tall, each fine branch holding a fuzzy seed. When the seed head is ripe, the plant cuts the sap and pinches a weak spot across its base. The panicles fade from purple to straw colored, and when the first norther blows, fall witchgrass is ready.

The sharp northeasterly gusts of late November lift the dehydrated, nearly weightless pinwheels, causing them to roll, bounce, and tumble across the grassland canopy, snapping the fragile branches and scattering their seeds far and wide. After a good blow the downwind sides of the sand dunes are matted deep in witchgrass chaff. More tattered panicles whip over the dunes and across the beach, joining the streamers of ghosting sand. The breakers gather them in, and high tide deposits a windrow of sodden whiskers.

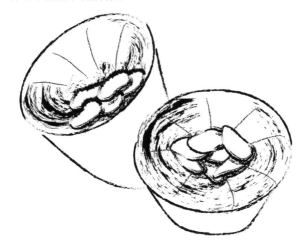

Splash cup

Even as the panicles of witchgrass run their race, the peridioles of splash cups (*Cyathus stercoreus*) take their one short dispersal leap. This intriguing fungus is found on wet sand enriched by nutrients from animal excrement. Fruiting cups appear in the fall, quarter-inch-high vases covered by a white membrane. Soon the membrane splits to reveal a nest of lead gray "eggs"—the peridioles. The pleated walls of a ripe goblet narrow toward the base, where the peridioles lie in a puddle of slippery mucilage, each one attached to the bottom of the vase by a thin cord coiled beneath the pile. A direct hit by a raindrop ejects the clutch of eggs with enough force to snap their cords. The missiles fly out, and their sticky cords snag the first solid object they encounter. There the peridioles dehydrate, split open, and release their packet of black dust. For every seed that witchgrass scatters, splash cup fires a thousand spores with the same purpose: to blanket the island with propagules and, by accepting horrendous loss, to exploit every spot favorable for germination.

How do you judge the number of speck-sized black beach beetles that swarm in the upper layer of sand on an expanse of undisturbed beach? They are too tiny, too secretive, too many to simply go out and count. So, we get kids to do the next best thing: they estimate their numbers by sampling.

First, we locate the beetle zone by finding their scribbles on the sand. Each team gets a plastic ring to delineate the boundary of a sample site. They pitch their ring into the beetle zone and go to work where it lands, using a hand trowel to excavate the area within the ring to a depth of two centimeters (the first joint of an index finger is a convenient gauge). They work the diggings through a sieve that lets the sand grains pass but holds back the beetles. Then, they count the scrambling little insects before they get off the mesh. This number goes on a tally sheet, the beetles are released, the hole filled in, and the team moves along to repeat the procedure several times. Finally, the numbers are fed into hand calculators to glean a population estimate.

So, how many black beach beetles are on the beach? An average of 1,150 per square meter in the scribble zone is a good estimate. It is astonishing to conceive of that many lives being lived out in tiny galleries gouged through the upper crust of this bleak microhabitat, nourished on nothing more than a green diatomaceous stain, with only luck and pluck to buffer themselves from the full force of the elements. On a mile of beach, the calculator claims there will be about 44 million beetles weighing thirty-six pounds. Thirty-six *pounds* of squirming black specks, and there are thirty-eight miles of beach on Matagorda Island!

We share living space on Matagorda Island with several species of ants, including southern fire ants (*Solenopsis xyloni*), the commonest of several kinds of native fire ants on the island. I do not believe that anyone or anything can tolerate the close company of these belligerent creatures. Their domain is the grassland, where they throw up irregular, flattened mounds of excavated soil over their nest. A quick kick across a mound will expose a seething mass of furious workers and hundreds of white grubs that had been comfortably toasting in the warmth of their upstairs chambers.

Southern fire ants are voracious and omnivorous in the wild. They seem to have scant taste for sweets but are eager for anything fatty. Now and then we discover a busy stream of southern fire ants hustling under the door to carry off toast or cracker crumbs, grains of cornmeal, and meat scraps. If the broom does not discourage them, we resort to a shot of insect spray.

We have a representative of the smallest of all ant species on the island. The workers are barely a millimeter long. We named them teeny-tinies. I have found teeny-tinies at the base of sea oats clumps in the sand dunes, where they seem to be in constant danger of sandblasting and wind tumbling. They seem more at home in litter beneath the grass canopy. Now and then a colony appears in the kitchen, thrives awhile, and then disappears. These ants are inherently cute, but they are so small that they can negotiate the threads of a closed jar lid. So, we have a running battle over who owns the sugar jar, and we get used to teeny-tinies in our coffee. They are either tasteless or too small to matter, so we drink them down.

Pharaoh ants (*Monomorium pharaonis*) are so easily transported around the world by humans that no one can determine their natural homeland more specifically than "the Old World." They are likely of tropical affinity; in the temperate zone they invariably live in human-made structures, making nuisances of themselves everywhere.

We occasionally have a rash of pharaohs on the kitchen counter, sometimes aligned in a neat ring quaffing from the margin of a sweet droplet, other times busy cleaning up a smear of jelly. Once I opened a collection box to find the wings clipped off all my pinned fly specimens. Pharaohs had made a nest in a seashell nearby, and the yellow workers, about half again as large as teeny-tinies, were easily slipping past the lid of the box, scaling the slick pins, entering the fly bodies through a hole where the wing had been. Then they scavenged the protein dust inside. I had to admire their tenacity.

Little black ants (*Monomorium minimum*) are related to pharaoh ants but are native Americans. A little larger than pharaohs but still small, on Matagorda Island they nest in upland soils, storm-heaved timbers, and dead mesquite branches. They are also among the most persistent and annoying invaders of dwellings, getting into the woodwork and forever after sending out bustling columns of foraging workers with a taste for almost anything.

Their numbers can be staggering. I once found a hustling trail of little blacks pouring from a door frame and running in a sinuous, unbroken stream to a garbage can seventy-five feet away (somewhat further via their wandering route). The ants were trotting three abreast, some heading for the can, and others returning with their booty of crumbs. I fed my calculator some numbers: one-sixteenth-inch long ants running three abreast end to end with virtually no space between individuals for seventy-five feet. I estimated over forty thousand little black ants! And those were just the workers in view at the time.

• • •

Halobates ("Hal-oh-bay-teez")! The only pelagic insects in the entire world, I never really expected to see one. Yet here they are, obviously disoriented but still kicking weakly among the fresh sargassum stranded on the beach.

Blown in from their limitless interface between air and sea; confused and perhaps perversely frightened by contact with solid substrate. Black, squinched-up bodies with raptorial front legs, ruddering hind legs and long, plumed middle legs suited for a lifetime of effortless rowing. Creatures of the surface film; completely waxed and water-proofed; so buoyant they seem levitated.

These unique bugs are homeless vagabonds, forever adrift on a boundless sea, eternally rocking, knowing nothing but wave, wind and sky. I cannot imagine an entire life expended "out there."

Rain! Rain for days, at times so torrential that even our island of sand cannot absorb it all. We had driven out an oyster-shell road to gaze in amazement at the nearly submerged grassland when we heard it—an explosive, agonized squall of abject despair repeated erratically from somewhere out there in the wet, answered now and then by similar anguished cries. We immediately looked at each other and lipped together as we strained to hear above the pounding rain: "anniversary toads."

Hurter's spadefoots (*Scaphiopus holbrooki hurteri*) are reclusive, largely subterranean amphibians that surface in numbers only during warm deluges. The piteous exclamations are the males' attempts to lure plump, ripe females to brief sexual orgy. These peculiar creatures ignore permanent ponds and await rains of the sort that would have puddled their arid ancestral Great Plains environment. Then they go into an erotic frenzy, spawning pollywogs that hasten through development before their ephemeral pools dry up. The creatures could afford to be more leisurely in this humid coastal zone, but their dryland genes refuse to take the risk and so drive them on.

In a day or two the exhausted adults will go back underground. Within two weeks the surviving tadpoles will have become toadlets, and they too will vanish. In a month the sand will absorb the puddles. Silence will reign. It will be as though spadefoots did not exist here.

Long ago we lay young together in our nuptial bed, anxious but hesitant to experience each other. It had rained hard. Outside our window a lusty chorus of anniversary toads was experiencing no inhibitions. They set the mood and gave us a fond aural memory to share for a lifetime.

Sifting through critters caught in sweeps of an insect net across the grass canopy, I found an intriguing little beetle huddled among the dregs. Only about 4 millimeters long, he is dumpy and covered with rounded bumps. Legs and head are neatly tucked into crevices precisely molded into his exoskeleton; even his pectinate antennae have their own furrows. The thin suture separating his elytrae is distinctively zig-zagged. The entire animal appears cast in copper and burnished with a purple sheen. What an absolutely exquisite, cryptic little creature! He was easy enough to track down—a warty leaf beetle (Chrysomelidae; *Neochlamisus* sp.). The books say these beetles avoid predation by mimicking caterpillar droppings. Beneath the microscope my specimen more resembles an exactingly graved medallion—a small fob for my eyes alone, a private token of a perfect day on Matagorda Island.

I put a postage stamp sized plug of blue-green algae under 20x magnification and see at least fifty pores riddling its surface, each with a pile of fecal pellets stacked nearby. With needles, I extract a thin red worm hardly an inch long from one of the holes. Isolated in a drop of water the beast constantly squirms and rhythmically gapes and swallows, as though determined to engulf its world. It is only by its gulping behaviour that I can readily tell which end is which and identify the creature as a capitellid thread worm (*Capitella capitata*).

I quiet its writhing with a drop of alcohol and rack up the magnification to see the tubular hearts still pulsing, sending burps of thin red blood on their vain course. Body wall muscles go into final tremors; the gulping movements begin to falter; short setae flick weakly from their sheaths. The intestine is yet wracked by peristaltic waves of contraction that push the queue of recently ingested food nodules rearward. I can read the assembly line digestive process by color: blue green fading smoothly into oil yellow and then to opaque brown— just the color of the fecal pellets. I am watching death creep through this worm.

• • •

How can one possibly describe an encounter with a dapple of fairy bells? They are so insubstantial they are best seen by watching their diaphanous shadows on the sand.

These are leptomedusae—little jellyfishes. Mine are *Blackfordia* sp. Each is a pulsing little bell half an inch across with a short veil of tentacles around its rim, four frilly ribbons fringing its mouth, and a thin white gonad lying athwart each of four radial canals that trace a thin cross beneath its clear pate. No head, no eyes, no front or back, no past or future, no substantial connection with the rest of their aqueous world; sprites casting fleeting shades as they wend their sylphidine way. Doubtless I profane them just by looking directly at them.

A stretch of backbeach claimed by a buzzing colony of sand wasps (*Bembix* sp.). Alert, fast-flying, hornetlike creatures. They zip over the beach faster than my eye can follow, then stop in an instant to hover over a small depression in the sand. I finally saw a wasp scratch a sand plug from her burrow and hastily drag something inside. A few minutes later she reappeared, and with a spate of furious terrier-like movements, she closed the entrance with sand and zoomed away.

Keeping my eye on the spot, I approached and excavated it with my pocketknife. The tunnel sloped down at an angle of forty degrees for seven inches until four inches below the surface, it swept up slightly and enlarged into a thimble-sized chamber. There, nestled in a dark, humid crypt, safe from predators and parasites, lay the wasp's horde of two horseflies, four soldier flies, and a sand wasp maggot. The maggot was busy nuzzling at the entrails of one of the horseflies; the remaining victims were alive but paralyzed, helplessly awaiting their turn to nourish the ravenous larva.

At least for the soldier flies (*Odontomyia cincta*), this was a case of beauty feeding the beast. Each was a luminous sea-foam green with a dark back furred with golden down, a flat abdomen crossed by black bars, and soft purple brown compound eyes. Although the sand wasp apparently had no trouble finding these green jewels, I have never seen one on the island outside these catacombs on the beach. I think the mercurial world of flies zips past leaving me groping unaware in its wake.

• • •

There is one fish that specializes in ravaging the subterranean community of creatures that wriggle-swims through the soupy sand where the waves backwash off the beach. Whip eels (*Bascanichthyes scuticaris*) are made to order for pursuit and assault in the innermost sanctums of this quasi-liquid domain. They are a sinuous, proverbially slippery rod a foot or so long. The pointed snout sports a pair of snorklelike nostrils and overhangs a mouth with a large gape and jaws armed with wicked teeth. Although they can slide forward with ease, whip eels are adept at darting backward, parting the sand purée with a cartilage-tipped tail tapered like a letter opener. I suspect that a succulent surf crab with a whip eel on its back trail is doomed.

A low tide on a warm summer night is the time to look for whip eels at the waterline. A flashlight held at a low angle now and then reveals a pencil-sized pit from which protrudes a sharp snout. If I can get to my knees without bumping, I can peer right into the face of a whip eel. It is always peering right back at me with surprisingly bright, ice blue eyes. Its mouth gapes rhythmically as it gulps water, and twin geysers of sand spew up beside its head as the water is expelled from the far end of the gill pouches. That's it. The eel regards me as long as I regard it, the curious and the curiouser, an alien encounter of the charming kind.

We have this day entered the ranks of the privileged few: we have found a living chiton! We were turning dead oyster shells in the bay searching for polychaete worms when suddenly there it was, clamped tightly to the underside of a shell, only half an inch long, with its distinctive armor of eight overlapping plates; unmoving, unassuming, and totally unexpected. Not the sort of creature to generate much excitement unless you have recorded its presence in college notebooks, looked long at its picture, read of its passive lifestyle, know of its ancient lineage, and long since consigned it to myth rather than reality. No matter that the animals are larger, more colorful, and more abundant in other seas. This one (*Ischnochiton papillosus*) exceeded them all because, by dumb luck, it was revealed exclusively to us with all its polyplacophoran mystique. Martha held the favored clump of oyster shell to the sun, and I snapped half a roll of photographs through the

Chiton

macro lens. We nudged our prize with a fingernail, but it only stiffened and did not budge. So we returned it to its sanctuary in the reef, one more pleasant revelation shared.

My trove of barn owl regurgitation pellets is no more. Over the weeks it has engaged in a silent, slow-motion explosion, and now the bits of shrapnel are hanging from the underside of the shelf above. Each of the shards is a tube half an inch long by one-eighth inch in diameter, closed at the upper end where it is attached to the shelf and open at the free-hanging end. The interior of each retreat is lined with silk, while the outer layers are a coarser weave heavily invested with hair, feathers, and snippets of bone purloined from my owl pellets. A strip of straw-colored parchment protrudes from the open end of each tube where a newly metamorphosed adult escaped its puparium.

What has happened here? Carpet moths (*Trichophaga tapetzella*) laid their eggs in my hoard of owl pellets. Their little white grubs thrived on the offal rejected by the barn owl's proficient gut. Each larva spun a protective case that it dragged around and later firmed into a tough cocoon by adding external debris. Finally, the full-term caterpillar affixed its domicile to the underside of the shelf. After hanging head down for two weeks while it worked its developmental magic, the transfigured creature struggled free, like Houdini working his way out of a straitjacket while suspended upside down by his ankles. Finally, it spread its wings and fluttered away, an inconsequential little being destined to expend its short life span never tasting food, scarcely resting, driven to find a mate to ensure that egg specks would be deposited on some bit of refuse to carry on the unobtrusive tradition.

Springtime is the best season to find ram's horns, fragile milky white tubes a quarter inch in diameter spiraled into a flat, inch-wide coil that merits its common epithet (and its Latin name), *Spirula spirula*. I can see that the end of the outer whorl is closed by an opalescent concave partition. Through the translucent walls, I see the edges of a series of such septa dividing the entire tube into chambers. The binocular microscope reveals that there is a thin canal traversing the length of the tube by passing from chamber to chamber through a pore in each septum. Although the outer wall of the coil appears quite smooth to the eye, the microscope shows an intricate pattern of minute, interlocking wrinkles that resemble the jigsaw-puzzle arrangement of sutures on an ammonite shell—an extinct Cretaceous ancestor of ram's horns.

But for books, these coils would remain a mystery to me. They are the internal shells of small deep-sea squid. The narrow canal conducts

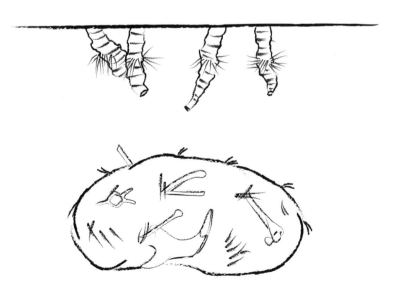

Carpet moth pupal cases

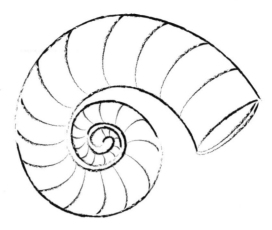

Ram's horn

gas secreted by the animal to maintain neutral buoyancy in the abyss. When the creature dies and decomposes, its calcareous air tank bobs to the surface, and the waves deposit it on the beach. There I find it, a fragile denizen of the deep come to final rest in the upper world.

The clean edge caught my eye and, once perceived, led to the entire smooth contour. A brace of perfectly symmetrical ovals master-crafted of eggshell porcelain and fired with a glaze of sun flecks, cast in a spare saucer scooped in a barren ridge of shell, starkly exposed to every manner of ill fortune. They lie invisible, shadowless, motionless, alone, pathetically vulnerable, each filled with hope and both likely foredoomed. So very many things can go wrong. How do least terns ever overcome the odds?

We have found that the strands of spent, parchmentlike egg cases of whelks are much favored as retreats by a variety of small marine fauna, which enter through the eighth-inch exit hole used by the emerged snailets. Some of the critters are inherently tiny; others are juveniles trying to get a start in a risky life. I wonder how many enter the pore as larvae, wax fat, and transform and then find they cannot escape through the small portal. Entire little assemblages must perish when their capsule is heaved onto the beach to parch and dehydrate.

Scale worms (*Lepidonotus sublevis*), young ones scarcely a quarter-inch long but with all the adult traits, including twelve pairs of flattened, papilla-fringed oval plates that cover the back. Because the worms prefer to live in tight crannies, the plates probably protect their gills; when annoyed with a pin, the creatures roll into a tight ball, their vitals protected by the shield of plates. As these worms are carnivores equipped with a grappling proboscis, I suppose they wreak havoc among the other creatures that share the confines of the capsule. Later I found inch-long adults in all sorts of nooks: among oysters on reefs and goose-necked barnacles on floating debris and inside snail shells occupied by hermit crabs.

Burrowing brittle stars (*Ophiophragmus moorei*), miniatures of the adults that we commonly unearth from the sand ridges in the surf. Their five bristly arms engage in the same slinky, flat contortions that characterize their kind everywhere. And a mere touch with my forceps causes them to throw off one or more appendages. Not to worry. The fabled echinoderm powers of regeneration from scant snippets will remedy the seeming tragedy in short order.

Sea pill bugs (*Sphaeroma quadridentata* and *Ancinus depressus*), squatty, flattened little crustaceans that resemble military tanks. These are all so tiny that they must be fresh from their mothers' brood pouches. Both kinds readily roll into a ball when threatened. The latter species maintains its defensive posture by snapping a protuberance on its head into a groove beneath its abdomen and erecting a pair of sharp spines.

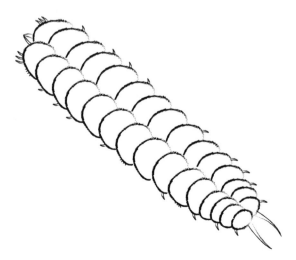

Scale worm

Crabs, all babies: gulf crabs (*Callinectes similis*), blue crabs (*C. sapidus*), speckled crabs (*Arenaeus cribrarius*), stone crabs (*Menippe adina*), and warty-backed little spider crabs (*Libinia* sp.) so ugly that they are cute. And smaller than any of the foregoing, adult pea crabs (*Pinnixa chacei*).

Acorn barnacles (*Balanus* sp.). Having arrived as spidery, scrambling nauplii and transformed into tiny white sessile prickles, they have made a poor choice for lifelong attachment. When the egg capsule deteriorates, they will be undone. But they do their thing, unfazed by premonition.

Long-eyed shrimp (*Ogyrides limicola*), peculiar little creatures with eyes on long slender stalks, antennae pepperminty with pink bands, legs flecked with clusters of red and greenish yellow chromatophores and bodies so clear as to reveal every internal organ, including the rapidly pulsating heart.

A passel of little bivalves. I can be certain only of blood arks (*Anadara ovalis*) covered in a hairy periostracum and coquinas (*Donax variabilis*) splashed with multihued pastels.

Several snails, the only one in numbers being fat doves (*Anachis obesa*), with plump fusiform shells scarcely a quarter-inch long, decorated with low spiral ridges and a beaded reticulum.

A flotilla of tiny boats blew ashore during the night, and this morning the beach is littered with its wrack! Each craft is a poker chip-sized wafer set with an erect diagonal sail and rimmed with a circlet of sky-blue tentacles. Crashed ashore, the vessels collapse into a flabby mess, their tackle thrown into disarray; but those still adrift ride the surface like the seamasters they are. They have a pretty name to match their trim lines—by-the-wind-sailors (*Velella velella*). The tragedy will be reduced to stacks of whitish, styrofoam-like hulls tomorrow.

No matter the horrendous attrition this day; somewhere out there in the vast pelagic there are other fleets of dauntless little frigates expertly trimming their sails in unison before the sea wind as they ply their abstruse maritime trade. They have no need for lodestone or star beam, for they chart their bearing by an inner urge honed to perfection by the ages. They routinely embark on voyages that by comparison would shame the boldest ventures of Phoenicians or Polynesians. These are seafaring folk through and through, not so much borne of the sea as never really disassociating from it, for each vessel is nothing more than a temporary and lightly congealed aliquot of azure sea water. Ravaged by ocean sunfish, engulfed by leatherback sea turtles, assaulted by purple storm snails, ripped asunder by sea slugs, tossed by combers, driven by tempests, unreckoned by the nonoceanic world— the brave little squadrons sail on.

One afternoon in late April I happened upon a coyote den dug into the west side of a well-vegetated sand dune, and there was a pup sound asleep in the sun at the entrance! I got a photo, but the click of the shutter roused the little creature, and it backed out of sight. I waited a bit, then squeaked through pursed lips and was almost immediately rewarded by the appearance of three pups' heads in the mouth of the burrow. What appealing little animals, with alert blue eyes, floppy ears, fat bellies, and unsteady legs. They turned their heads quizzically at the repeated snaps of my shutter and then all faded back into the dark interior.

Two hours later Martha and I were back at the den. It looked deserted, and I feared an alarmed Mom had hauled her offspring to an alternate dig. However, when I squeaked, all three pups came bounding out of the burrow. Two soon went back, but the third little fellow came right toward us. I am sure he thought Mom had returned, ready to regurgitate a meal. The pup waddled right between our legs, and we could not resist picking him up and petting him. He nuzzled us and licked our hands, his thin tail wagging, like any joyous and loving puppy: pudgy, velvety, wet nosed, clean smelling, innocent, trusting.

If we ever wanted a pet coyote, this was the time and place, but we refrained. Better enjoy the moment, keep the memory.

Sitting on a bench on the boardwalk this afternoon, watching oysters spit and listening to pistol shrimp snap. Everyday events, inscrutable creatures. There is no way I can view the universe from their dim submarine perspective, but it is challenging to poke around the edges, to give them anthropomorphic motives to satisfy my own desire for sense of direction, even though these humble creatures are doubtless quite content to do their thing simply because that is what they do.

Oyster

Why *does* an oyster spit? To rid itself of pseudofeces—the inedible particles that come in on the feeding current. After being sifted by fine hairs lining special grooves on the gills and sorted by banks of sensitive fibrils on the liplike palps, the inorganic sludge is wrapped in a pellet of slime and diverted away from the oyster's mouth. It slides on ciliary currents to the margin of the shell, and there, in a precisely synchronized effort, the gill hairs swish, the mantle puckers, the adductor muscle twitches, and the packet of offal is burped out. An impressive show of coordination for a creature with neither brain nor cord. In animals at the upper edge of a reef, this ballistic expulsion breaks the surface, creating a fleeting fountain and a soft splash. So I sit here, half awake in the muggy heat, trying to catch the next geyser in the act and musing over which of us—the oyster or I—is engaged in more lofty purpose.

Why does a pistol shrimp (*Alpheus heterochaelis*) snap? The books say that it sends out a short-range shock wave, a concussion that stuns prey and deters predators. I don't doubt it, but I think there must be something more. As I sit here idly watching for oyster spittle, I hear a continual patter of underwater popcornlike reports across the reef. One discharge usually elicits a series of bursts from the same vicinity, as if the shrimp were hallooing each other. I think they are doing just that—keeping in touch, reinforcing boundaries, establishing status, identifying gender, passing along alarm or signaling all's well, binding their separate retreats in the reef into an intimate aural commune via their palpitating grapevine.

How does a shrimp fire its pistol? First, its handgun is a specially modified and enlarged pincer. The immovable claw has a deep socket precisely bored to receive a peg on the movable claw when the pincer is closed. To cock its gun, the animal opens the pincer wide. Then—much too quick for the eye to follow—the pincer snaps shut, and the peg plunges into the socket, displacing a jet of water. Enter Daniel Bernoulli, an eighteenth-century Swiss physicist who proclaimed that the faster the moving stream of a fluid, the lower the pressure within that fluid. The shrimp's water jet is so fast that its pressure drops enough for bubbles to form inside the water stream (literally, the water begins to boil!). With the peg fully seated, the jet stream abruptly slows, the pressure quickly rises, and the bubbles implode, producing the distinctive detonation.

Down to the pier on a rare, still night. The bay was a silent, black mirror, only the occasional flare of a comb jelly marking its third dimension. The humid air was so heavy we had to push forcibly through it, moving in slow motion, breathing with difficulty. A fit night for a happening. And then we heard it. A low, penetrating, musical twang, like a banjo string thrummed and damped. Haunting! Eerie! At first it seemed distant, perhaps from a barge on the Intracoastal Canal away across the bay. But no. It was nearby, beneath us, underwater!

We discovered that by putting an ear against the top of a piling, we could hear the sound much better, and so we located half a dozen sources along the pier. After a silent interlude, one minstrel might pluck his instrument regularly once every twenty seconds or so for a couple of minutes, and his euphony stimulated strumming up and down the pier.

What sort of cabalistic concert of trolls had we stumbled upon? Much of the rapture of that night and the poignant memory of it is that we did not immediately resolve the mystery. We went to bed talking and signifying, accounting and recounting, proposing and counterposing, and finally drifting off utterly captivated by the spell of this barrier island.

Toadfish (*Opsanus beta*) are bottom-living fish, flabby, big headed, evil eyed, prickly finned, ugly. They are grouchy creatures that open huge mouths wide to snap at unwary fingers and emit guttural croaks when they are brought to the surface. Although local fishermen proclaim ignorance of its musical ability, I eventually learned that on the

Chesapeake Bay, watermen know of the boatwhistle fish (*O. tau*), a close relative.

During April and May, male toadfish spruce up their mucky retreats and emit their evocative strains as they attempt to entice a ripe female in to spawn. The instrument is their swim bladder. This gas-filled buoyancy chamber makes a resonator for a clump of special muscles that vibrate against its walls at two hundred times per second, fast enough to produce the peculiar harmonic that not only draws in a female but at least once also enthralled a naive pair of terrestrial barrier island residents.

If I had not been looking closely, I would never have noticed the mesquite twig with the oddly swollen tip and perceived that the thumbsized blob was not the bird plop it resembled but a fat spider with its legs tucked beneath its lumpy abdomen. I had to poke the impassive creature several times before it finally came to life just enough to drop on a drag line into the open container that I held ready for it. Even as I snapped the lid in place, I felt that inner thrill that all naturalists get at the suspicion of something special, something heretofore known only vicariously, something so rare and wonderful that they were resigned to accept it on faith for they could never aspire to have a firsthand encounter. Could it be? Could it *really* be? Here on a barrier island, of all places? I headed directly back to the house and the books.

It was for sure—an adult female bolas spider (*Mastophora cornigera*)! If not actually rare, the species is rarely encountered because of its cryptic nature. Its habitat is reported to be lofty forest, not wind-pruned chaparral, but there was no doubt about my specimen.

Rather than spin a web to snare prey, this enterprising arachnid rouses at night to dangle a viscid droplet from a short strand of silk held by the tip of one front leg. Detecting air currents from fluttering wings of a flying insect, the spider raises its throwing arm. When the prey comes within its two-inch range, the bolas spider adeptly flicks its leg forward to fling out the strand with its tacky blob, thus earning its name. If the spider's aim is true, the ball smears out and sticks to the prey, which begins to sputter and twirl at the end of the tether. The spider drops down on a line to its catch, paralyzes it with a venomous bite, trusses the weakly struggling carcass in a silken sheet, and proceeds to suck its juices.

This may not be all of the bolas spider's wiles. Recently, a South American relative was found to release a chemical akin to that emitted by certain female noctuid moths to attract male suitors. The spider was apparently using the ruse to lure amorous male moths in for the kill. Fall armyworm moths were the favored prey, and this is a very abundant moth locally. So, who knows what intriguing ambushes get set and sprung in the dark among the mesquites on Matagorda Island?

In August, cabbagehead jellyfish (*Stomalophus meleagris*) appear in great spectral squadrons in the bays and in the Gulf. Ghostly luminous in the dark waters, they pump silently, rhythmically, obstinately. Pale as death yet vigorously alive, wending their eerie and enigmatic way, primordial beings doing their primordial thing in a primordial realm, disjunct from all the rest.

Worn out by summer, cabbageheads begin to strand in piles on the bay shores and in great windrows along the beach. Their smooth pates are pummeled, plundered, pecked, and plucked. Sometimes their corrugated cores last the day, rolling forlornly up and down the beach in the swash. Many carcasses heaved beyond reach of the waves seem to simply sublimate rather than decompose, leaving behind an ephemeral, odorless, slickened imprint in the sand. They are gone then, as though they never were, until next year.

Always the cabbageheads return—from where?—and no one but me regards it as a miracle. Cabbageheads come from "out there," and it takes familiarity with the peculiar scyphozoan life cycle to imagine

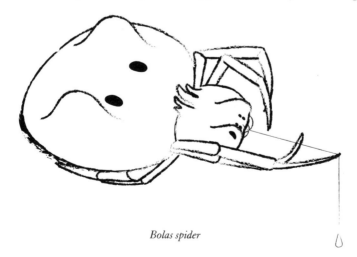

Bolas spider

how. Sperm ejected by a male are incidentally taken in along with planktonic food by a female, and these are diverted to fertilize ripe eggs waiting in her body cavity. She then casually spews out her impregnated brood, most of which stick to her own tacky underside. With this unimpassioned beginning, cell division surges, and immediately microscopic ciliated blobs of protoplasm called planulae squirm away, each with no more than an infinitesimal chance of fulfilling its destiny.

Even as the parental population is dying, a small fraction of their offspring beats the odds and settles down somewhere on something hard. A seated planula transforms into a scyphistoma, a stalked cup with tentacles around its rim. So the cryptic, vaselike creatures pass the submarine winter. Come spring, each scyphistoma develops a series of creases that constrict into close-set annuli until the segments resemble a stack of upside-down saucers. Finally, the terminal disc pops free to become an independent ephyra, a tiny pinwheel complete with central mouth, pulsing habit, and cnidarian determination. Others follow sequentially. A given scyphistoma may live for several years, pumping out hundreds of aspiring ephyrae each spring.

Those ephyrae that survive the gauntlet begin to ball up into spheres and to inflate rapidly on planktonic fare. By June they appear along the beach and motor around in bay inlets, some hardly as large as marbles, others already golf ball–sized, all as cute as can be. Some will balloon into cabbage-sized medusae, and a few of these will, in their turn, produce sperm and eggs to keep the cycle turning and the miracle recurring.

Diamondback, or just rattler (formally, western diamondback rattlesnake, *Crotalus atrox*). From the human point of view at least, no other creature has so impressed itself upon this island or indeed upon this state. You do not do anything here outdoors without unconsciously "watching out," especially in April (the month of arousal) and on summer nights (foraging time). But even during cold spells you never quite let your guard down. A cooled-down diamondback coiled in the winter sun is an invitation to a close encounter of the worst kind. See a rattler, even a dead one, and you walk gingerly for the rest of the day. Hear one and your skin prickles. The buzz of a cicada or the movement of a wind-blown turkey feather in the grass is enough to bring on a full startle.

The horned lizard (*Phrynosoma cornutum*) is the designated state reptile of Texas, and it is hard to argue against such a charming and unique mascot, but I think the western diamondback more closely matches the mythic proportions that macho Texans are so proud of. Perhaps we should have both: the horned lizard the state lizard, the rattler the state snake.

Respect. Rattlers deserve not just our healthy respect generated by fear of being bitten but merit genuine esteem for their unflinching, fierce dignity. Given a chance, most rattlesnakes that I have encountered beat a hasty retreat; but even when they dodge for cover, I have never seen one "run scared." They are not that kind of critter. On this refuge, at least, I am honored to give them their due.

MARCH '97: *Observing tufts of cochineal on prickly pears on an oyster-shell ridge when I became aware that what I had taken for a mesquite limb on the ground nearby was in fact an enormous diamondback. It was stretched out straight, head slightly raised, motionless, no buzzing rattles, not even a tongue flick. It was looking right at me. I backed up and moved on. Passed the same spot five minutes later, watching carefully. It was gone, as though it had never been. My nerves continued to register the diamondback's magnificent presence for the rest of the morning.*

MAY '97: *From the boardwalk I noticed a large rattler moving through the thin vegetation below. He was moving slowly, effortlessly, in a nearly straight line; head up, pausing occasionally to peer alertly from side to side, black tongue flicking repeatedly. He glided out of the fringe of glasswort onto an expanse of bare oyster shell to the edge of an inlet where he paused, and I could see the water ripples when his tongue tipped the surface. He confidently set off then, swimming with strong lateral undulations, his thick body riding high in the water. He held his head and neck up, but his string of rattles was submerged, thus dispelling myth to the contrary. The snake easily gained the far shore some fifty feet distant and melded into the gloom beneath the bank of cordgrass.*

NOVEMBER '97: *A large rattler dead on the road. Run over. It had a prominent bulge amidships, so I slit it open with my pocketknife. Two cotton rats and a mourning dove, the hair and feathers already dissolving.*

APRIL '99: *Walking beside the Environmental Center early this morning when, in a crack in the siding at ground level, one coil of a large diamondback looped into view. I clamped the coil in a mechanical snake catcher, but the snake felt so limp and compliant I thought he was dead. When I dragged him out, it was obvious that he was not only quite alive but very much preoccupied. As his tail cleared the crack, I saw that it was firmly attached to the tail of a second large snake. The two were vent to vent, caught in the act; and before I realized it, my interference caused them to uncouple, thus briefly exposing the male's finger-long, prickly, opalescent hemipenis before he retracted it. I set the male aside and pulled the female out. She, too, was uncommonly passive. I left both snakes there in the grass, and a short time later they had disappeared, probably back beneath the building, perhaps to return to business.*

MAY '99: *Twice this month near sunset we have halted our bikes to let a large diamondback have the right of way on the road near the water tank. I am almost certain this is the female snake that I found copulating at the Center in April. Something about her tone of brown and smudged diamonds.*

JUNE '99: *Saw "our" rattler crossing at her accustomed spot this evening. She never rattles—just freezes when we approach, then slides on across. Definitely no pet, but we have come to regard her as an acquaintance.*

JULY '99: *Too bad! Found our rattlesnake dead beside the road at her usual spot beside the water tank. Apparently she had just started to cross when a vehicle ran right over her head. No one's fault, I suppose, but a tragedy nonetheless. She was so corpulent that I decided to open her up. Inside were thirteen large eggs, each containing an early embryo. Glad at least to see that she was impregnated despite my bumbling intrusion back in April.*

CHAPTER 10

LAND

Tired old mesquite tree
back bent, arms stretching downwind
Sea breeze unflagging.

I CANNOT WANDER this barrier without wondering who has roamed this strip of land before me and why. What aspirations brought people here, and what desperations sent them packing? When? How much planning? How many plans gone awry? How much happenstance? How much is worth knowing? I have pieced together what I can.

Here is a thumbnail overview of the seven sovereigns of this land. It includes the aborigines plus an annotated history book list of the "six flags over Texas." The Indians waved no banner, so their dominion overlaps that of interlopers.

ca. 8000 B.C.–A.D. 1800	Karankawa Indians
1519–1685	Spain
1685–1690	France
1690–1821	Spain
1746	Province, Nuevo Santander

1821–1836	Mexico
1824	State, Coahuila and Texas
1836–1845	Republic of Texas
1838	Refugio County
1840	Victoria County
1845–1861	State, USA
1846	Calhoun County
1862–1865	State, Confederate States of America
1865–present	State, USA

Aboriginal Inhabitants (ca. 8000 B.C.–A.D. 1800)

We do not know when the first paleohunters arrived on the local Gulf Coast or where they came from. No matter; they surely antedated Matagorda Island. The Indians were living along the mainland shore in 3000 B.C. and were already possessed of a well-tuned littoral hunting-and-scrounging Karankawan culture when the rising sea began to pile a shoal of sand just offshore. Doubtless, even as the new barrier was forming, the neat pattern of its fresh sand ripples was disarranged by questing trails of bare human footprints.

The emerging island was merely an unquestioned extension of a communal roaming ground; a place to pole a pirogue in the wintertime when the mosquitoes were down, the oysters were fat, redfish by the thousands were tailing in the marsh, and waterfowl blackened the sky; a supplement to the more consistently inhabited river bottoms and moist prairie on the mainland; communally "yours," if you bore the charcoal-packed facial welts and blood ties of the Cujanes band.

Why go across the bay to the spit of sand? Adventure. Exploitation. Why else? Feather-bedecked noble Indians filled with reverent awe of Nature? Hardly. Just ever-hungry and nearly naked people trying to make the day. That is the way it was, and it must have seemed the way it would always be.

Just as they registered no formal claim on their land, the Karankawas probably had no cognizance of losing it. Incomprehensible aliens arrived. (I wonder how truly unexpected the first Europeans were, whether their occasional flotsam had not already alerted the Indians that there were strangers across the sea.) Cultural differences fanned into quarrels and killings. Clans split up; old ways dissolved; strange, lethal diseases raged; spirits sagged. By 1750 the Indians were hiding out, sniping and thieving and coming into the missions occasionally to endure unintelligible catechism in exchange for more meaningful handouts. Their social fabric was already irrevocably rent; they were no longer lords of their homeground. I have given them until 1800, but by that time their only claim was their degenerate presence. By 1852 the last of them gave that up.

Exploration and Early Settlement (1519–1828)

This island was indisputably Karankawa country when Alonso Álvarez de Pineda sailed past in the summer of 1519 and imperiously claimed what he saw in the name of King Charles I of Spain. In 1528 Cabeza de Vaca strengthened Spain's right of possession but reaffirmed by his tenure as a slave that the Indians were still very much in control.

Thinking he was hard on the mouth of the Mississippi River, René Robert Cavelier, Sieur de La Salle, fatefully sailed into Matagorda Bay in February 1685. Although he eventually realized that he was off course, the indomitable explorer nevertheless proclaimed for King Louis IV the barren island on which he camped and the adjacent mainland, where he eventually established a ragged settlement, as well as the interior, in which he was soon to be murdered by his own men. As they did with the Spanish, the Karankawas soon showed the French who actually reigned in this inhospitable coastal strip.

Internal strife, the Indians, and the elements had finished off the French colony by the time anxious Spanish soldiers arrived from Mexico to reaffirm their long-neglected title to the coastal country. This time, presence and persistence paid off: soldiers, priests (the latter the more potent force by far), charity, chicanery, bribery, pathogens, technology, and unrelenting disassembly of aboriginal customs and beliefs finally reduced the once-proud Karankawas to chattel. At last, Matagorda Island was indubitably Spanish, even if all the Spaniards were on the adjacent mainland.

In the early decades of the eighteenth century, the invigorated landlords began to explore and exploit their domain. A tenuous nucleus of civilization attended the Zacatecan mission established to convert the Karankawas on Garcitas Creek, about thirty-five miles north of the island. In 1746 Don José de Escandón was commissioned to settle the coastal country from deep in Mexico as far north as the Guadalupe and

San Antonio Rivers, and the old campaigner proved good at getting the job done. Although most of Escandón's land grants were issued south of the Nueces River, people began to filter north on their own into the upper Coastal Bend. So did their livestock. Released or escaped onto the virgin prairie, the animals proliferated and transformed: horses turned mustang, cattle turned longhorn, and hogs turned ugly.

Meanwhile, people of Mexican descent were infiltrating the land. Some, the *paisanos* (people of the land), tried scratch-stick farming; most ranched; yet others simply lived off the land. Like the Karankawas, they hunted, fished, and foraged. In so doing, they learned the coastline and its biota, gave names to landmarks, felt out passageways between oyster reefs and around mud flats, poked up the river deltas. Although they did not settle there, they surely hunted and fished their way along Matagorda Island; crude vintage maps reveal as much. But the people were few, and their accoutrements were impotent. So, as it had done with the Indians, the island merely shrugged them off.

Preoccupied with problems at home and abroad, Spain was forced to relinquish its troubled territories, and an independent Mexico took over in 1821. On Matagorda Island, nothing much changed at first. But by the 1820s Anglo-Americans were moving out of the forests of East Texas onto the coastal prairie, and they would not be ignored. These were people of vision—personal vision—and their every aspiration was founded on individual title to land. As it so happened, the first individual owner of Matagorda Island was not one of these. He came by sea; but he was cut from the same ambitious mold and was more capable than most.

Unsettled Years (1828–1880)

James Power was a transplanted Irishman who did well in the mercantile business in New Orleans and then moved south to Saltillo to see what investments presented themselves in the new Republic of Mexico. There he met fellow countryman James Hewetson, and the two were soon scheming together. Under the Mexican land grant system—modeled on Spanish colonization laws—Power and Hewetson were commissioned in 1828 to bring in and settle one hundred upstanding Irish Catholic colonists and an equal number of Mexican settlers along a sixty-mile stretch of Texas coastline lying between the Guadalupe and Nueces Rivers. For such service Power and Hewetson would receive liberal personal grants of land, but the enterprising pair did not stop there. Out of pocket they bought twenty-two leagues within their allotment for themselves.[1] These came on generous terms directly from the Mexican government, and they could be sold on less accommodating terms for a handsome profit. Thus, the two gained title to the entire local shoreline with all its potential ports and townsites, plus the offshore barriers—Mustang, Saint Joseph, and Matagorda Islands. Old-country chauvinists, perhaps; shrewd entrepreneurs, for sure.

So, James Power and James Hewetson acquired Matagorda Island. Throughout their partnership, Hewetson would remain a silent partner in Saltillo, while Power made his home on Live Oak Point at the entrance to Copano Bay, smack in the center of the Coastal Bend. We can regard James Power, as he himself did, the man to follow.

Power's trail was one of success, prestige, influence, adventure, two wives, seven children, some peace, much frustration, and final disillusionment. He brought in the earliest Irish colonists, fought Comanches, signed the Texas Declaration of Independence, battled Urrea, lived through the Republic and into early statehood. James Power touched many lives and opened and closed a lot of deals in the Coastal Bend in his time, including the founding of the port town of Saluria on the north tip of Matagorda Island in 1847. But he was dogged by adverse litigation for having personally purchased his land titles from the State of Coahuila and Texas without following all of the convoluted legal curlicues. Land speculators noticed the oversight, and they hired lawyers to make the point. In the end Power's titles were voided. He lost Live Oak Point, the homeplace, and all the rest, including Matagorda Island. In 1852, worn out at the age of sixty-three, James Power responded by dying.

Power's land reverted to public domain at a time when first the Republic and then the new state were looking desperately for vacant lands to validate the great quantity of land scrip and head rights shuffling through the hands of veterans, immigrants, deserving residents, and a large contingent of conniving usurpers. All Mexican land grants were thrown under suspicion, and fresh boundary surveys were called for. The Civil War brought more chaos and added another category of veteran to the long queue at the land-certificate window. Speculators bought up land certificates by the fistful. Contradictory ownership titles were issued, inadvertently or otherwise. Some deeds were forged, while many were burdened with concealed or unanticipated encum-

brances. For four decades (1840–80), surveyors, attorneys, bankers, and
a huge array of shysters enjoyed an open season in Texas real estate.

Despite its remove, property rights on Matagorda Island were not
spared the fluster of the latter nineteenth century, so much so that I
shall here narrow my focus to the ownership of the one square mile
(640 acres) surrounding our current FWS headquarters on the south
end of the island.

In the confused decades following the attainment of statehood,
William Little was a pettifogging lawyer who specialized in locating
and claiming vacant lands along the Texas coast. For a time he worked
for the law firm of Bryan and Hall in Galveston. When William Bryan
died, Edward Hall settled up with Little by transferring a load of fi-
nagled land certificates to his name. In 1851 William Little had thirty
surveys conducted on the south end of Matagorda Island, including
Survey #6, which encompassed the current USFWS headquarters site.
Little eventually laid claim to thousands of acres of land on the barrier
islands and adjacent mainland, much of which he forfeited to delin-
quent taxes.

Although William Little and his nephew John lived and ranched on
both St. Joseph and Matagorda Islands just after the Civil War, and
William continued to dabble in local real estate into the 1880s, there is
no indication that either of them ever fenced, developed, or lived on the
640 acres in Survey #6. William did finally receive his patent for the
tract on November 14, 1882.[2] Then in 1883, he sold all his holdings on
Matagorda to John.

As the original grantor under current state land law, William Little
was responsible for bringing this previously nondescript stretch of barrier grassland into the archives and onto the tax rolls of the State of
Texas; and he became the first in an unbroken chain of individuals or
corporations who would enjoy fee simple estate in this particular par-
cel of land: the guaranteed right to absolute dominion thereon over
everything on the surface and to the center of the earth (for there were
no separate mineral rights in those days) and to the heavens above (nor
air space restrictions), along with the unqualified prerogative to be-
queath all or part of his property to whomsoever he pleased. His was
the highest estate in land a person could hold, a near-sacred covenant,
but one rendered plebeian by its ease of acquisition, attended by no
stewardship responsibilities whatsoever. The American way: all take,
no give.

Survey #6 of 640 acres of land for William Little situated on Matagorda Island in the County of Calhoun District of Victoria about 29 miles S.W. from the Pilot House it being the quantity of land to which he is entitled by virtue of Land Scrip #8 dated at Columbia Dec 10th 1836 issued to William Bryan and by him transferred to said Little[3]

Beginning on the shore of Espiritu Santo Bay and at the north corner of Survey #4 made for said Little a stake from which a mesquit [*sic*] tree 6 inches in dia marked "x" bears N5°E 156 varas and 3 palmettos bears N15°15°W[4]

Thence N55°E 1359 varas to stake in a salt pond from which 3 palmettos bears S81°45°W[5] and the southernmost of 5 palmettos bears N15°15°W

Thence S35°E 2593 varas to the Gulf shore a post

Thence with the Gulf shore S49°30°W 1366 varas to the east corner of survey #5 a post

Thence N35°W with the N.E. boundary of surveys #5&4 2723 varas to the place of beginning

Surveyed June 10th 1851

[Signed] Francisco Escobar & Ignacio Cuellas, Chairmen

[Signed] Edward Linn District Surveyor Victoria District

Recorded Dec 22nd 1851

So there it is, Survey #6, the location and boundaries of a plot of virgin barrier island, stretching from bayside to gulfside; a designated place of beginning and a boundary line succinctly laid out in four calls; a square mile squinched into a rectangle three-quarters of a mile long and about a mile and a third wide; the elegant penmanship supplemented with a tiny scale drawing, cleanly inked in the upper left corner of page 311 of Book K in the Surveyors Records in the Victoria County courthouse. With an original grantor about to patent his claim, for better or for worse, the site was no longer on its own.

Then, from out of nowhere appears one Henry Lewis, who stays on the scene only long enough to sell two leagues (sitios) of former Power and Hewetson land—the lower nine miles of Matagorda Island, including the future headquarters site. Apparently William Little had neglected to pay the annual $27.26 tax bill due on his more than 11,000-acre hodgepodge of land parcels on the south end of the island, and Lewis probably bought up the entire tract at a sheriff's sale. So, our square mile goes from one absentee speculator to another. However, in June 1877, when Henry Lewis sold the two leagues to John McOscary

Brundrett for thirty-seven hundred dollars (seventeen hundred dollars cash in hand plus promissory note), the property transformed from a paper commodity for quick resale into a family holding that would nurture hard-earned insular subsistence living for the next half century.

Firmer Ground (1880–present)

The local Brundrett clan began with George: born and orphaned in Scotland; immigrated to Detroit where he took up boiler making, married, and began a family; hied off with Hannah and three young children toward better prospects as a Texian in the latter years of the Republic; moved into a rustic setting on Cape Carlos,[6] bought a schooner and took up transferring freight among the busy local ports; got conked on the head by a swinging yardarm and was "lost at sea," or at least his body was never recovered from the shallows off Mud Island in the lower reach of Aransas Bay; departed this world in 1846.

George seeded a hardy and prolific lineage, and Hannah Hollingsworth upgraded the stock. After her husband's untimely death, she moved to the primitive settlement on the southern tip of St. Joseph Island with six little Brundretts in tow, the youngest less than a year old. She lived through two more husbands, bore three more children, and raised one grandchild whose mother died in childbirth and another whose mother died in a kerosene stove explosion. Others spooked when shells from Yankee gunboats crashed into the defenseless cluster of clapboards and wharves, but Hannah refused to budge. She also defied the cyclone of 1875 but finally moved to the mainland after the devastating storm of 1886. At last, crusty Hannah Hollingsworth Brundrett Thompson Gaston, born in England and tempered in Texas, died in 1901 at the age of eighty-four.

The patriarch's two eldest sons, George Albert and John McOscary, were reared on St. Joseph Island. They were hardly out of their teens before they became landholders and joined the small cohort of men who introduced cattle onto the virgin barrier grassland. George Albert matched his mother by living to age eighty-four; John McOscary made it to ninety-three. Each married twice, and each sired eighteen children, most of whom carried on the fecund familial tradition. There were soon Brundretts and Brundrett kin all over the Coastal Bend and still are.

The two brothers lived and ranched on St. Jo until the big storm of 1886. After that they moved across the bay to Lamar and sailed back and forth to the island occasionally to tend their cattle. Just after the turn of the century, several families of Brundretts (they were always clannish), including George Albert and John McOscary, moved onto Blackjack Peninsula on the shore of St. Charles Bay.[7] When they finally weakened in old age, both brothers moved to Rockport to die, George Albert in 1920 and his brother in 1932.

To pick up the tale of the square mile of land on Matagorda Island, we found John McOscary extending his ranching enterprise on St. Joseph Island by buying the lower nine miles of Matagorda from Henry Lewis in 1877. It was a natural expansion. The two islands were barely separated by narrow and shallow Cedar Bayou. On a low tide, anyone on horseback could haze cattle across the pass; stock frequently swam the cut on their own.

In 1882 George Albert bought an undivided half interest in John's Matagorda property, and the two fenced and ranched the tract together, riding over from their homes on St. Joseph now and then to look after the cattle.

At the time of John's death intestate, the Matagorda ranch, still in undivided joint ownership, was parceled among the numerous heirs. The square mile of interest was included in the 7,383-acre tract that went to John McOscary's eight children by his first wife, Hannah Sophia.

After several quick deals among siblings and cousins, two brothers—Jed Albert and James William Brundrett—gained undivided half interests in 4,190 acres of Matagorda Island that encompassed the square mile where our FWS headquarters is now situated. Like their father and uncle before them, the two ran cattle on the land but did not live there. When they could not make ends meet with cattle, they shifted to sheep.

So in 1932, as the darkness of the Depression deepened, it was essentially back to life as usual on the remote island. But Adam Smith's invisible hand has a long reach. No one could foresee how quickly the Brundrett dynasty on south Matagorda was about to end.

Clinton Williams Murchison (1895–1969) of Dallas liked to make and spend money, Texas style, and he was good at it.[8] His forte lay in swinging deals with a minimum of cash outlay and a daring risk with credit and collateral. He made and lost several fortunes in the rough-and-

tumble oil fields of his boyhood stomping grounds in East Texas during the unregulated boom days of the 1930s, and throughout his life he
enjoyed gambling with and diversifying his estate.

Along with his friend Dudley Golding, Murchison incorporated the
independent petroleum operating and production company American
Liberty Oil and was involved in everything from wildcat drilling to
running hot oil in the days when even deployment of the National
Guard could not enforce proration of gushing production. With a
shrewd eye always out for an untapped petroleum reservoir, Clint
Murchison noticed the barrier islands strung along the coast tantaliz-
ingly close to subterranean salt domes known to be likely petroleum
traps and lying just east of the booming Refugio oil field. He decided
to give the barriers a try. On a typical Murchison-style impulse, he set
out not merely to buy up a few insular oil leases but to finagle himself
an entire island.

In 1933 Clint Murchison boldly tried to buy Matagorda Island lock,
stock, and barrel, but he was surprised to find that even in the dismal
economic throes of the day, his overtures could not entice the second-
and third-generation subsistence ranchers to let go their land. Their
rebuff only piqued Murchison's desire, so he sniffed around for vulnerable spots.

The many heirs of George Albert and John McOscary Brundrett
had just been doled their fractional interests in the Matagorda property.
Most of the children felt no keen attachment to the land and were
willing to sell their estates to the highest bidder. Murchison was there
at the right time. In November 1933 he negotiated his first island transaction when he bought an undivided one-eighth interest in a 5,009-acre
Brundrett tract just north of current FWS headquarters. The next
summer, July 1934, Murchison acquired his first warranty deed on
Matagorda Island when he induced Jed Albert and James William
Brundrett to sell him a 6-acre sandy knoll out of their sheep pasture
with a couple of squatter's shacks on it, located one mile from the Gulf
and about four and a half miles up the island from Cedar Bayou, the
tidal pass that marks the south end of Matagorda. The spot was within
the square mile we are following, precisely where headquarters is located today. I am sitting there as I write.

Meanwhile, hard times were dogging the brothers Brundrett. James
William took out a mortgage lien on his half interest in their 4,190-acre
tract (now less 6 acres). Clint Murchison quickly acquired the lien. In

1934 the Brundretts mortgaged their property for $27,425. The next year they lost the land to foreclosure and sold off the livestock. By January 1936 guess who owned 4,190 acres of Matagorda Island, including our focal square mile? American Liberty Oil, aka Clinton W. Murchison. The oil tycoon was on his way to island fiefdom.

Once their reticent shield was pierced, the other Brundrett heirs began to sell out. By 1941 Clint Murchison owned over 8,000 contiguous acres, including most mineral rights, on south Matagorda Island and was satisfied that was about all he could easily acquire. ALO drilled at several sites on the property, but they all came up dry. No matter. By that time the new owner had turned to ranching the land for profit and building a recreational retreat for fun.

By the early 1940s the original 6-acre hillock had sprouted a scatter of ranch outbuildings, a small bunkhouse for resident Mexican cowhands, a foreman's house, catch pens, corrals, cross-fences, cattle guards, a water well and water storage tank, electrical generators, a landing strip of packed oyster shell, and the centerpiece—the labyrinthine, one-story lodge, a richly furnished twenty-bed weekend retreat for family and friends. There was a small boathouse and shellcrete dock on the nearby bay shore to receive boats out of Rockport.

Now, whenever they felt like it, Murchison and his entourage flew down from Dallas for fun and games: hunting everything from geese to rattlesnakes; laying bets on greyhounds trained to run down jackrabbits; fishing the bay, the pass, and the surf; enjoying the solitude of miles of public beach inaccessible to the public; tooling around the island paradise in stripped-down Ford touring cars; wining, dining, and conniving on the breezy veranda; indulging their every fancy; living the good life. With Clint Murchison on the premises, the square mile was roused from its customary dream state.

Since the early days in the oil fields, fellow East Texan Toddie Lee Wynne (1896–1982) had been legal counsel, business associate, and trusted friend of Clint Murchison. Both were innate wheeler-dealers. Following Dudley Golding's untimely death in an airplane crash in 1938, Wynne acquired 50 percent of ALO, and thereafter he and Murchison were involved in a welter of far-flung deals and enterprises ranging from oil leases and cattle ranches to life insurance and racehorses.

Then in 1943, at age forty-seven, Wynne suffered a serious heart attack that drained him of his fast-paced business ambitions. In 1946 he and Murchison decided to divvy up their assets, and by the flip of a coin Wynne got the option to take over ALO and the Matagorda property that went with it. He took it.

Wynne immediately swung a deal that Murchison had never attended to. He bought the 3,193 acres that Brundrett heirs were still ranching on the southern tip of the island. With that transaction, the Star Brand Ranch was complete: 11,502 acres, the lower nine miles of Matagorda Island.[9] Our square mile was distinguishable only as the area surrounding ranch headquarters.

Wynne continued in Murchison's lavish tradition. He came down with family, friends, and hangers-on in his customized DC-3 from Fort Worth/Dallas when he wanted to enjoy The Island. He added to the lodge until it sprawled over thirteen thousand square feet. He surrounded the place with a large irrigated lawn neatly trimmed with a white board fence and flanked by rows of stately palm trees. He paved the airstrip and built a yawning hangar to house his airplane.

Wynne brought in top-grade Santa Gertrudis stock (Murchison had run Herefords), sank one or more windmills in each pasture, built new shipping pens, bought a hundred-foot barge to haul his stock to market, and leased nearly 14,000 acres of barrier grassland for grazing beyond the limits of his ranch.

In 1982, while awaiting the liftoff of a privately financed space satellite from the south tip of the island, Toddie Lee Wynne suffered his second major heart attack and died aboard his DC-3 en route to a Dallas hospital. It was time; he was eighty-six.

With the old man gone and family interests turning elsewhere, Toddie Lee Wynne, Jr., was ready to unload the Star Brand Ranch. Fortunately, he retained enough feel for the land to negotiate a sale with the nonprofit Nature Conservancy rather than with private land speculators, who undoubtedly would have turned the property toward resort development. In December 1986 ALO conveyed the surface rights on the 11,502 acres to the Nature Conservancy for $9 million, and TNC immediately began transactions to sell the land piecemeal to the Department of Interior for inclusion in a national wildlife refuge.[10] In November 1988 the final payment was made on the purchase price of $13 million, and the warranty deed was issued.[11] The Star Brand Ranch, or "the old Wynne Ranch" as it is usually called today, became the property of the Department of Interior. Our square mile was now in the public trust.

The sale of the Wynne Ranch to the federal government did more than give the lower nine miles of Matagorda Island a lease on perpetuity. Because of prior transactions on the rest of the island, once this last tract of private property was conveyed, Matagorda Island became the first, and so far the only, Texas barrier to fall entirely into public ownership.

Briefly, the rest of the story is this. In 1942 the federal government used its power of eminent domain to buy the upper twenty-eight miles of Matagorda Island from a swatch of unwilling private landowners for use as a conveniently remote practice bombing range by the U.S. Air Force. The deal did not sit well with either the landowners or with Texans in general. As they saw it, it was their land but not their war.

By 1975 the military mission was finished, and the land went up for grabs. Both the State of Texas and the Department of Interior applied for the tract. Texas, through the Texas Parks and Wildlife Department, wanted to establish a state park and state natural area on the island; Interior, through the Fish and Wildlife Service, wanted to create a Matagorda unit of the Aransas National Wildlife Refuge complex. In 1982 an amazingly sensible and amicable compromise was reached: the state and the feds would manage the island jointly. Better yet, the two would exchange one-hundred-year conservation easements so that not only the federally owned island proper, but the surrounding state-owned marshes and fringing beach would be included in the management plan. In effect, the entire barrier ecosystem would be monitored and protected as one integral unit. TPWD was given lead responsibility for public access while FWS would attend the natural resources. In 1992 Secretary Manuel Lujan signed the deal for Interior; Governor Ann Richards signed for Texas in 1994.

Meanwhile, Matagorda Island exists in blissful limbo. With congressional approval, the 56,000-acre insular ecosystem will be designated the Matagorda Island National Wildlife Refuge and State Natural Area, and it is already being jointly managed as such. The 7,300-acre Matagorda Island State Park is situated on the north end, while the 37,000-acre Wildlife Management Area occupies the remainder of the northern two-thirds of the island. Both are overlaid atop the refuge and are also part of the state natural area. The old Wynne Ranch is set aside as a conservation and education area where there is no hunting and little human traffic other than education groups and an occasional graduate student doing fieldwork.

So our square mile has come nearly full turn. It began boundless, free, secure, doing nothing in particular. It came to know the stride of foraging Cujanes, probably felt the staggering tread of poor old Cabeza de Vaca, glimpsed the topmast of one of Jean Laffite's corsairs gingerly wending through the treacherous shallows of Cedar Bayou, figured in James Power's unfulfilled aspirations for a world-class seaport, winced when Ed Linn drove in his survey stakes, saw the Matagorda light blink on, heard the rattle of Charlie Johnson's stagecoach, held steady beneath the measured tread of twenty-eight hundred Yankees marching up the beach to take Fort Esperanza, succored Brundrett livestock for over half a century, luckily avoided being bombed and strafed by trainee aviators, tolerated the commotion of Murchisons and Wynnes at play, listened bemused as I extolled its virtues to visitors, cast about uneasily as things quieted down, and finally drowsed off—still boundless, nearly free, hopefully secure, and once again doing nothing in particular.

I can look out my window and see the headquarters compound, a 15-acre patch of weathered buildings and crumbling roadways set amid an impassive, sweeping natural grassland that from this vantage seems infinite but which, I know, shortly slopes down to the sea at every quarter. An anthropomorphic islet astride a natural barrier island, the duo a serene galaxy apart from the harried mainland world.

There is a sprinkling of modernity among the old structures: radio and cellular telephone antennae; gleaming solar panels; in the office, file cabinets filled with multiple copies of long-forgotten reports, a couple of outmoded computers, and a fax machine that refuses to fax. Mostly, however, the place continues in its sixty-odd-year somnolence. When the site shifted over from the hub of a working ranch to the headquarters for a national wildlife refuge, things really did not change that much. We got rid of the livestock and took down the wire fencing but left the posts; now the old cross-fence lines are marked by rows of weary cedar posts stretching from bay to Gulf, convenient perches for white-tailed hawks, rubbing poles for feral hogs, reminders of days gone by.

At headquarters we did not brusquely tear down the old and erect the new. We just moved in. Actually, there *were* grandiose plans, but they fell through. The money did not come down from Albuquerque; there was static from the Historical Commission in Austin; because of

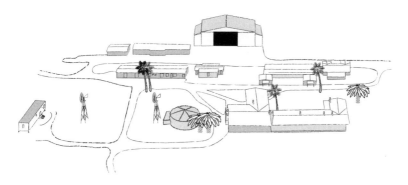

Headquarters compound

difficult access, the anticipated influx of visitors did not materialize; the omnipresent threat of a wipe-it-all-out hurricane instilled uncommon prudence in usual federal obstinacy; and in the interim it became obvious that the sturdy ranch buildings not only served quite well in their new capacity but that they lent an unparalleled charm to the place. So with quiet insistence, the island had its way.

I like to wander around this haunted place. Despite its bad roof and listing foundation, the lodge is still the centerpiece. Boarded up and empty now, with torn screens singing mournfully along the gulfside veranda, weathered shingles sloughing into the yard after each norther, and its interior ravaged by creeping mildew and splattered with barn owl droppings, the sprawling building still reeks of past grandeur. Here in imported luxury the Dallasites and their guests partied in the grand brick room, hatched deals around the well-stocked bar, supped in the elegant dining room, sipped iced drinks on the breezy piazza, watched the kids romp in the yard, retired to their airy bedrooms, and generally whooped it up as only the idle rich can afford to do.

It is all quiet there now except for raccoons scratching in the garret, barn swallows nesting under the eaves, the hum of mud dauber wasps, and the reflected wink of restive old Sambo's lantern when I shine the beam of my flashlight at a window on a dark night. (Sambo was Mr. Tot's faithful servant whose shade is reputed to still stalk the house.)

Across the yard from the lodge is the Environmental Education Center, spruced up but little changed from its sojourn as the bunkhouse for Mexican cowhands who resided there. Minus the grease and grime, faded pinup calendars, cigarette stains, and scarred pool table, it still sports the original heavy kitchen tables, sturdy benches, and fine old propane cook stove. We added a screened back veranda, a good place to have lunch and discuss what we saw on our field trip. One room is converted into a classroom that I seldom use because I prefer to keep groups busy outside. We replumbed the bathroom and divided it into men's and women's. The spacious pool room now contains bunk beds for overnighters. Our FWS offices are tucked into two small back bedrooms.

And our house trailer—our thin-walled, leaky-roofed, much-cursed but ever-beloved domicile for four years—now lies in the grass with wheels in the air, spare siding and meager entrails strewn to the south, a victim of a vicious little whirlwind spawned by tropical storm Charley in the summer of 1998. Not by planning but by dumb luck, Martha and I had just moved into the Pilot House. The Pilot House—so-called because that is where the DC-3 pilot stayed until the return flight—is a stout, five-room bungalow with a roof that does not leak and walls that do not shudder in a moderate sea breeze. But the place has yet to provoke either the feeling or the memories of the house trailer. In time it will.

There is a scatter of outbuildings that still emit the fragrance of livestock feed and manure and now serve as a maintenance shop and storage sheds. Martha and I commandeered the room with the best roof for a museum. There the old pool table displays an array of labeled seashells, and the shelves are overloaded with the fruits of Martha's near-daily sorties to the beach.

The lone new building, built like a cement bunker, houses the 16-kilowatt diesel generator that powers the shop. Hands down, it is ranked by the maintenance crew as the structure most likely to survive a hurricane's wrath. So, there I built a "storm shelf" beneath the ceiling. If we have to evacuate, that is where we will stash our books, sewing machine, and microwave, all twist-tied in garbage liners. Our computers and floppies will go with us, off to the mainland to security and worry. The rest of our belongings will take their chance in the Pilot House.[12] Personally, I would rather wedge into the generator house to safeguard my books and experience the thrill of either riding the weather out or succumbing to it, but the Service will not hear of it. They have a patronizing image to protect and lawsuits to beware of, so I must forgo any thought of premeditated risk while in uniform. Safe but dull.

The onshore breeze whishes through the crowns of five tall Washington palms, the hardy remnants of a guardian ring of over a hundred such trees that once graced this place with the aspect of a tropical oasis. Over half a century of Texas northers culled the rest.

Jackrabbits crop grass and dig dust basins in the yard; they hardly bother to move aside when we walk past. Wild turkeys stop by for an early-morning handout of kitchen scraps, while squadrons of brown pelicans silently soar past, headed for breakfast in the surf. An aplomado falcon playfully drives a flock of great-tailed grackles into panic. A diamondback rattler shows its fat coils now and then in the secure gloom under the edge of the house. The sun rises in splendor and sets in matching grandeur. Gulf clouds swell up into pile upon billowing pile or scud across, gray, low, and ominous. At night coyotes wail, deer bed down in the yard, the moon seems close enough to touch, the heavens beckon. The seasons come around, the tide turns. You can hear the silence, feel the stillness, revel in the isolation, get to know yourself, reflect on your good fortune.

We try to stay in the background, enthralled observers. We do not belong, can never truly belong, but we can coexist and commingle. Close enough.

NOTES

Preface

1. W. H. McAlister and M. K. McAlister, *A Naturalist's Guide: Matagorda Island* (Austin: University of Texas Press, 1993).
2. Norman's fishing rules:

   > If'n the fish are bitin', fish. If they ain't, fish anyway. They might start.
   > If I ketch him, no matter *how* I ketch him, he's mine.
   > You don't look in my cooler box, and I won't look in your'n.
   > A fish ain't rightly caught 'til he's gutted an' et.

Chapter 1

1. Some declare that it was the setting sun that enthralled the Indians (reread the evocative commentary by Roy Bedichek in Karankaway Country), but all agree that their gaze was directed "over the sea." Unless "the sea" can be construed to include the bay—not a common usage—it must have been the rising sun that captivated them, for nowhere in Karankawa country can one see the sun set in the Gulf of Mexico.
2. I am speaking here from the anthropomorphic edge. After even a severe storm the island itself is largely unperturbed, even gratified. Tidal passes and bays are cleansed, nutrients are redistributed, green shoots poke up, animals venture forth from sundry hideaways to repopulate. A manifest vigor ripples through the insular ecosystem, driven by a primal inspiration untainted by any sense of injustice or deprivation.
3. At my latitude of 28 degrees north, the sun should appear to rise at a shade under 23.5 degrees. As we say out here, "close enough for government work."
4. Robert A. Morton et al., *Living with the Texas Shore* (Durham, N.C.: Duke University Press, 1983). There is a precursor volume containing more entertaining Pilkeyisms (from both Orrin, Jr., and Orrin, Sr.) and additional shoreline insights, all quite applicable to the Texas Gulf Coast: Orrin H. Pilkey, Jr., et al., *From Currituck to Calabash: Living with North Carolina's Barrier Islands,* 2d ed. (North Carolina Science and Technology Research Center, Research Triangle Park, North Carolina, 1980).

Chapter 8

1. Paul Edwards, ed., "What I Believe," in *Why I Am Not a Christian* (New York: Simon & Schuster, 1957).

Chapter 9

1. Harold Oldroyd, *The Natural History of Flies* (New York: W. W. Norton, 1964).
2. Calvin McMillan, "Environmental Factors Affecting Seedling Establishment of the Black Mangrove on the Central Texas Coast," *Ecology* 52, no. 5 (1971): 927–30.
3. W. Frank Blair, "Some Aspects of the Biology of the Ornate Box Turtle, *Terrapene ornata*," *Southwestern Naturalist* 21 (1976): 89–103.

Chapter 10

1. This is just popular shorthand. A Spanish *league* is a linear distance equivalent to 2.63 miles. A square league encloses 6.92 square miles, or 4,428 acres, and such a square is properly called a *sitio*. Power and Hewetson actually bought twenty-two sitios, just over 150 square miles, not far short of 100,000 acres.
2. A *patent* is a conveyance, usually a deed, from the Sovereignty of the Soil (in this case, the State of Texas) to the first owner, the *original grantor*. Once surveyed, recorded, and service fees paid, the land is said to be *patented* to the owner, and from that time its fate is scrupulously documented through public registries. Actually, the grantor here was the deceased William Bryan, but his entitlement—his Land Scrip #8, surely bought for cash from some eligible recipient—was transferred to William Little. Then Little had Survey #6 performed and finally received Patent #13, as recorded in Volume 34 among the old patent records filed in Austin.
3. Columbia, briefly one of several sites of the capital of the Republic, on the lower Brazos River in Brazoria County; the scrip bearing the signature of President Sam Houston.
4. Espiritu Santo Bay is modern Mesquite Bay; I have looked for the mesquite tree and cannot find it—at this remove, no surprise; a *vara* (literally, a stick or rod) is equivalent to 33.33 inches in early Texas surveys; as there are no palmettos (*Sabal minor*) on the island today, Linn was probably referring to Spanish daggers (*Yucca treculeana*).
5. Surveyors have their own peculiar way of describing direction. They use either N or S as a baseline, then indicate the declination as either E or W of that line. Here, for instance, is a bearing almost due west.
6. In George Brundrett's day, Cape Carlos was an oyster-shell promontory poking into Carlos Bay from the edge of Blackjack Peninsula opposite the north end of St. Joseph Island. Today the Gulf Intracoastal Waterway slices through the margin of the peninsula and isolates Cape Carlos on a strip of shell called Bludworth Island.

7. The foundations of their homesites are today on the Aransas National Wildlife Refuge.

8. Not to be confused with his son, the late Clinton, Jr., once flamboyant owner of the Dallas Cowboys professional football team.

9. In the early days the two Power and Hewetson leagues were sometimes regarded as encompassing over 18,000 acres because surrounding marshes and beaches were included. Today the beach and tidelands are owned by the General Land Office of Texas, their inland boundary somewhat vaguely described as "the mean higher high waterline."

10. It says something for the expertise and resourcefulness of private initiative over the inertia of big government that TNC not only could see the opportunity and swing the deal but could come up with the cash before the window of opportunity closed. Congress appropriated land and water conservation funds during fiscal years 1987–89 to buy the land from the Nature Conservancy. The purchase was specifically justified for the protection of resident and migrant endangered species, especially whooping cranes, which had begun to visit the island from their traditional wintering haunts on the adjacent Aransas refuge.

11. Of passing interest, when J. M. Brundrett bought the two Power and Hewetson leagues in 1877, he paid $0.32/acre. When the U.S. government bought much of Matagorda Island at the onset of World War II, it paid the going price of $7/acre. The Nature Conservancy bought the Wynne land for $783/acre and sold it to the U.S. government for $1,130/acre.

12. We did just that in August 1999 when Hurricane Bret threatened before swerving inland south of Corpus Christi, leaving Matagorda Island unperturbed.

INDEX

Acacia cornigera, 179

Acartia tonsa, 105

accordion alga, 104

Acetes americanus, 106

Aedes sollicitans, 91; *taeniorhynchus,* 91

Agalinis maritima, 138

Agelenopsis naevia, 123

alligator, 158

Alpheus heterochaelis, 210

American avocet, 69

amphioxus, 128, 132–33

Anachis obesa, 208

Anadara ovalis, 208

Anchoa hepsetus, 146

Ancinus depressus, 207

angelwing clam, 71

ant: army, 119; carpenter, 123, 196; curious, 179, 180; fire, 118; fungus gardener, 119; leaf cutter, 119; little black, 199; pharoah, 199; pyramid, 118; southern fire, 198; teeny-tinies, 199; valentine, 80, 118

Aphaenogaster texana, 123

Aphonopelma steindachneri, 120

Arctosa littoralis, 122

Arenaeus cribrarius, 208

Arenivaga bolliana, 118

arrowworm, 108

Atalopedes campestris, 124

Atlantic needlefish, 72

Atlantic winged oyster, 171

Atta texana, 119

Augchloropsis sp., 124

auger snail, 47

Aysha gracilis, 196

bacteriorhodopsin, 89

badger, 181

Balanoglossus aurantiacus, 129

Balanus sp., 208

barnacle: acorn 208; giant, 183; gooseneck, 182; seawhip, 184; turtle, 183; whale, 183

barnacles, 182–84

Bascanichthyes scuticaris, 203

Batis maritima, 138

bay anchovy, 72

bay wiff, 72

beach hopper, 50

beetle: beach tiger, 47, 49; black beach, 52, 197; brown marsh, 90; carabid, 54; click, 117; darkling, 117; firefly, 188; ground, 117; ladybird, 195; lantern click, 188; predaceous diving, 151; rainbow dung, 184; rove, 117; scarab, 117; snout, 117; soft-winged flower, 82; spiny-legged rove, 90; warty leaf, 201

Bembix sp., 202

Berlese funnel, 111

Beroe ovata, 107, 187

bird grasshopper, 118

bird rookery, 166–69

blackcheek tonguefish, 73

black drum, 72

Blackfordia sp., 202

black mangrove, 189

black-necked stilt, 148

Bledius, 53, 90

blood ark, 208

blue cactus borer, 195

bluefish, 146
blue-green algae, 53, 70, 85–88, 116
bobwhite quail, 155
Borrichia frutescens, 138
Bowmaniella sp., 106
Brachymyrmex depilis, 123, 199
Branchinecta, 171
Branchiostoma caribaeum, 132
brown sea cucumber, 153
Brundrett, 224–27
Brunner's mantis, 80
Bufo valliceps, 123
bull's-horn acacia, 179
burrowing brittle star, 207
burrowing sea cucumber, 68, 108
by-the-wind-sailor, 208

cabbagehead jellyfish, 213
Cabeza de Vaca, 219
Callianassa jamaicense, 70
Callichirus islagrande, 46
Callinectes: sapidus, 121, 208; *similis,* 208
camphor daisy, 138
Camponotus: abdominalis, 123; *rasilis*, 123,
        196
Capitella capitata, 201
Cardisoma guanhumi, 135
carpet moth, 204
Cedar Bayou, 6, 15, 163
centipede, 120
Centruroides vittatus, 120
Ceratinopsis interpres, 122
Chaetognatha, 108
Chelonibia testudinaria, 183
chiton, 203
Chrysaora quinquecirrha, 149
cicada, 81
Cicindela dorsalis, 47
ciliate protozoan, 70
clam shrimp, 124
clapper rail, 89, 157
Clathrus columnatus, 192
Clausidium caudatum, 46
Cnemidophorus sexlineatus, 123
coachwhip, 155
cochineal, 194

Collembola, 113
Collops sp., 82
colonial rotifer, 124
comb jelly, 72, 107, 149
common nighthawk, 184
Conocephalus, 164
Conochilus sp., 124
Conomyrma flavus, 118
Conopea galeata, 184
constricted macoma, 67
copepod, 46, 70
coquina, 41, 208
cordgrass bug, 81
cotton rat, 123, 156
coyote, 148, 156, 209
crab: blue, 121, 146, 152, 163, 208; ghost,
        54–59; ghost, megalops, 57; ghost
        shrimp, 46; great land, 121, 134–43;
        Gulf, 208; marsh, 79; mole, 44; mud,
        79; mud fiddler, 83, 121; pea, 46, 208;
        sand fiddler, 89, 121; speckled, 208;
        spider, 208; stone, 208; surf, 47; wharf,
        121
Crematogaster: laeviuscula, 80, 118;
        lineolata, 118
crested caracara, 152
Crotalus atrox, 214
cryptozoa, 112–15
cumacean, 108, 162
cyanobacteria, 85
Cyathus stercoreus, 197
Cybister fimbriolatus, 151
Cynoscion: arenarius, 146; *nebulosus*, 146
Cyrtopleura costata, 71

Dacylopius confusus, 194
decomposition, 172–75
deer, 156
desulfovibrios, 65
detritus, 64
diatom, 53, 70
dipluran, 114
Distichlis spicata, 138
Donax variabilis, 43, 208
double-crested cormorant, 157
Dugesiella hentzi, 120

dunes grasshopper, 118
dunlin, 160
dwarf olive snails, 47
dwarf surf clam, 71

eastern narrowmouth toad, 123
Echeneis naucrates, 180
Eciton nigrescens, 119
Elops saurus, 146
Emerita portoricensis, 44
ephyra, 214
Erigone autumnalis, 122
Erythrodiplax berenice, 81
Escandón, Don José de, 219
estuary, 63
Eulimnadia texana, 124

fairy bell, 202
fairy shrimp, 171
fall armyworm, 164, 213
fall witchgrass, 196
fat dove snail, 208
feral hog, 148
field cricket, 117
firebrat, 122
flatworm, 70
fly: anthomyiid, 51, 154, 163; blow, 51;
    brine, 87; dance, 81; deer, 80; dung,
    185; flesh, 51; green-head, 80; horse,
    80, 81, 123; long-legged, 70, 80; pic-
    ture-winged, 81; robber, 81, 154; sea-
    weed, 51; shore, 51, 165; soldier, 123,
    202; stable, 51
foraminifera, 106, 186
fulvous harvest mouse, 123
fungus gnat, 114

Gastrophryne carolinensis, 123
gastrotrich, 124
ghost shrimp, 46, 70, 162
glasswort, 89
Glycera americana, 47
great-blue heron, 148
great southern white butterfly, 89
green-head, 80
ground cricket, 118

ground skink, 123
Gryllus pennsylvanicus, 117
Guadalupe River, 6, 62
Gulf coast ribbon snake, 123
Gulf coast toad, 123
gulf killifish, 72
gulf menhaden, 72

halictid bee, 124
Halobacterium salinarium, 88
Halobates, 200
Hargeria rapax, 161
harvestmen, 120, 122
Hastula salleyana, 47
Haustorius sp., 47
Heliastus subroseus, 118
Heteromastus filiformis, 68
Hewetson, James, 220
horned lizard, 215
hurricane, 19
Hurter's spadefoot toad, 200

Ischnochiton papillosus, 203
Ischnodemus falicus, 81
isopod, 121

jackknife clam, 71

Karankawa, 12, 218

Laeonereis culveri, 67, 161
Laetilia coccidivora, 195
lancelet, 127, 132
Laphygma frugiperda, 164, 213
larvacean, 109
LaSalle, René Robert, 219
Latrodectus mactans, 120
Lepas anatifera, 182
Lepidonotus sublevis, 207
Lepidopa websteri, 47
Leptochelia rapax, 70
Leptogenys elongata, 123
Leptogorgia setacea, 184
Leptoloma cognatum, 196
Leptosynapta inhaerens, 68, 108
Leptysma marginicollis, 124

Lewis, Henry, 223
Libinia sp., 208
Limonium carolinianum, 138
Lithobius sp., 120
Little, William, 222
lizard fish, 72
long-billed curlew, 84, 162
long-legged centipede, 122
long-nosed killifish, 72
Loxosceles devia, 120
Lumbrinereis parvula, 47

Machaeranthera phyllocephala, 138
Macoma constricta, 67
maritime saltwort, 138
Marmara opuntiella, 196
marsh periwinkle, 79
marsh rice rat, 89, 123
massasauga, 123
Masticophis flagellum, 155
Mastophora cornigera, 212
meadow frog, 150
meadow katydid, 164
Mediomastus californiensis, 87
Megabalanus antillensis, 183
megalops, 57
Melampus bidentattus, 164
Melitara junctolineella, 196
Menippe adina, 208
Mesosoma nigrum, 122
midge larvae, 161
millipede, 121
Misumenops asperatus, 124
Mnemiopsis mccradyi, 149, 188
Molgula manhattensis, 130
Monanthochloe littoralis, 138
Monomorium: minimum, 199; *pharaonis*,
   199
moon snail, 45
mosquito: black salt marsh, 91; elephant,
   92; golden salt marsh, 91; purple rain,
   91; shaggy- legged, 91
mosquitoes, 91–99
mosquito fish, 93
Mugil cephalus, 73
Murchison, Clint, 226–28

Mutinus caninus, 192
myriapod, 120
Myrmekiophila fluviatilis, 120
mysid, 161
Mysidopsis almyra, 106, 161

naked goby, 72
nematode, 70
Nemobius sp., 118
Neochlamisus sp., 201
Nepthys bucera, 47
Nitzschia, 104
Noctiluca scintillans, 109, 187
northern harrier, 157

Ocypode quadrata, 54
Odontomyia cincta, 202
Ogyrides limicola, 208
Oikopleura, 110
Oligembia sp., 115
oligochaete, 70
Olivella minuta, 47
Onuphis eremita, 47, 164
Ophiophragmus moorei, 207
Ophisaurus attenuatus, 123
Opsanus beta, 211
Opuntia engelmanii, 194
Orchestia grillus, 121
Orchilium, 164
Oribatei, 113
ornate box turtle, 152, 193
Oryzomys palustris, 123
ostracod, 70
owl fly larva, 122 145
Oxyurostylis: salinoi, 108; *smithi*, 162
oyster, 210

Pachychondyla harpax, 123
Palaemonetes pugio, 106
Parcoblatta fulvescens, 117
Pass Cavallo, 15
Peckhamia picata, 120
Pelagia noctiluca, 188
peregrine falcon, 154
perennial glasswort, 138
Phallus, 192

Phanaeus difformis, 184
Phidippus audax, 120
phosphorus jelly, 187
Phrynosoma cornutum, 215
Pineda, Alonso Álvarez de, 219
pinfish, 72
Pinnixa spp., 46, 208
plankton, 100
Polinices duplicatus, 45
Polydora ligni, 69
Pomatomus sal-tatrix, 146
Porcellio laevis, 121
Power, James, 220
prairie-lined racerunner, 123
protochordates, 127
psammobionts, 41
Pseudomyrma: ferrugineus, 180; *gracilis*, 179; *pallida*, 123
pseudoscorpion, 114
Psorophora: ciliata, 91; *cyanescens*, 91
Pteria columbus, 171
puffer fish, 73
purple bacteria, 88
purple jellyfish, 188
Pyractonema angulata, 188
pyralid moth, 195, 196
Pyrophorus sp., 188

ram's horn, 205
Rana sphenocephala, 123, 150
rapier katydid, 80
rattlesnake: diamondback, 165, 214; massasauga, 123
razor clam, 71
red-eared slider, 159
redfish, 73, 153, 157
red tide, 170
Reithrodontomys fulvescens, 123
remora, 180
Renilla mulleri, 188
ribbed mussel, 79
rough sea squirt, 131

Saccoglossus kowalevskii, 130
sachem skipper, 124
sailfin molly, 93

Salicornia virginica, 138
saltgrass, 138
saltmarsh beach hopper, 121
saltmarsh dragonfly, 81
saltmarsh grasshopper, 80
saltmarsh katydid, 80
saltmarsh snail, 164
sand, 38
sand-digger amphipod, 47
sanderling, 154, 163
sand roach, 118
sand trout, 146
sand wasp, 202
Scaphiopus holbrooki, 200
Schistocerca americana, 118
Scianops ocellata, 157
Scincella lateralis, 123
Sclerodactyla briareus, 153
Scolelepis squamata, 47
Scolopendra sp., 121
scorpion, 120
scorpionfly, 81
Scutigera coleoptrata, 122
scyphistoma, 214
Scytodes perfecta, 160
sea grape, 130
sea-lavender, 138
sea nettle, 149
sea ox-eye, 89, 138
sea pansy, 188
sea pill bug, 207
sea robin, 73
seaside gerardia, 138
sea squirt, 130
sea walnut, 187
seawhip, 183
seed mite, 113
seepweed, 138
Sesarma cinerea, 121
sharksucker, 180
sheepshead killifish, 72, 93, 152
shore-grass, 138
shrimp: brown, 157; grass, 106; long-eyed, 208; opossum, 106; pistol, 210; sergestid, 106
Sigmodon hispidus, 123

Sistrurus catenatus, 123
skipjack, 146
slender glass lizard, 123
smooth cordgrass, 75-80
Solenopsis: geminata, 118; *xyloni*, 118, 198
songbird migration, 169
southern flounder, 73
southern meadow frog, 123
sowbug, 121
Spartina alterniflora, 75
speckled kingsnake, 146
speckled trout, 73, 146
Sphaeroma quadridentata, 207
spider: ant-mimic, 120; black widow, 120; bolas, 212; brown recluse, 120; crab, 80; dwarf, 119, 122; flower, 124; funnelweb, 119; ghost, 196; ground, 119; jumping, 80, 119; long-jawed orb weaver, 80; meshweb weaver, 80; sac, 119; spitting, 160; tarantula, 120; trap-door, 120; wolf, 80, 119, 122
spider mite, 113
Spirula spirula, 205
splash cup, 197
spot, 72
springtail, 113
stinkhorn, 191
Stomalophus meleagris, 213
Streblospio benedicti, 70
striped anchovy, 146
striped mullet, 73–75, 148
Styela plicata, 131
Suaeda linearis, 138

Talorchestia sp., 50
tanaid, 70, 161
tarantula, 120
Texas prickly pear, 194
Thamnophis proximus, 123
Thermobia domestica, 122
tidewater silverside, 72

toadfish, 211
toothpick grasshopper, 124
Toxorhynchites rutilis, 93
Trachymyrmex: septentrionalis, 119; *turrifex*, 119
Trichocorixa, 165; *verticalis*, 192
Trichophaga tapetzella, 204
tube-building amphipod, 79
tunicate, 110

Uca: panacea, 89; *pugnax*, 83

Velella velella, 208
veliger, 105
virgin nerite, 79

water boatmen, 165, 192
waterspout, 8
wave signature, 39
webspinner, 115
western pygmy blue butterfly, 89
western sandpiper, 67
whelk egg case, 206
whip eel, 203
white ibis, 84, 164
whooping crane, 176–78
willet, 152, 163, 165
Wilson's plover, 51, 147
wood roach, 117, 144
worm: acorn, 128, 129, 130; bamboo, 71; bar-gilled mud, 70; blood, 47, 71; capitellid thread, 68; clam, 71; Culver's sand, 67, 161; medusa, 71; mud whip, 69; nematode, 70, 124; palp, 47; plume, 71; red thread, 47; red-gilled, 71; sand parchment tube, 164; sand tube, 47; shimmy, 47; thread, 201; trumpet, 71; yellow paddle, 71
Wynne, Toddie Lee, 227–28

Xenobalanus globicipitis, 183